D0084707

THE WEST AND EASTERN EUROPE

The West and Eastern Europe

ECONOMIC STATECRAFT AND POLITICAL CHANGE

Thomas A. Baylis

Foreword by Richard C. Leone

A TWENTIETH CENTURY FUND BOOK

Westport, Connecticut
London

The Twentieth Century Fund sponsors and supervises timely analyses of economic policy, foreign affairs, and domestic political issues. Not-for-profit and nonpartisan, the Fund was founded in 1919 and endowed by Edward A. Filene.

Library of Congress Cataloging-in-Publication Data

Baylis, Thomas A.
The West and Eastern Europe : economic statecraft and political change / Thomas A. Baylis ; foreword by Richard C. Leone.
p. cm.
"A Twentieth Century Fund Book."
Includes bibliographical references and index.
ISBN 0-275-94676-2 (alk. paper).—ISBN 0-275-94734-3 (pbk. : alk. paper)
1. Europe, Eastern—Economic policy—1989- 2. Post-communism—Europe, Eastern. 3. Europe, Eastern—Foreign economic relations.
I. Title.
HC244.B35425 1994
338.947—dc20 93-14139

British Library Cataloguing in Publication Data is available.

Library of Congress Catalog Card Number: 93-14139
ISBN: 0-275-94676-2
0-275-94734-3 (pbk.)

First published in 1994

Praeger Publishers, 88 Post Road West, Westport, CT 06881
An imprint of Greenwood Publishing Group, Inc.

Printed in the United States of America

The paper used in this book complies with the Permanent Paper Standard issued by the National Information Standards Organization (Z39.48-1984).

10 9 8 7 6 5 4 3 2 1

Contents

Tables

Foreword

Over the last four years the Trustees of the Twentieth Century Fund have made a substantial commitment to projects exploring the implications of the end of the Cold War for U.S. foreign and economic policies. This area of inquiry obviously is vast, and it is further complicated by the fluidity of political circumstances within and among many of the relevant nations involved. This turbulence means that we are asking for more than is usual from our authors. They must reinterpret the recent past in light of sweeping changes in Europe. And, more precariously, they must think out loud, putting their reputations on the line with immediate reactions to what these changes mean for American policymakers.

In the pages that follow, Thomas Baylis of the University of Texas at San Antonio meets the challenges posed by the "new world order" with intelligence and candor. *The West and Eastern Europe* is certainly the most comprehensive work so far on the economic policy issues raised by the aspiring capitalist democracies formerly known as "satellites" of the former Soviet Union. Baylis provides a detailed history of Western, especially American, policies toward these nations during the post–World War II period. He draws crucial distinctions among the nations involved, in both their internal development and in their relations with the West. He reports in depth on the economic relations of the Eastern bloc countries with one another, with the former Soviet Union, and with the West in general.

The book places special emphasis on the late 1980s and the beginning of the 1990s. These years, reinterpreted in retrospect, set the stage for the variety of internal conditions and international issues currently facing Eastern European nations in their relations with western democracies. The special role of Germany, of course, is discussed in detail. Baylis's historical material is valuable both for understanding what happened and as a foundation for his forward-looking approach to Western policy.

The author offers strong and specific policy recommendations for the United States. He argues forcefully for a bold American response to the needs, both political and economic, of the region. His reasoning demands the attention of the new administration in Washington, for it is built not only on a strong historical and factual foundation but also on a clear and consistent view of the self-interest of the United States.

Baylis's work adds an important volume to recent Fund-sponsored work in this area, complementing Elizabeth Pond's *Beyond the Wall,* Jeffrey Garten's *A Cold Peace,* Richard Ullman's *Securing Europe,* James Chace's *The Consequences of the Peace,* and Bennett Kovrig's *Of Walls and Bridges.* In addition, it balances projects under way, such as Steven Burg's examination of nationalism and the democratization of Eastern Europe, Jonathan Dean's analysis of European security in the 1990s, Robert Art's study of America's grand strategy after the Cold War, David Calleo's exploration of Europe's future, Henry Nau's examination of America's foreign policy after the Cold War, Sylvia Ostry's study of the new international economic order, and Richard Ullman's new work for the Fund—a look at the international aspects of the war in Yugoslavia.

On behalf of the Twentieth Century Fund, I thank Thomas Baylis for his contribution to the critical and still-evolving debate on America's new place in world affairs. His book deserves serious attention from those who hope to understand, let alone shape, the new choreography of the United States, the West, and Eastern Europe.

Richard C. Leone, *President*
The Twentieth Century Fund

Acknowledgments

When I began this project in 1987, Eastern Europe was still firmly under Communist rule, or so it appeared. The epochal changes in the region in the intervening years have required a good deal of rethinking and rewriting on my part, and they have lengthened substantially the list of those to whom I owe thanks for various forms of assistance. In many respects, the most important are the scholars and officials I interviewed in Washington, Berlin, Budapest, Warsaw, Prague, London, and Austin,Texas, although there are too many of them to name individually. Most were themselves seeking to make sense of the extraordinary and rapid changes that were transforming Eastern Europe, and often to influence the direction of change; without their generosity in sharing their diverse perspectives, my own understanding of the process would have been much poorer.

I owe particular thanks to the Institute for Sino-Soviet Studies of The George Washington University, and to Professors Carl Linden and Michael Sodaro for accommodating me as a Visiting Fellow when I first began this project. I also made profitable use of the facilities of the American Institute for Contemporary German Studies in Washington; the director of the institute, Robert Gerald Livingston, was very helpful in putting me in touch with East German officials and academics. In Berlin, I owe special thanks to Hartmut Zimmermann, Gert-Joachim Glaessner, Irmhild Rudolph, and other staff members of the GDR Division of the Free University's Institute for Social Science Research; sadly, the division, for years the leading center of serious research on the GDR, has become a victim of the end of the Cold War.

I want to thank a number of other colleagues who helped me find informative contacts in Eastern Europe: Kazimierz Poznanski, Jack Bielasiak,

Peter Rutland, Milan Reban, and Henry Krisch. At the University of Texas at Austin, the Center for Post-Soviet and East European Studies and its director, Michael Katz, and at my own university the director of the Division of Social and Policy Sciences, David Alvirez, helped me in a variety of ways as I worked to complete the manuscript before changing events in Eastern Europe rendered it obsolete. The staff of the Twentieth Century Fund provided a running critique of the manuscript as I wrote and rewrote it; I want to thank Nina Massen, Pamela Gilfond, and John Samples especially, together with the fund's anonymous outside reviewers, for their help.

My warmest appreciation goes to my wife, Theresa Kelley, for her many-faceted support, and to both her and my son Patrick for their patience as I struggled to complete an undertaking that demanded far more time and adaptability than I could have guessed when I first began it.

INTRODUCTION

1

The Political Objectives of Economic Policy

> For more than 40 years the Cold War imparted a clarifying logic to American foreign policy that now will be missing.
>
> Charles William Maynes[1]

The end of Communism in Eastern Europe[2] has altered the terms of the Western debate over policies toward the region, but the outlines of a new set of competing assumptions and objectives are just beginning to appear. Old habits and frameworks of analysis, shaped during the cold war and giving primacy to considerations of military security and ideological rivalry, find themselves in retreat but resist their displacement. Self-indulgent Western interpretations of the changes in Eastern Europe and the Soviet Union as the "triumph of democratic capitalism" or even as the "end of history" obscure the difficult choices that now must be made. The collapse of Communist rule in Eastern Europe is irreversible, but the shape of the future political, social, and economic order in the area is anything but clear.

This book is concerned with the West's choices in the realm of economic policy, and with the impact of these choices on the ability of Eastern Europeans to build stable, prosperous, and democratic political orders. Its emphasis is thus on the intersection between economics and politics. It argues that the West must pay greater attention to the political dimension of economic reconstruction in Eastern Europe if its policies are to succeed. And it suggests that the United States, in particular, must alter its policies and perspectives toward Eastern Europe if this country is to avoid being reduced to political irrelevance in the region and losing much of its influence in the new Europe as a whole.

After the tumultuous fall and winter of 1989 that swept the Communist regimes of Eastern Europe from power, the foreign economic policies of Western states toward the area, once the concern of a relatively small number of specialists, came to command much broader attention. Proposals for direct Western aid and technical assistance to Eastern Europe—which, at their most ambitious, amounted to a "Marshall Plan" for the region—and for stimulating large-scale private investment came to occupy much of the terrain for debate. As we shall see, the subsequent disintegration of the Soviet Union has greatly complicated this debate, even while threatening to overshadow it. The policy questions that had dominated Communist-era discussions—questions revolving around trade rules and practices, finance and debt service, technology transfer and technological security, and support for economic reform—did not lose their relevance, although the terms of discussions about them necessarily shifted.

The precondition for addressing these issues of economic policy, however, is the clarification of the overarching political goals that such tools of economic statecraft might now serve. What does the West, or individual Western nations, now wish to achieve in Eastern Europe? What have become the underlying geopolitical stakes at issue in the region? Earlier, the choice of policies toward Eastern Europe was derived largely from Western goals and strategies with respect to the Soviet Union. The yardstick by which measures toward Eastern Europe were judged, especially by Americans, was their impact on Soviet power or on Soviet-Western relations. Even the German Federal Republic, while giving priority in its East European policies to its relations with the German Democratic Republic (GDR), was convinced that the path to significant change in the GDR would have to lead through Moscow.

Russia and the other former Soviet republics remain important, if highly uncertain, factors in the future of Eastern Europe, but the hegemony enjoyed by the USSR from 1945 until just a short time ago is now a thing of the past. Still formidable in terms of its population and resources, Russia faces internal afflictions so severe that it is not likely to regain its dominating position in the region in the foreseeable future. Western policymakers are now obliged to view the East European states more in their own right, as potential models for the former Soviet republics rather than vassals of them. The West must also view the East European states in the context of the economic and political transformation of Western Europe and its individual states, particularly Germany. The potential for divergence between American and European views and the likelihood that American influence will recede are both substantially greater than before.[3]

OLD ALTERNATIVES

Lincoln Gordon, writing in 1987, succinctly characterized the policy alternatives of the West at that time as falling along a spectrum ranging from "accommodation" to Soviet control over Eastern Europe, through the gradual "transformation" of that control into something less all-embracing and restrictive, to its total "dissolution."[4] He noted that the consensus view centered on varying forms of transformation, with only unrepentant right-wingers viewing dissolution as a realistic objective and only a leftist minority, mostly in Western Europe, finding full accommodation to Soviet rule acceptable. That the total disintegration of Soviet control might come in the way and at the pace that it did was not anticipated by any of the three groups.

It is nevertheless worth examining the three alternatives briefly in order to understand the reasoning behind each and the degree to which they remain relevant today. Accomodationists were concerned above all with stability in East-West relations, reasoning that a Soviet Union bordered on the West by a number of states that it viewed as friendly and domestically peaceful would be more willing to engage in serious arms control negotiations and would find it easier to permit political and economic liberalization within its own borders. What seemed at the time to be the irresoluble domestic turmoil and economic paralysis of Poland, combined with the Reagan administration's confrontational response to the imposition of martial law, were viewed as an example of how the unleashing of Eastern European aspirations could lead to heightened international tensions and provoke still harsher domestic policies in the region itself.

At the other extreme, dissolutionists favored uncompromising policies toward Eastern Europe in order to raise the "costs of empire" to the USSR while that country simultaneously had to cope with the expensive task of responding to the American arms buildup and the uncertain threat of the Strategic Defense Initiative. Thus they argued that the West should have forced Poland into default in 1982, because this, they believed, would have required the Soviet Union to pick up the tab. Any trade that might conceivably benefit the East European economies, much less the Soviet military, was to be forsworn. Dissolutionists viewed with suspicion policies singling out for favorable treatment East European states that seemed to be pursuing more liberal domestic policies than the USSR, or that deviated from it modestly on foreign policy questions; such deviations, they suggested, were only tactical. The dissolutionists were willing to accept the risks entailed in an unrelenting confrontational posture in order to advance the goal of weakening or destroying the Soviet "enemy."

The predominant transformationist view, in its many variants, sought to encourage incremental changes through a combination of carrots and sticks that did not frontally challenge Soviet interests or provoke uncontrollable turmoil in Eastern Europe. The goal—expressed best by the felicitous phrase of Willy Brandt's advisor Egon Bahr, *Wandel durch Annäherung* (change through rapprochement)—was to loosen Soviet control gradually and expand the autonomy, personal freedom, and economic well-being of East Europeans, while simultaneously reducing the hostility between East and West. The possibility that such modest policies might lead to the total unravelling of East European Communism was not seriously entertained.

Ironically, the maximalist goals of the dissolutionists have now been realized, even though the policies of the transformationists were by and large those that were followed. While the premises of the accommodationist view, notably the immediacy of the threat of nuclear war, have lost much of their force, the concern with stability associated with it has become, if anything, more urgent. Emphasis on the East-West conflict has been replaced by worries over a united Germany, contagion from revived East European nationalisms, and unmanageable waves of migration. Western triumphalism over the demise of the erstwhile Communist enemy has given way to the growing realization that a stable democratic future for the region is by no means assured.

NEW ALTERNATIVES

The reformulated debate over Eastern Europe centers around the place of the region in an emerging new European order—and, by extension, any new world order. As yet, much of the debate is loosely defined, and the critical question of the respective roles of the United States and the former Soviet republics in such a European order has yet to be answered. Nearly all parties agree that the West should assist Eastern Europe in the difficult tasks of political and economic reconstruction (any objections to such assistance are based on considerations of fiscal stringency and/or the fear that aid will be squandered), but they do not agree on the goals reconstruction should serve. We can distinguish among several emerging foci of concern; these are not mutually exclusive, but represent different emphases or preoccupations. All parties agree that assistance is desirable in itself to help create more autonomous, democratic, and prosperous societies in Eastern Europe, but for most states this concern ranks behind the considerations of perceived national interest expressed in other objectives.

Many continue to favor policies that, consciously or unconsciously, reflect ideological and strategic assumptions persisting from the bipolar worldview that characterized the cold war. To the degree that they are moved to support aid to Eastern Europe, those favoring this perspective do so primarily to ensure that the region's states renounce their past and become uncompromisingly capitalist, antisocialist bulwarks, a reversal of their former status as Soviet buffers. Implicit in this course is a sharp differentiation among the East European states according to their willingness to turn Westward in their choice of political and economic models[5] and in their foreign and defense policies. The successful insistence of the United States that a unified Germany remain in NATO and that some strategic trade barriers be maintained and U.S. efforts to concentrate Western aid on assistance to private entrepreneurs and foreign capitalist investors reflect in part the continuing influence of this view.

A rival perspective gives primacy to the former Soviet Union, but not as a still-menacing foe. Rather, it argues that the need to overcome the appalling economic disarray of the former Soviet republics and prevent their further disintegration and possible descent into civil war must take precedence among Western concerns. The West, in this view, must be willing to commit at least a substantial fraction of the resources it devoted to fighting the cold war to assisting Russia and the other republics. For Eastern Europe, the implication, usually unspoken, is relative neglect. While the experience of the region since 1989 may be cited as a precedent or cautionary example for reforms in the former USSR, the urgency of the crisis in the latter, in this view, overshadows the stubborn but less spectacular problems of its smaller neighbors.

From another perspective, the primary concern is for stability in Eastern Europe, reflecting a fear of revived nationalisms, political fragmentation, unmanageable levels of migration, and economic disorder (e.g., rampant inflation and unemployment) that might infect the West, especially if coupled with similar difficulties in the former Soviet Union. The vision of Eastern Europe as a potential "vast, grim Lebanon"[6] has been given new credibility by the violence in Croatia and Bosnia-Herzegovina; however exaggerated with respect to the northern tier states (the former GDR, Poland, the Czech Republic, Slovakia, and Hungary), such a vision is not inconsistent with the earlier history of the region. There is no gainsaying the extent to which nationalistic impulses compete with liberal democratic tendencies among the new parties and movements that have emerged in the wake of Communism's demise. The policy implications of this concern are not obvious, but most outbursts of nationalist fervor are clearly related to perceptions of economic deprivation or simply to the newly available opportunities for political expression. Thus possible policy responses might include broad economic assistance or pressures for some sort of constitutional engineering designed to heighten political stability (even at the cost of short-term democratic accountability), along with improved regional security arrangements.

From still another perspective, the overriding motivation is the fear of a (re-)united Germany, viewed either as a historically malevolent force or as a dominating and irresistible economic power. Some commentators suggest that the new Germany, because of its economic strength and the previous extensive involvement of both the Federal Republic and the GDR in Eastern Europe, could dominate the entire region while developing a special relationship (with overtones of Rapallo) to a weakened Russia and other components of the former USSR.[7] Adherents of this view are concerned with rebuilding Eastern Europe and reconstructing East-West European relations in such a way as to contain Germany militarily and economically. They do not agree, however, on the best means for doing so. Some have advocated new balance of power arrangements that would include certain East European states, such as a new European security system in which Germany could be permanently enmeshed;[8] others have advocated a revamped NATO; still others, a "widened" or "deepened" European Community.

For its part, the Federal Republic has displayed a new assertiveness in its international role even while responding to pressures to shape its East European policies so as to allay the fears of a resurgent German threat. The idea of a new Western "security partnership" with the East has long had an attraction for Germans, and was promoted by the West German Social Democratic Party (SPD) even before the collapse of Communist rule. The terms and precise functions of a post-Communist European security system and its implications for NATO are by no means clear, however.[9] German efforts to multilateralize assistance to Eastern Europe and to negotiate new economic and political agreements with the region's states must also be seen in the light of its desire to assuage historic fears.

Another important perspective links (or subordinates) the emancipation of Eastern Europe to the process of European integration and seeks to transform the economies and governments of the region as quickly as possible so as to make them acceptable candidates for full membership in the European Community.[10] Within this perspective, however, the significant differences between the partisans of an outward- and an inward-looking Europe are likely to influence the views of each on the terms of Eastern Europe's admission to the EC "club." Few Western Europeans publicly favor the inward-looking variant, in spite of the suspicions of the United States and other economic rivals, but the established pattern of hard-nosed bargaining on the basis of national self-interest within the Community (displayed, for example, in the EC's negotiations with Hungary, Poland, and Czechoslovakia over treaties of association) is apt to propel the organization in such a direction in the absence of a strong commitment to the contrary.

Finally, there is what we may term an economically instrumentalist perspective, which supports the reconstruction of Eastern Europe largely as an adjunct to Western capitalist economies, as a source of low-cost labor and new markets for Western goods. We are not likely to hear such a course advocated openly, since it contains overtones of neocolonialism and is apt to evoke memories of Eastern Europe's pre–World War II peripheral economic status.[11] Indeed, it may not even be the conscious goal of those whose policies would in practice produce such a result. But the logic of unrestrained Western investment in Eastern Europe, especially if unaccompanied by a regional development policy or a social charter like those of the EC but on a grander scale, could produce something of a "Latin Americanization" of the region more or less by default.[12] Timothy Garton Ash has invoked the unhappy but all too plausible vision of Eastern Europe as an "intermediate zone . . . exporting tin saucepans, bottled fruit, cheap shoes, and cheap labor, importing German tourists and Japanese capital."[13] Others put the case still more bluntly: "The East," Adam Przeworski writes, "has become the South."[14]

The objectives of the United States and those of Western Europe toward Eastern Europe have in the past sometimes diverged, in spite of efforts on both sides to minimize the differences. Broadly, Americans were more attracted to the dissolutionist and Europeans (especially Germans) to the accommodationist deviation from the central transformationist position. We can expect the divergence to reappear in a different form and to grow under the changed circumstances of East-West relations in the 1990s, as the bond that united the two, a common fear of Soviet power, recedes into the past. Americans might be expected to place greater emphasis than Europeans on the first goal discussed here (modified bipolar), and perhaps the second (primacy of the needs of the former Soviet republics) and sixth (economically instrumental) objectives, while Western Europeans are likely to be more concerned with the implications of German unity and the dangers of East European instability, as well as more preoccupied by the question of integration of Eastern Europe into the European Community. Americans and Europeans could conceivably find common ground in supporting the integration of the countries of the region into an outward-looking Europe whose economy would complement rather than rival that of the United States, a Europe that would offer expanded opportunities for American-based multinational business. But such an optimistic scenario could easily be frustrated by growing EC–United States tensions and by pressures toward the regionalization of world trade.

Over time, the United States is likely to come to feel it has less at stake in Eastern Europe than it did during the days of the cold war. The attention of the U.S. media, always fickle, has already moved on to other places and events, notably the Persian Gulf and post-Soviet crises. Even the publicity given the Yugoslav tragedy has not rekindled American interest in the less dramatic struggles of the other East European states. In the future, American foreign policy concerns will probably be focussed on the economic challenge represented by the European Community and East Asia, along with the recurring problems of U.S. relations with the Middle East and Latin America. Western Europe, on the other hand, may become increasingly preoccupied with its Eastern neighbors as the problems of economic adjustment, ethnic conflict, and political transformation mount. The consequences of a possible disengagement of the United States from Eastern Europe, a ceding of the area as a sphere of influence to Western Europe, may not be entirely happy ones.[15]

In formulating its goals, the West will need to take into account the priorities of the East Europeans themselves and of the leaders of the republics that formerly belonged to the Soviet Union. The new East European leaders made clear from the outset their aspirations for full economic and political membership in "Europe," as quickly and on as nearly equal terms as possible. But time has brought a somewhat more sober assessment of their chances of achieving this goal quickly, as well as a heightened concern over their future relations with the former Soviet states. The fear of instability and, especially for the Poles and to some extent the Czechs, the wish to contain Germany[16] are significant secondary themes; all also fear economic colonization, even as they compete for Western investment. Overall, there is some tension between the objectives of Eastern and Western Europeans, while the United States must already seem to the former to have become a somewhat marginal player.

The former Soviet republics are likely to have varying priorities toward Eastern Europe. The structures and trading relationships built up over more than forty years that created a high level of economic interdependence between Eastern Europe and the Soviet Union now lie in tatters. Both sides have an interest in reconstructing them, at least in part, because of geographical proximity, some complementarity of needs, the rough similarity of levels of development, and the difficulty both have in breaking into Western markets. Ukraine, Belarus, the Baltic states, and Moldova will want to have especially close relationships with their East European neighbors for historic and cultural as well as geographic reasons; Russia, because of its size, its ownership of the bulk of the former Soviet Union's oil and other resources, and the needs of its industries and consumers, will continue to cast its shadow over the region. Eastern Europeans will unavoidably feel ambivalent over Western aid to these states: while they have reason to fear that assistance that might have come to them will be diverted, they have no interest in seeing an economic collapse in the former Soviet states that would end any possibility of reviving their Eastern trade and threaten them with a flood of desperate refugees.

THE USES OF ECONOMIC STATECRAFT

Long before the issue of the effectiveness of economic sanctions animated discussions over policy in the Persian Gulf, the use of economic means to achieve foreign political objectives had been a matter of intense controversy. During the cold war, Europeans sharply criticized the United States for its belief in the efficacy of economic sanctions to punish the Soviet Union and its Eastern European allies for alleged international misbehavior. American conservatives regularly questioned the value of positive economic incentives—trade concessions, state-guaranteed credits, and so forth—for promoting political liberalization in Communist societies. Communist officials often argued that trade and other economic relations should be carried out on the basis of mutual economic advantage and nothing else, a position that accorded well with the classic free trade position of many Western businessmen and some economists.

Western governments, however, have generally accepted the view of David Baldwin that "economic statecraft" can be a highly useful policy tool—indeed, that it is often the most practicable and effective of the four classic instruments of foreign policy (diplomacy, force or "military statecraft," and propaganda are the others) for the pursuit of their goals.[17] In the past, the argument seemed to apply particularly well to Eastern Europe: there the use of force, or the threat of it, was virtually precluded by the Soviet Union's military presence. The argument that the Western arms buildup of the late 1970s and early 1980s was largely responsible for the revolutionary changes in Eastern Europe (and the USSR) has little merit, but to the extent that the buildup did have influence, it was through the additional economic strains it placed on the Communist states.

In retrospect, one can make a strong case for the effectiveness of certain Western economic policies in influencing changes in Eastern Europe in the last decade and a half. Above all, the generous policies of the German Federal Republic toward the GDR brought concrete political concessions from the latter's regime and helped foster a level of consumerism and a Western orientation that contributed significantly to the regime's downfall.[18] The economic pressures applied to Poland by the West, especially with respect to managing the country's debt, visibly influenced the Jaruzelski regime's policies, for example, the easing of martial law, the release of political prisoners, and the ultimate relegalization of Solidarity. The gradual economic opening to the West pursued by Hungarian reformers was encouraged by the response of Western governments and helped make possible the dismantling of the iron curtain in that country, which quickly influenced events in the GDR and Czechoslovakia as well as in Hungary itself. To be sure, not all Western economic initiatives were successful—the favorable treatment of Ceausescu's Romania, for example—and the results produced were not always those intended (as in the German case). Nor is the catalytic role of Mikhail Gorbachev in stimulating East European reform to be explained by Western policy choices. Still, there are ample grounds for believing that in the 1980s Western economic policies had far-reaching effects in the region.

Whether the same will be true in the 1990s cannot easily be predicted. Employing economic means to promote the construction of stable democratic political institutions and functioning market economies is much harder than was using them for the more limited goals of the past. But the economic needs of Eastern Europe are overwhelming, and all the region's regimes are eager to accept Western assistance in almost any form. All are fragile politically, and their survival is likely to be closely linked to their economic performance. Under such circumstances, the West's choice of economic policies may well prove to be decisive for Eastern Europe's future development—and thus, indirectly, that of the new European and world orders.

THE PROBLEM OF POLICY COORDINATION

The "West," of course, is unlikely to make a single choice, or a consistent set of choices, since it is composed of numerous different actors with differing goals and interests. In a time of growing international economic interdependence, it is customary in studies like this one to call for measures to assure effective policy coordination among Western governments. One should not underestimate the difficulty of such an endeavor, based as it is on a somewhat romantic and not entirely accurate view of an essential Western unity of purpose. In the past, Western policies toward Eastern Europe could be seen as part of a complex, quadrilateral relationship among the United States, Western Europe, Eastern Europe, and the Soviet Union, each of which had its distinctive agenda with respect to each of the others. If the importance of one of these participants, the former Soviet Union, has now diminished, a new one has entered the equation: Japan, or, more accurately, East Asia.[19] Moreover, with the unification of Germany and its attendant difficulties, it can no longer be assumed that Western European interests themselves are necessarily aligned, even though the Western Europeans have stronger mechanisms available for coordination among themselves, through the European Community, than do the United States and Japan with them. What we have, then, is a series of diverse bilateral relationships among the different actors, relationships that enormously complicate the task of forging a common Western policy toward one of them.

It hardly need be added that even individual nations do not always speak with a single policy voice. Partisan divisions may be so severe as to imply significant policy changes with a change of government. Institutional divisions within individual governments, for example, between the American executive and the Congress as well as within the executive, may produce inconsistent policy. Private sector actors, especially banks and corporations, may, in pursuing their own economic goals, subvert the policies of the public sector. Such problems are especially severe in the United States but are also present elsewhere.

Is it, then, futile even to speak of policy coordination? On occasion, one might argue, diverse policies can produce a fruitful division of labor, or a productive competition. But competing policies probably more frequently nullify one another or lead to consequences not desired by any party; the reckless competition among Western financial institutions and governments for lending to Eastern Europe in the 1970s is a notable, cautionary example. It is also worth emphasizing that policy coordination is not a zero-sum affair. If total coordination is impossible, partial coordination is not, and in most cases is preferable to anarchy. To the extent that Western governments can reach some agreement on overall policy goals, of course, the possibility of coordination will be enhanced.

CHOOSING PRIORITIES

In foreign policy-making, we normally expect specific economic policies to reflect broad political objectives. These policies, however, are always subject to more narrowly focussed political pressures at home. In the post–cold war era, the overall objectives themselves are likely to remain more ambiguous than they were at the height of the East-West conflict, national differences over them are likely to be greater, and the policies, correspondingly less comprehensive and coherent.

The West faces multiple dangers in shaping its policies toward Eastern Europe. One is that the area will fall victim to not-so-benign neglect, especially on the part of the United States, because of what seem to be more urgent concerns at home and elsewhere. Another is that the European Community will sacrifice its professed intent of integrating Eastern Europe fully into its ranks to the more parochial interests of its present members. A third is that the means chosen to assist Eastern Europe will be so narrowly "economistic" as to assure their failure—that is, they will be based too uncritically on the advice of Western economists, with an insufficient sense for the political and social context in which their recommendations must be implemented.

In this book I recommend a different course. The disintegration of the Soviet Union makes it more imperative than ever that the United States, the European Community, and other Western nations give high priority to helping Eastern Europe overcome its present difficulties. Doing that successfully requires that the West place special emphasis on the political requirements of economic reconstruction and maximize the participation and mutual cooperation of the new Eastern European polities in shaping their countries' own economic future. The United States must resist the decline of its engagement in Eastern Europe, and Western Europe must reject self-serving policies that are destined to become self-defeating. Both must recognize the pivotal position that the region will occupy in the shaping of the much-invoked but still inchoate new world order.

NOTES

1. Charles William Maynes, "America without the Cold War," *Foreign Policy* (Spring 1990), 5.

2. "Eastern Europe," in this book, refers primarily to the six East European states that belonged to the Warsaw Pact and the Council for Mutual Economic Assistance (CMEA): the German Democratic Republic (GDR), Poland, Hungary, Czechoslovakia, Bulgaria, and Romania. Even though the GDR is now part of a united Germany, Czechoslovakia is divided, and several of the post-Soviet states can now be regarded as part of an independent Eastern Europe, I have chosen not to alter this selection, since this study emphasizes as its background the more than forty years of postwar development of Western economic relations to an "Eastern

European six" viewed as a bloc. For similar reasons, I have not included the states of the former Yugoslavia in this study, even though much of my analysis and several of my recommendations would also apply to them.

I have retained the term "Eastern Europe" instead of the more fashionable, and culturally and geographically more accurate, alternatives "East Central" or "Central Europe," since for those forty-plus years "Eastern Europe" was the political term defining the Communist-ruled lands between Western Europe and the USSR.

3. See Jenonne Walker, "Keeping America in Europe," *Foreign Policy* (Summer 1991), 128–42.

4. Lincoln Gordon et al., *Eroding Empire: Western Relations with Eastern Europe* (Washington, D.C.: Brookings Institution, 1987), 85–90.

5. "Once the fear of Communism has been somewhat allayed, the right will focus on its dislike of state interference in the economy" (Walter Russell Mead, "The United States and the New Europe," *World Policy Journal* 7 (Winter 1989–1990), 65.

6. See Mead, 47–50.

7. For a polemical statement of this view antedating the Eastern European revolutions of 1989, see Ferenc Feher and Agnes Heller, "Eastern Europe under the Shadow of a New Rapallo," *New German Critique* 37 (Winter 1986), 7–57, and the replies in the same issue. More recently (and soberly), see Andrei S. Markovits and Simon Reich, "Should Europe Fear the Germans?" *German Politics and Society* (Summer 1991), 1–20.

8. See, e.g., Richard Helms, "Hold your Horses, Helmut," *Manchester Guardian Weekly*, March 4, 1990, 8; Michael Howard, "Prison that History Built Comes Tumbling Down," *Manchester Guardian Weekly*, March 25, 1990, 11.

9. See, however, Malcolm Chalmers, "Beyond the Alliance System," *World Policy Journal* 7 (Spring 1990), 215–50.

10. See "Survey—Eastern Europe," *Economist*, March 13, 1993, 20–22.

11. See Andrew C. Janos, "The Politics of Backwardness in Continental Europe, 1780–1945," *World Politics* 14 (April 1989), 325–58.

12. "What's going on in Eastern Europe is truly incomprehensible without an understanding of the current plight of Latin America. . . . Poland, for example, has to understand what international capitalism has in mind for it, which is not that it become Sweden but rather that it serve as a sort of Mexico for the emerging post-1992 European powerhouse." Lawrence Weschler, "The Media's One and Only Freedom Story," *Columbia Journalism Review* (March-April 1990), 29. Whether a reified "international capitalism" has quite so conscious a program for Eastern Europe may be questioned, but as an actual outcome, what Weschler describes is far from improbable.

13. Timothy Garton Ash, *The Uses of Adversity* (New York: Random House, 1989), 300.

14. Adam Przeworski, *Democracy and the Market* (Cambridge: Cambridge University Press, 1991), 191.

15. See Mead, 64–69; Michael J. Brenner, "Finding America's Place," *Foreign Policy* (Summer 1990), 25–43.

16. See Stephen Engelberg, "Eager if Uneasy, East Europe Accepts German Investments," *New York Times*, January 23, 1992, 1, 6.

17. David A. Baldwin, *Economic Statecraft* (Princeton, N.J.: Princeton University Press, 1985).

18. I have made this argument at greater length in my "Conflict and Collaboration: The Evolution of Inter-German Economic Relations" (Paper delivered at conference on "After Forty Contentious Years: The Two Germanies since 1949," University of Southern California, February 16–18, 1990).

19. See, e.g., Karoly Okolicsanyi, "Japanese Prime Minister Brings Large Loan Package," *Report on Eastern Europe*, February 23, 1990, 8–11. Japan is now said to be Hungary's largest creditor, holding some 40 percent of the country's foreign debt. Ibid., 9. However, Japanese investment in the region has been small, and trade actually declined 13 percent in the six months ending in September 1990. Hiroko Yamane and Paul Blamire, "Japan and Eastern Europe—the Case for Patience," *The World Today* 47 (April 1991), 61–64. South Korea has also become an active lender to and investor in Eastern Europe, and Taiwan has similar plans. See "Taiwan stellt Fuss in Tür des Osthandels," *Neues Deutschland*, May 4, 1990, 7.

2

Crisis and Opportunity: Eastern Europe Enters the Post-Communist Era

> Our society is still in a state of shock. It could have been predicted, but no one predicted that the shock would be so profound.
>
> Václav Havel, January 1991[1]

> In no instance of a revolution is the break with the past culture total.
>
> Robert Tucker[2]

The difficult transition to democratic rule experienced by the East European states has been marked by the recurrence of forms of protest much like those that earlier helped bring down their Communist governments. Strikes and demonstrations similar to those that had shaken the foundations of the old regimes are now often directed against the new ones. Now, as before, such protests convey a lack of faith in the avenues of political expression deemed legitimate by those in power. They are symptoms of a crisis of political authority that by no means ended with the fall of the old regimes. In this respect as in others, the legacy of the Communist era weighs heavily on the prospects of the region's new democracies.

In the first months of 1988, East European citizens took to the streets in unprecedented numbers to call for fundamental changes in the relationship between themselves and their Communist rulers. In almost every case, the Communist regimes responded to the protests with police arrests and sometimes with brutality.[3] Yet the size and frequency of the demonstrations suggested that something fundamental had changed in Eastern Europe. Many Eastern Europeans were evidently no longer intimidated by the coercive powers of their regimes—and no longer regarded such demonstrations as futile exercises. They had also come to believe, it appears, that the reaction from the authorities was not likely to be draconian; in East Germany, for example, the demonstrators may have anticipated that the response would be more or less what they wanted—immediate expulsion to the West.

Without question, this remarkable outbreak of public protest was inspired in part by the rhetoric and reform ventures of Mikhail Gorbachev. But it also was the consequence of a process that had been unfolding in Eastern Europe over a longer period of time, foreshadowed by the 1968 "Prague Spring" and the rise and dramatic, if fleeting, successes of Solidarity in Poland in 1980. The demonstrations—and the hesitant response of the Communist regimes to them—reflected a rising self-consciousness among East European publics and the multifaceted erosion of the authority and self-confidence of the ruling parties. They culminated barely a year and a half later in the massive protests in East Germany, Czechoslovakia, Bulgaria, and Romania that in a matter of weeks brought down seemingly entrenched Communist regimes that had once appeared to be impervious to effective challenge.[4]

By mid-1990 all six East European states had elected democratic parliaments, and governments responsible to them had taken office.[5] Within just a few weeks, however, thousands of East Europeans took to the streets again, pressing political and economic demands on the new regimes. In East Germany, farmers protested against lost markets and railroad workers against the loss of their jobs. In Czechoslovakia, Slovak nationalists demanded an independent state, and other demonstrators called for the expulsion of former Communists from the government. In Hungary, taxi and truck drivers blocked traffic across the Danube in Budapest, and then across the entire country, in response to a sharp increase in gasoline prices.[6] In Poland, hunger strikers called for the withdrawal of Soviet troops from the country, farmers demanding minimum price guarantees blocked roads, and once-coddled miners struck for higher wages. In both Romania and Bulgaria, turbulent street demonstrations called for the removal of governments chosen in democratic elections only a few months earlier. In Sofia, the Socialist (former Communist) party's headquarters were set ablaze in the wake of a demonstration demanding removal of the building's red star.[7] Popular tolerance for the deliberate, compromise-ridden processes of parliamentary government and for painful economic measures had manifestly worn thin in a very short time.

The return of protest to the streets underscores the tenuousness of the authority of the new East European regimes. Their weakness has both proximate and more fundamental causes. All suffer from the severe fragmentation of what political scientists call their countries' "political cultures," the fundamental attitudes toward politics and the ways of acting in the political sphere that are characteristic of a people and its elites.[8]

Simultaneously, they suffer from a crisis in leadership, a product of the forty years of political monopoly enjoyed by the Communist party and its consequences for the character and experience of the new elites. Finally, they suffer from the severity of Eastern Europe's dual economic crisis: a crisis in part rooted in the failures and omissions of the now-defunct central planning system, and in part resulting from the unprecedented complexity of transforming such systems into functioning market economies and from the unavoidable mistakes and hardships accompanying this process.

THE CRISIS OF POLITICAL CULTURE

The concept "political culture," while developed by Western scholars, acquired a surprising popularity among East European and Soviet writers and even government officials in the 1970s and 1980s, perhaps in implicit recognition of the profound cultural obstacles that frustrated the efforts of the Communist regimes to achieve full legitimacy and to bring about many of the changes they desired in society.[9] While Western states are often assumed to possess more or less uniform political cultures, supportive in greater or lesser degree of democratic institutions and values, the countries of Eastern Europe can be said to have suffered, and to suffer today, from the presence of conflicting and sometimes incompatible political traditions, the product of checkered historical experiences and the variety and fervor of ethnic, religious, and linguistic attachments found in the region.[10]

There is much remaining in Eastern Europe of political traditions dating from the interwar period and earlier, including elements of authoritarianism, bureaucratic dominance, and intense nationalism.[11] The violent, anti-Semitic culture of fascism left its mark particularly on those countries and regions that belonged to the World War II Axis, Germany, Hungary, Slovakia, Bulgaria, and Romania. The official culture of Communist rule was itself divided between an idealized Marxist-Leninist model and the more opportunistic culture of de facto or "real" state socialism.[12] Based on a dogmatized ideology and the dominance of a single Leninist ruling party, the official culture co-existed uneasily with the semioppositional countercultures, which emerged in especially developed form in Poland and Hungary but elements of which could also be found elsewhere. Situated especially among the intelligentsia and young people, these countercultures had by the mid-1980s acquired an impressive degree of autonomy. In Poland, and to a lesser degree elsewhere, one could also speak of distinctive working class and peasant cultures far removed from the proletarian ideal celebrated by the official ideology. Religious and ethnic subcultures, often with distinctive political overtones, also survived (and in the case of Polish Catholicism, flourished) under Communist rule, and reemerged with surprising vigor after the collapse of the old regimes.

The ruling Communist parties were able to take advantage of some elements of the earlier political traditions, particularly those that supported the role of an interventionist state vis-à-vis a weak and divided civil society, but they found their authority subverted by others. Especially in the last decade of Communist rule, the ruling elites repeatedly had to yield ground to social forces they were no longer able to dominate: the churches, the intelligentsia, youth. They found themselves obliged to make concessions to the Western values and tastes that especially the latter two groups often embraced—as well as to indigenous feelings of nationalism. Thus, the East German regime harrassed but ultimately tolerated the independent peace and environmental movements protected by the Evangelical Church; the Polish and Hungarian regimes made little effort to eliminate a flourishing underground culture or the remarkable flood of samizdat journals and books it produced. Even the Czech government sought to co-opt rather than suppress annual commemorations by the young of the death of John Lennon at the "Lennon Wall" in Prague, although the irony of the displacement of Lenin by Lennon could not have been lost on them.[13] As their weaknesses became increasingly evident, the regimes sought to reconstruct the bases of their authority. They attempted to negotiate ever-new versions of the "social contract" under which they offered their populations such things as attractive consumer goods, generous social benefits, blue jeans, rock music, and greater opportunities for Western travel in exchange for political quiescence. But this effort to strike a bargain with rival cultures and subcultures only seemed to whet popular desires for more fundamental changes, and ultimately to hasten Communism's demise.

Unfortunately, the new democratic regimes formed after the upheavals of late 1989 have also been unable to find much either in their countries' earlier political traditions or in their Communist or alternative cultures that could provide a reliable foundation for their authority. Instead of democratic experience and values, they have found authoritarianism and nationalism, and a lust for settling scores with Communists and their presumed collaborators, and with other ethnic and social groups. Instead of market instincts and entrepreneurial skills, they must contend with strong attachments to state-guaranteed security (in spite of the overt rejection of the Communist political and economic systems), and a pent-up consumerism disinclined to be tolerant of calls for patience and sacrifice. "We have clearly defeated the monolithic, visible, and easily identifiable enemy," Václav Havel has remarked, "and now—driven by our discontent and our need to find a living culprit—we are seeking the enemy in each other."[14]

Long-suppressed nationalisms have emerged with an unexpected virulence, seemingly moving into the political vacuum left by the rapid collapse of Communist social controls and the absence of democratic norms and partisan structures ready to replace them. Nationalist ambitions and hostilities have been intensified by economic grievances. Romanians have attacked ethnic Hungarians, Hungarians have demanded better treatment of their kinsmen in Romania and Slovakia, ethnic Turks continue to leave Bulgaria because of discrimination and unemployment in spite of the end of the Zhivkov dictatorship's notorious assimilation campaign, Slovaks complain of Czech arrogance, Poles blame Jews (now a tiny minority in Poland) for their difficulties,[15] East Germans cheer on skinhead attacks upon migrant hostels, and gypsies are victimized almost everywhere.[16] Nationalist aspirations and resentments have become fodder for ambitious politicians and parties.

It was understandable that East Europeans would blame the former ruling parties for the "forty lost years" that—they believed—had laid waste to their economies and prevented them from becoming "normal" European societies. The pervasiveness of the secret police and its network of informers has left a legacy of institutionalized distrust that has deepened the desire for revenge and threatened the credibility of anyone associated with the old regime. But the resultant scapegoating endangers political stability and the achievement of a minimum civic consensus, and has also come to serve as a convenient alibi excusing the indecision and mistakes of the new rulers.

Eastern Europe faces a particularly critical problem of democratic institution building in its need for the creation of a viable system of political parties. As in the West, such parties are indispensable for channelling and focussing public sentiment, offering the newly enfranchised voters meaningful and comprehensible choices, and providing an orderly framework for political conflict. In the heady atmosphere created by the changes of 1989 and 1990, new parties sprouted like mushrooms, but they were greeted with distrust both by the public and the broad social movements that had carried out the East European revolutions; for many, "party" was still associated with the old ruling Communist establishment or with its docile satellites. More fundamentally, the new class system that had been created by four decades of Communist rule did not readily lend itself to the building of a traditional left-right party spectrum along Western lines. The greatly enlarged educated class, made up especially of bureaucrats and economic functionaries, lacked much of a sense of social or political identity, and an independent bourgeoisie, the social basis of European liberalism, was almost entirely absent.[17] The large, relatively skilled working class, often concentrated in very large enterprises, had been alienated from leftist parties by years of hollow Communist rhetoric. Thus neither Social Democrats nor liberal parties fared well in the first post-Communist elections;[18] Christian Democratic, peasant, and nationalist parties won somewhat greater support, but for many the choice they offered was unsatisfactory. Social movements like Civic Forum and Solidarity entered into electoral competition but tried to avoid redefining themselves as parties; they soon found themselves dividing in response to increasingly deep internal fissures.

East European intellectuals and officials have spent a good deal of time searching for foreign political and economic models that might plausibly be applied to their countries' situations. They have found them almost entirely in Western Europe, reflecting long-standing historical inclinations that were if anything strengthened by four decades of Communist rule, but also based on an admiration for their Western neighbors' ability to combine prosperity and freedom with social security and political stability. Such admiration has been coupled with an understandable tendency to minimize the differences among Western systems and to overlook Western failures. The advocacy of a "third way" between Soviet-style state socialism and Western capitalism, so prominent a feature of the Prague Spring and of the ideals of the East German reformers who played a catalytic role in that country's nonviolent revolution, almost entirely disappeared by early 1990. But the obstacles to installing a "West European" type of system—the depressed economic level, the existing "socialist" class structure, the cultural inheritance of state socialism—have proven daunting, and the emergent politics of post-Communist Eastern Europe remind some observers of the region's unhappy interwar experience.

Thus in Poland, the Mazowiecki government, which launched the boldest and perhaps most consistent program of economic reform in the area, was forced to resign after the prime minister himself finished an embarrassing third in presidential elections behind Lech Wałęsa and a little-known Canadian-Polish millionaire eccentric. Wałęsa's campaign and his personal magnetism recalled for some Poles the popularity of the interwar dictator Marshal Piłsudski; unlike Piłsudski, however, once elected he met frustration in his efforts to strengthen the presidency's political influence. Wałęsa's attacks on the government seemed to express the growing estrangement between ordinary Poles and many intellectuals, whose alliance had been vital to the success of Solidarity. Subsequent parliamentary elections produced a fragmented body in which twenty-nine parties were represented and a shaky minority government that survived only until June 1992.

The region's other states have suffered comparable afflictions. In Bulgaria, the reform Socialist (former Communist) government of Andrei Lukanov resigned shortly after its installation in response to a general strike; new elections in September 1991 led to the formation of a minority government under the former opposition, which itself fell a year later. The Romanian government led by Petre Roman was forced from office in the same month by strikes and demonstrations, and the Hungarian government has been rent by internecine warfare between two of its coalition partners. In Czechoslovakia, Havel and the federal government proved unable to compromise Czech-Slovak differences, and the ideologically polarized winners of the June 1992 elections were able to agree only on the terms for dissolving the federation.[19]

EXCHANGING OLD LEADERSHIP FOR NEW

The political predicament of the new Eastern Europe has also found expression in the replacement of the region's leadership. The swiftness with which the East European revolutions swept the old Communist leaders from office was by no means an unalloyed advantage, since new leaders were for the most part unprepared to take their places. The new elites suddenly found themselves, sometimes to their own surprise, in possession of power, but they had at best an incomplete notion of what to do with it. Below the top levels of power, moreover, they were obliged to deal with a stratum of officials and managers who had been employed under the old regime and who combined uncertain democratic loyalties with often badly needed experience, training, and skills.

The feeble resistance the old Communist leaders had managed to muster in response to the democratic revolutions of 1989 was testimony to the profound loss of self-confidence and of ideological conviction they had experienced in the period leading up to them. By the time the upheavals took place, two veteran leaders whose political careers dated to the prewar years had already been forced to retire: Hungary's János Kádár (age 77) and Czechoslovakia's Gustáv Husák (age 76). Two other aging leaders, the GDR's Erich Honecker (age 77) and Bulgaria's Todor Zhivkov (age 78), were pushed hurriedly off the stage by their erstwhile comrades as the crises in their countries mounted. In all four cases the immediate successor chosen was younger but wholly inadequate to the task of reestablishing the party's authority; indeed, long-suppressed divisions and discontents within the party welled up and the leadership, increasingly irresolute, drifted from crisis to crisis. Communists with plausible credentials as reformers, such as Hungary's Pozsgay, East Germany's Modrow, or Bulgaria's Lukanov, found themselves caught between the inflexible instincts of many of their party's functionaries and rank-and-file members, and the hostility and distrust of opposition leaders and much of the public toward anything associated with the old regime.

The new, non-Communist leaders had little in common apart from their inexperience at governing.[20] Their ranks included an electrician and a blacksmith, but most were intellectuals or professionals: playwrights, doctors, churchmen, historians, and engineers. Especially in Poland and Czechoslovakia, several had years of experience in the political opposition, some of it spent in prison; neither Solidarity (and its intellectual supporters in KOR—the Workers' Defense Committee) nor Charter 77, however, could be described as homogeneous political organizations with clearly defined programs for post-Communist rule. Such intellectual dissidents for the most part fared poorly in the second round of elections held in 1991 and 1992, or in the reconstruction of governments; they were replaced by figures who had quietly pursued politically unobtrusive careers under Communist rule.

Some of the new leaders were associated with minor political parties that had survived for years as docile satellites of the ruling Communist parties. Some with apparently authentic credentials as opposition figures had in fact served as agents of or informants for the secret police; once unmasked, they were forced to resign from their new posts, but their discovery fanned popular apprehensions that similar figures still occupied key positions. Economic (and other) specialists who had served under the former regimes and who had in many cases been Communist party members were sometimes placed, or remained, in important posts under the new governments, the economists of the Prague Institute for Prognostics being a notable example. Lawyers, some of whom had defended dissidents under the old order, also assumed a number of important positions.

The unhappy fact that all the new regimes have had to face was that, apart from the courageous few who had openly proclaimed their opposition, few men and women of ability who rose to positions of even modest importance under Communist rule could have avoided being compromised politically at least to some degree.[21] The distinction between regime apologists and opportunists, on the one hand, and those who had genuinely sought to retain their integrity while making unavoidable concessions to the system as it was, on the other, has not always been easy to make in retrospect. Popular frustrations over the survival of members of the former *nomenklatura* in administrative and managerial positions has led to indiscriminate efforts to exclude all former Communist officials from such roles, most notably in Czechoslovakia through its "lustration" law,[22] but also in Poland and East Germany. Such measures, apart from their dubious presumption of collective guilt, are likely to diminish still further the already meager stock of skilled personnel.

Thus the new regimes all but unavoidably combine inexperience, ideological diversity, and great discrepancies in competence, and have been obliged to act in an atmosphere thick with distrust.[23] Such regimes could have been expected to have enormous difficulties maintaining for long public confidence and support or internal cohesion. Accordingly, their effectiveness has been severely impaired even as they begin the unenviable tasks of simultaneous political and economic reconstruction.

THE ECONOMIC PREDICAMENT

What had seemed in most countries to be a slowly rising economic malaise in the last days of Communist rule suddenly took on the proportions of a rapidly mounting crisis once the old regimes had been overturned. Fundamental economic weaknesses, some of which had been hidden behind faulty statistics, now stood revealed as the new governments took office. Each of them soon concluded that the actual economic situation of their country was far worse than they had imagined. The old institutions of the central planning system, their political support structure gone, crumbled well before new mechanisms tailored to the needs of emerging market economies were ready to take their place. Many of the measures hastily undertaken by the new regimes have proven to be inadequate, ill-conceived, or premature; others have been blocked by political infighting, the resistance of affected interests, or the fear of hostile public reaction. Thus the euphoria that at first accompanied the East European revolutions has quickly given way to deepening economic pessimism and social discontent.

The immediate origins of the economic difficulties that the departing Communist regimes turned over to their successors can be traced to the beginning of the 1980s. In the first half of the 1970s production levels and living standards had risen significantly in most of the East European states, but this apparent prosperity depended heavily on Western imports financed largely by generous Western credits. Growth rates declined sharply in the second half of the decade as hoped-for Western markets failed to materialize, increased world oil prices began to drive up the price of Soviet fuel imports, and rising interest rates made the burden of hard-currency debt increasingly oppressive. The Polish crisis of 1980–1981 brought matters to a head: it led to an abrupt cutoff of Western credits to all the East European countries and forced several to the edge of default. The regimes responded with frantic efforts to slash both their hard currency and ruble trade deficits, scaling back imports and seeking to increase exports, largely at the expense of domestic investment and consumption. Even when nominal economic growth resumed in 1984 and 1985, living standards continued to fall or at best to stagnate.

Especially in Poland and Hungary, and less visibly in the GDR and Bulgaria, the sheer size of the outstanding external debt became a serious obstacle to economic recovery. Export surpluses were devoured by the cost of debt servicing; there was no money for the imports needed to modernize plant and equipment and strengthen export industries over the longer run. The problem was apparent in particularly dramatic form in Poland, where foreign debt rose sharply, owing largely to the capitalization of interest in the process of debt rescheduling and to the fall in the value of the dollar, in spite of high levels of repayment and the achievement of a modest export surplus.[24]

Consumers, above all in Poland, Hungary, and Romania, but to a lesser extent elsewhere, felt the resultant pinch in the form of mounting shortages, rationing (in Poland and Romania), and, especially in Poland and Hungary, inflation, a malady once thought to be confined to capitalist economies. Government budgetary deficits and wage increases put money into citizens' hands not matched by increases in supply, feeding consumer frustrations and further reducing confidence in the state's nonconvertible currency. Under such conditions, the partly illegal "second economy" and black markets in foreign exchange flourished. Heightened consumer expectations, stimulated by the East European regimes in the previous decade and fed by the Western media and more widely available Western travel, intensified the discontent.

The international economic position of the six states also worsened. Western markets had become more intensely competitive for East European producers, who saw their share of the market for manufactured goods drop particularly because of the success of the so-called NICs (newly industrializing countries) of East Asia and elsewhere in selling their often superior products at lower prices. Falling prices for fuel and expanded world food production made the export of refined oil products, which had become a staple of East European trade with the West, and of agricultural products, especially important for Hungary and Bulgaria, more problematic. In their economic relations with their most important customer and supplier, the Soviet Union, the East European economies were confronted with new demands that they cut their trade deficits, provide more and higher quality manufactured goods, and make new investments in Soviet energy projects. On the other hand, the prices the Soviet Union asked East Europeans to pay for oil and other fuels and raw materials continued to rise even when world prices began to fall; the Soviets also cut back their oil deliveries to their allies in 1982 by some 10 percent, forcing them to scramble for alternative sources of supply. In short, the terms of trade of the East European states substantially worsened in both East and West.

The obstacles to expanded trade reflected in large measure the structural weaknesses of the East European economies. Productivity levels were generally low; machinery was typically aged and outmoded; fuels, raw materials, and manpower, though in short supply, were used inefficiently. Better economic organization and improved work discipline—persistent themes to which the Communist regimes had already devoted considerable attention—would have enhanced productivity, but the larger problem implicated in productivity figures was Eastern Europe's technological lag behind the West.

The hard currency needed for importing Western technology was scarce, and Western strategic trade rules blocked many potential imports. But even when the technology was available domestically or within the CMEA (Council for Mutual Economic Assistance), funds for investment were inadequate and were often employed wastefully. One painful casualty of the credit crunch of the early 1980s in the East European states was the rate of investment: because of the need to increase exports while curtailing imports and because of the political risks inherent in reducing domestic consumption too drastically, almost all regimes had to cut back investment sharply. Moreover, the GDR and even the Czechoslovak regime, which had avoided the heavy foreign debt obligations of its neighbors, were forced by domestic inefficiency and rising oil prices to devote much of their restricted capital spending to the energy sector, especially expanded brown coal production and, in the Czechoslovak case, nuclear power generation.

Cumulated, and exacerbated by corruption, these problems brought three types of responses. In Hungary, and more haltingly in Poland, the Communist regimes committed themselves to market reforms and actively solicited Western investment and assistance. The Czechoslovak and Bulgarian regimes, pressed by the Soviet Union, promised more limited *perestroika*-style reforms but did little to implement them. The East Germans and Romanians openly resisted reform and sought to circle the wagons against their critics. None of these responses saved the regimes from the extraordinary events that swept them all from power in 1989 and 1990.

The post-Communist governments have inherited nearly all the economic problems of their predecessors. If they enjoyed greater initial public support, the promise of substantially greater Western aid and investment, and greater access to Western technology, they faced new obstacles as well. These included the breakdown of the old systems of centralized foreign trade and domestic distribution, the further erosion of work discipline with the elimination of the old instruments of persuasion and coercion, the disruption of supplies from markets in the Soviet Union, and the loss of alternative fuel sources in Iraq and Kuwait.

The answer that all the new governments have proposed to the economic crisis has been the same one that the more enlightened of their Communist predecessors offered (or, in the cases of the Czechoslovaks, Bulgarians, and East Germans, at least debated): fundamental economic reform. Unrestrained by the ideological considerations or fears for their power that had inhibited their predecessors, the new, mostly moderate-to-conservative regimes have committed themselves to building true "market economies" and to rapid "privatization." These terms have become virtual shibboleths that seem to promise far more than they are likely to be able to deliver to East European citizens for years to come. The explosion of democratic politics, which has given new or greater voice to, among others, enterprises reluctant to give up their subsidies, workers (justifiably) fearing for their jobs, and consumers hostile to price increases, has made the task still more difficult.

When, nevertheless, East European governments began at varying speeds to implement certain pivotal reform measures—freeing prices, slashing subsidies, closing at least a few hopelessly obsolete or highly polluting enterprises and turning others into joint stock companies, subjecting the currency to limited forms of convertibility (or, in the case of the GDR, replacing it with the convertible West German mark)—the short-term costs were not long in making themselves felt. Production fell by as much as 25–30 percent in 1990 and continued its sharp decline in 1991 and 1992;[25]

unemployment and inflation mounted; living standards fell. The United Nations' Economic Commission on Europe has characterized conditions in the region as a "depression."[26] East Europeans, told that such sacrifices are unavoidable if decades of Communist mismanagement are to be overcome, nevertheless have found diverse ways of making their displeasure felt. Everywhere, the new regimes are in danger of losing the race to carry out economic reconstruction before the modicum of political authority they enjoy vanishes.

VARIETIES OF CRISIS

Specialists on Eastern Europe agree that the countries they study are very different from one another culturally, politically, and economically. Yet nearly all seek to generalize about them, just as I have done to this point. Such an approach allows the writer to identify broad trends and avoid immersion in details of interest only to specialists; the disadvantage is that it may blur significant differences and lead the reader to assume a degree of homogeneity that does not really exist. It is now time to disaggregate the previous discussion and single out some of the distinctive elements of each country's economic cum political crisis.

Because of the incorporation of the former GDR into the Federal Republic, many writers no longer treat it as a part of Eastern Europe at all—a mistake, in my view, given the close resemblance of its problems to those of other countries in the region and their common sources. Poland, Hungary, the Czech Republic, and Slovakia are often grouped together, in part because of their more advanced economies and their ostensibly better prospects for success. Romania and Bulgaria, sometimes together with the former Yugoslav republics and Albania, are relegated to a subordinate position and, unjustifiably, often ignored in Western discussions, owing to their presumed backwardness and geographical and psychological remoteness from Western Europe. Even within these conventional groupings, however, national differences remain substantial.

East Germany

East Germany, the former GDR, is of course distinguished by no longer existing as a separate political entity. Yet the five new eastern *Länder* (states) of the Federal Republic share many economic agonies with the remaining East European states, and in some respects offer a cautionary example to them of what a precipitous and inadequately prepared plunge into market capitalism might bring. The former GDR did benefit in certain ways from its economic annexation by the wealthy Federal Republic, although Western commentators often exaggerated its advantages. Its foreign debts were absorbed, its citizens became eligible for the generous West

German social safety net and could migrate freely, and it enjoyed special access to Western investment. The West Germans moved especially quickly to repair the creaking eastern German economic infrastructure. The problem of building strong and legitimate political authority was largely solved by the West German takeover, although filling the leadership vacuum in the five new *Länder* and East Berlin required that large numbers of West German politicians, bureaucrats, and managers be sent in.[27]

None of this has warded off economic crisis. Production figures have fallen sharply, and unemployment has reached levels unanticipated by even the most pessimistic observers. By January 1992 it had reached 1,340,000, some 17 percent of the labor force; when others on "short-time work" (which in many cases meant no work at all) and in government-funded job-training or temporary make-work programs and those who have retired early are added, the total reaches 40 percent or more.[28] The East to West migration that had brought about the opening of the Berlin Wall resumed at an alarming rate, as the economic gap between the two parts of the country widened; public morale declined apace. "In economic terms," remarked a former East German economist, "Germany is more divided than before unity."[29] Private investment in the East has remained well below expectations, in spite of government exhortations and subsidies. The conversion to hard currency devastated the once-heavy trade between eastern Germany and the USSR and the rest of Eastern Europe, at the expense of production and jobs on both sides. By the end of 1991 industrial output had fallen to just one-third its level at the beginning of 1990; in 1991 the East produced less than 7 percent of Germany's total GNP.[30] Although the sheer quantity of western German support, some $100 billion in both 1991 and 1992,[31] has kept living standards from sharply declining and will in time probably bring some recovery from the deeply depressed conditions of 1992, the likelihood seems great that most of the former GDR will remain a poor, dependent backwater of the Federal Republic (and of the European Community) for decades to come.[32]

Poland

In Poland, the first government led by non-Communists benefitted from the reputation and organizational strength of Solidarity and its popular leader, Lech Wałęsa, as well as from the support of the Roman Catholic Church. The thoroughly discredited Communist party, reorganized in two rival social democratic groups, quickly lost what little remaining influence it might have had. But a year of economic hardship and growing divisions in Solidarity, nurtured in part by the discontent and ambitions of Wałęsa himself, culminated in the defeat of Prime Minister Mazowiecki in presidential elections and the resignation of his government in November 1990.

The new president, Wałesa, and government promised to continue and even accelerate the economic reform plan named for the Finance Minister Leszek Balcerowicz. Viewed as a model by many Western officials, the "shock therapy" of the Balcerowicz plan reduced Poland's runaway inflation and stabilized the zloty. Store shelves and street vendors offered goods in quantities and of a variety not seen for years in the country, but the ability of Poles to buy them was sharply constrained by high prices and the government's effort to freeze wages. Industrial production and the gross national product fell sharply in 1990 and 1991, but appeared to level off in 1992; inflation in that year was still 45 percent, however, and by November unemployment had reached 13.5 percent. Repeatedly, Polish governments faced shortfalls in expected revenues and, under pressure from the international financial community, were forced to seek painful reductions in spending.[33] President Wałęsa's battles with parliament and his wavering support for successive prime ministers and for economic reforms reinforced rising public disaffection with Poland's new political class.

In elections in October 1991, only 40 percent of eligible voters bothered to go to the polls. Those who did produced a parliament splintered among the representatives of twenty-nine parties, none of which had won more than 12.5 percent of the vote.[34] The first postelection government expired in June 1992 in a firestorm of controversy over "decommunization"; its more pragmatic if embattled successor, under Hanna Suchocka, succumbed to a no-confidence vote in May 1993.

Hungary

A poll taken toward the end of 1990 showed Hungarians to be the most pessimistic people in the world over their economic future.[35] Their pessimism reflects the steady decline of the Hungarian economy throughout the 1980s in spite of the pioneering role of the country's Communist leadership in promoting market-oriented economic reform. The former ruling party, renamed the Hungarian Socialist party, was rewarded for its efforts with a crushing defeat in the March 1990 elections; it remains, however, a significant opposition force, and some of its former leaders retain considerable personal popularity.

The government constituted after the elections and led by Jozsef Antall, a historian and former museum director, is a coalition of the Hungarian Democratic Forum, or HDF (a right-of-center party with Christian Democratic and moderate nationalist overtones), with the smaller Smallholders' and Christian Democratic People's parties. From the beginning, the coalition has been burdened with internal disagreements (notably over the issue of returning land to the peasants from whom it was seized after 1947) and has been taxed by its opponents with indecision and ineffectualness. Hungarian voters rendered an early, negative electoral judgment on the coalition's work in the local elections of September and October 1990, when the HDF came in second to its major rival, the Association of Free Democrats; in later polls, the standing of both parties declined. Nevertheless, the Antall government was the only one in the region still in power three years after its installation.

In its economic program, published in September 1990, the government emphasized "entrepreneurship, private initiative, government noninterference in economic affairs, and . . . privatization as the key features of [its] economic ideology and its key priorities."[36] But it also pledged to avoid "shock therapy." Critics noted the program's lack of clarity and internal contradictions, and events proved that the government could not meet the timetable outlined in it. Meanwhile, although Hungary has continued to attract more Western investment than the other former East bloc countries and still seems to Western visitors to offer more Western-style comforts, most economic indicators have continued to fall. Unemployment had risen to 12.2 percent by the end of 1992,[37] and industrial production was down 19 percent in 1991 and another 10–12 percent in 1992, while prices rose 36 percent and an estimated 22–25 percent in the same two years.[38] Government deficits have reached record levels.[39] Some 270,000 private businesses, most of them small, were already in operation by mid-1990, but the privatization of large state firms has proceeded slowly.[40]

Czechoslovakia

Czechoslovakia benefitted initially from the extraordinary popularity of its president, Václav Havel, and from the country's reputation as the only East European country with a relatively successful democratic experience during the interwar period. In the June 1990 elections, Civic Forum, the umbrella movement that had led the country's "velvet revolution," and its Slovak counterpart, Public Against Violence, won a strong mandate. Havel reappointed a Slovak and former Communist, Marián Čalfa, as prime minister. Ideological differences within Civic Forum, however, eroded the unity of the movement. Václav Klaus, the finance minister chosen over Havel's nominee as chairman of the Forum, sought consciously to move it to the right and purge it of its leftist components; his efforts led to a formal split in February 1991. Public Against Violence also splintered, and a Christian Democrat became Slovak prime minister.

From the outset, the demands of Slovak politicians for autonomy or full independence threatened to divide the fledgling democratic state, even though only a minority of Slovaks appeared to favor complete separation. The failure of protracted negotiations between the two sides to achieve a settlement and the ideologically incompatible governments produced by new elections in June 1992 made that outcome certain. Apart from longstanding cultural differences, the resistance of Slovaks to radical economic reform, which they correctly believed would damage them disproportionately, and the unwillingness of Czech leaders to moderate such reform persuaded both sides to accept the country's division.

In his 1991 New Year's message, Havel remarked gloomily that, economically, "what a year ago seemed to be a dilapidated house is, in fact, a ruin."[41] Nevertheless, Czechs and Slovaks began to experience the pains of economic transition somewhat later than their neighbors, primarily because extensive economic reform began only in January 1991 with the freeing of most prices. The determination of the controversial Klaus, an avid student of Milton Friedman's works, to press forward with such reforms and with privatization, together with the near-collapse of Czechoslovakia's Soviet trade, increased the level of economic hardship rapidly; although inflation levelled off after an initial leap, industrial production and the GDP plummeted. The pain, however, was not evenly distributed, and the discrepancy grew with the country's division. Unemployment has thus far remained low in the Czech Republic, while reaching 11 percent in Slovakia; most Western investment has gone to the former. By mid-1993 the new Slovak government, its popularity tumbling, was facing a serious economic crisis.

Bulgaria

The Bulgarian elections of June 1990 were won, more or less fairly, by the Communist party, now ostensibly reformed and rechristened the Bulgarian Socialist party (BSP). It did not long enjoy the fruits of its victory, however; mass demonstrations and a general strike orchestrated by the opposition alliance Union of Democratic Forces (UDF) brought down the government of Andrei Lukanov in November 1990. Earlier the popular UDF leader Zhelyu Zhelev had replaced a Communist as the country's president. The BSP was afflicted with deep internal divisions, with a conservative majority resisting its reformers, including Lukanov. For its part, the UDF, a fractious coalition of sixteen groups, discovered in its moment of triumph that its chairman, Petar Beron, had been a secret police informer; he quickly resigned. New elections, held in October 1991, produced a narrow victory for the UDF, but it was able to form a government only through the support of the predominantly Turkish Movement for Rights and Freedom (MRF). That government fell a year later in the wake of attacks by President Zhelev; following two months of political wrangling, an odd coalition of the MRF and BSP, supported by dissident UDF deputies, emerged to elect a fragile government of "national responsibility" headed by a nonparty economist.[42]

Bulgaria's political turmoil has taken place against the background of nearly catastrophic economic difficulties. In March 1990, the country stopped payment on its foreign hard-currency debt of over $10 billion. The gross domestic product is reported to have fallen by 40 percent in the eighteen months following January 1990 and continued its sharp decline through the end of 1992. Foreign trade, heavily dependent in the past on the country's close ties with the Soviet Union, all but collapsed. Unemployment reached 13.3 percent by September 1992.[43] Price reform early in 1991 drove up the cost of food severalfold, but eased the severe shortages that had produced hoarding and local rationing of such goods as sugar and vegetable oil; inflation continued at a rate of about 100 percent in 1992.[44]

Successive Bulgarian prime ministers have promised a rapid transition to a market economy, and several important reform measures have been approved. But the deep fissures in both major political camps and a debilitating wave of strikes have delayed their effective implementation. In February 1992, the International Monetary Fund (IMF) suspended the second payment of a $250 million credit because of its dissatisfaction over the pace of privatization and financial reforms. The country did, however, resume some payments to its commercial creditors in exchange for their willingness to consider a substantial debt reduction.

Romania

Romania's National Salvation Front (NSF), the body of ostensible reform Communists that took power in the popular uprising that ended the despotic reign of Nicolae Ceauşescu and his family, transformed itself into a political party in order to compete in the country's May 20, 1990, elections. In spite of winning an overwhelming victory—its presidential candidate, Ion Iliescu, received some 85 percent of the vote—the NSF's right to rule was immediately challenged by the political opposition, concentrated heavily among students and the intelligentsia in Bucharest and other major cities. In June, Iliescu's use of miners from the Jiu Valley to brutally suppress the protests further estranged the opposition from the regime, and earned the latter international opprobrium. Only gradually did the reform efforts of the prime minister, Petre Roman, restore some modicum of international respectability to the government.

By imposing devastating hardships on his people, Ceauşescu had left Romania free of foreign debt, but otherwise in desperate economic straits. His restrictions on imports "led to a pervasive technological backwardness in practically every sector of the economy," in the words of a Western expert.[45] Romania ranked at the bottom of the six East European CMEA members in GNP per capita and almost every other index of economic well-being.

Yet industrial output has dropped 54 percent since the revolution, and inflation in 1992 was some 250 percent.[46] Foreign debt has mushroomed, but Western assistance has been modest, and the government's reform efforts have been blamed for mounting hardship. The reforms contributed to growing fissures and ultimately a split within the NSF as well as a bitter personal conflict between Iliescu and Roman.[47] In September 1991, the miners returned to Bucharest—under whose auspices is still unclear—and forced the Roman government from office. Elections in September 1992 produced a minority, pro-Iliescu government, which almost at once had to face the harshest winter since the days of Ceauşescu.

OPPORTUNITIES

The generally dark portrait I have sketched in the preceding pages is reflected in the widespread pessimism of East Europeans. Economic discontent and the public wrangling and apparent ineffectualness of the new governments have bred a renewed popular cynicism. Voting turnout has fallen sharply, and some grumble that things were better under the Communists. The former Communist parties, now ostensibly reformed, still capture a significant proportion of the vote—12 percent even in Poland, where the party was especially discredited, 14 percent in both the Czech and Slovak republics, nearly 33 percent in Bulgaria.

The opening to the outside world, however, has given others a new sense of possibility. The hundreds of thousands of newly established private businesses are testimony to the presence of such hope; to be sure, many such ventures fail, owing partly to the depressed incomes of their potential customers, but there are also notable successes. Consciousness of opportunity is most heavily concentrated among the young, the educated, and the mobile; the outlook of the middle-aged and elderly and the unskilled, especially in smaller towns and rural areas, is much bleaker.

Seeking to mobilize and enlarge the sense of opportunity while confronting a dispiriting mixture of protest, petty squabbling, and apathy, East European governments find themselves caught in a classic "devil's circle." They need to strengthen their authority in order to undertake and carry through necessary economic measures, but they must demonstrate some degree of economic success if they are to gain public confidence and remain in office long enough to implement their programs. They possess no proven formulas for righting their economies; the pressures of international lending agencies and the advice of many of their own economists run directly counter to many of the demands they face from their workers and electorates.

Only the West seems to offer a possible avenue of escape from this dilemma. The continuing parade of Western officials, businessmen, academics, and ordinary tourists through East European capitals in the period since the region's revolutions is testimony to their lively interest in its future prospects. In spite of the pervasive economic and political uncertainty, both public and private Western entities, from a variety of motives, have sought involvement in the region's transformation.

Private Western investors have come into eastern Germany and Hungary in substantial numbers, and have ventured more cautiously into Czechoslovakia and Poland, while largely ignoring Bulgaria and Romania. Overall Western investment has failed to rise to the level of East European expectations. Western entrepreneurs find themselves frustrated by persistent bureaucratic bottlenecks, frequent uncertainty as to the locus of decision-making authority in rapidly changing economic and political systems, and in some cases lack of clarity over property ownership. Western banks, which have virtually halted nonsubsidized loans to Eastern Europe, are also often reluctant to support Western ventures there. High inflation, rapidly changing laws and regulations, and the difficulty of repatriating profits furnish additional obstacles.

However great the importance of private investment, the policies and actions of Western governments and other public and nonprofit institutions will be still more critical. Only they are in a position to contribute significantly to political as well as economic reconstruction; yet the latter, as I argue throughout this book, is heavily dependent on the former. (Such institutions also risk weakening the authority of the new regimes if they pursue ill-advised policies.) International lending agencies—the International Monetary Fund, World Bank, and the new European Bank for Reconstruction and Development—have greatly expanded their commitments to Eastern Europe, with Poland and Hungary benefitting disproportionately to date, but in doing so they have imposed conditions that have not always been helpful politically. Bilateral government aid, with the exception of West German support for its new eastern provinces, has been relatively modest, and has also been concentrated on Poland and Hungary. Governments, international agencies, and private groups have offered diverse forms of technical assistance, in such areas as management training, privatization, and financial reform. The contribution of the United States government has to date been unimpressive, although American nonprofit institutions, such as charitable foundations and universities, have lauched a large number of often admirable small-scale initiatives. In most cases, the emphasis has been on economic reconstruction in isolation from its political context.

Nevertheless, there are some grounds for optimism, especially if we compare Eastern Europe's present situation with its plight during the 1930s. Unlike conditions at that time, Western economies are fundamentally strong, and Western governments stable and unambiguously democratic. Thus both as a model and as a source of material assistance, the West is in basic respects better positioned to help the East move toward economic growth and political maturity. For their part, the East Europeans have thus far retained a surprisingly tenacious commitment to democracy in spite of its evident frustrations. The tasks that remain are formidable enough, however, and delay is likely to strengthen the forces resisting their completion. The West must work together with Eastern Europeans to identify the region's real needs, mobilize the necessary resources, and use them effectively to help bring about the political and economic transformation that both desire. Western policy will have to be generous, informed, and imaginative; unfortunately, that has not always been the case in the past.

NOTES

1. Václav Havel, "The New Year in Prague," *New York Review of Books*, March 7, 1991, 19.

2. Robert Tucker, *Political Culture and Leadership in Soviet Russia* (New York: Norton, 1987), vii.

3. See Vladimir Kusin, "East European Police Impair Independent Action," *Radio Free Europe [RFE] Research*, March 18, 1988.

4. For two of the best accounts of the fall of the Communist regimes in Eastern Europe, see J. F. Brown, *Surge to Freedom: The End of Communist Rule in Eastern Europe* (Durham, N.C.: Duke University Press, 1991), and Timothy Garton Ash, *The Magic Lantern: The Revolution of '89 Witnessed in Warsaw, Budapest, Berlin and Prague* (New York: Random House, 1990).

5. A small qualification is necessary for Poland, whose elections in June 1989 were held under special rules negotiated between the Communist leadership and Solidarity, guaranteeing the Communists a certain number of seats in the lower house; after the elections, the two parties agreed to form a Solidarity-led government that included Communist ministers. In Bulgaria, elections were held in June but a new government was not sworn in until September 21.

6. See Alfred Reisch, "The Gasoline War: Order or Chaos," *Report on Eastern Europe*, November 9, 1990, 6–11.

7. Mark Baskin, "The Politics of the Attack on the BSP Headquarters," *Report on Eastern Europe*, September 20, 1990, 8–12.

8. A great many definitions have been offered for this term, and many more for the parent concept of "culture." The one given here is my own; unlike some, it includes aspects of behavior as well as attitudes. See Archie Brown, "Introduction," in Archie Brown, ed., *Political Culture and Communist Studies* (Armonk, N.Y.: M. E. Sharpe, 1984), 1–12. See also Tucker.

9. See Archie Brown, "Soviet Political Culture through Soviet Eyes," in Brown, ed., 100–14. Brown notes that the term was used by Lenin in the 1920s, in a passage frequently cited by Soviet writers on the subject. Ibid., 104.

10. "Indeed, the persistence and resilience of distinct and diverse political cultures within the matrix of common Communist institutions is quite striking." Joseph A. Rothschild, *Return to Diversity* (New York: Oxford University Press, 1989), 225.

11. See George Schöpflin, "The Political Traditions of Eastern Europe," *Daedalus* (Winter 1990), 55–90; see also Rothschild, 222–25.

12. For a similar distinction, see Jack Gray, "Conclusion," in Archie Brown and Jack Gray, eds., *Political Culture and Political Change in Communist States*, 2nd ed. (New York: Holmes & Meier, 1979), 260.

13. "John Lennon and Pacifism in Czechoslovakia," *Radio Free Europe Research*, March 25, 1988, Czechoslovak SR5, 27–29.

14. Havel, 19.

15. See Abraham Brumberg, "Polish Intellectuals and Anti-Semitism," *Dissent* (Winter 1991), 72–77.

16. See Irene Runge, *Ausland DDR: Fremdenhass* (Berlin: Dietz Verlag, 1990); Zoltan D. Barany, "Democratic Changes Bring Mixed Blessings for Gypsies," *RFE/RL Research Report*, May 15, 1992, 40–47.

17. See János Mátyás Kovács, ed., "Rediscovery of Liberalism in Eastern Europe," special issue of *East European Politics and Societies* 5 (Winter 1991).

18. In the second Czechoslovak elections of June 1992, Václav Klaus's Civic Forum Party, a conservative party advocating liberal economic reform, won one-third of the vote in the Czech Republic; the self-consciously liberal Civic Movement was unable to win the 5 percent of the vote needed to enter parliament, however. The two Polish parties supporting the liberal Balcerowicz reforms won just 20 percent of the vote between them in the October 1991 elections.

19. Paul Wilson, "The End of the Velvet Revolution," *New York Review of Books*, August 13, 1992, 57–64.

20. Biographical information on the new political leaders can be found regularly in the *RFE/RL Research Report* and its predecessor, *Report on Eastern Europe*. See also Rudolf L. Tökes, "Hungary's New Political Elites: Adaptation and Change, 1989–90," *Problems of Communism* (November–December 1990), 44–65; Ákos Róna-Tas, "The Selected and the Anointed: The Making of the New Parliamentary Elite in Hungary," *East European Politics and Societies* 5 (Fall 1991), 357–93; Thomas A. Baylis, "Leadership Change in Eastern Germany: From Colonization to Integration?" in Peter H. Merkl, ed., *The Federal Republic at 45* (New York: New York University Press, forthcoming 1994).

21. Rita Klimova, Czechoslovakia's first post-Communist ambassador to the United States, has remarked that during the years of Communist rule "most people compromised, except for a handful of dissidents who wouldn't, and who went to prison. I was never in prison myself. So I count myself among those who, although I was fairly active in the dissident movement in the final years, have made compromises during my life that I probably shouldn't have made, that were not healthy." "Interview: Rita Klimova," *Europe, Magazine of the European Community*, December 1990, 11.

22. See Jiri Pehe, "Parliament Passes Controversial Law on Vetting Officials," *Report on Eastern Europe*, October 25, 1991, 4–9; Jeri Laber, "Witch Hunt in Prague," *New York Review of Books*, April 23, 1992, 5–8. On page 7, Laber remarks that "those most actively seeking vengeance are not, I found, the former dissidents," but those who, "on the whole, come from the 'gray zone'—neither Communists nor dissidents, they sat back, did nothing to incur disapproval, and were not persecuted. They suffer now, some say, from a guilty conscience and are taking revenge for their own humiliation."

23. For a suggestive analysis of the problems of creating elite consensus in post-Communist regimes, see John Higley and Jan Pakulski, "Revolution and Elite Transformation in Eastern Europe," *Australian Journal of Political Science* 27 (March 1992), 104–19. It has been argued that consensus among Southern European elites during the transition period helps account for their countries' success in building

stable democratic institutions. Robert Fishman, as cited in *Report on Eastern Europe,* December 14, 1990, 38.

24. See Paul Marer and Włodzimierz Siwiński, eds., *Creditworthiness and Reform in Poland* (Bloomington: Indiana University Press, 1988).

25. Some economists have argued that available statistics tend to overstate the fall in production, or that much of the lost production represents low-quality goods for which there was little or no demand, and thus should not be mourned. But the magnitude and persistence of the reported decline (as well as collateral evidence) suggest that the figures reflect real economic hardship.

26. *New York Times,* December 3, 1991, C6.

27. Fourteen of the fifty-two government ministers named after the October 1990 elections in the five east German states were from the West, including the minister-president of the most populous state, Saxony, and three of the five finance ministers. *Informationen* (Bundesminister für innerdeutsche Beziehungen), December 7, 1990, 15–24; December 13, 1990, 13–15. Subsequently west Germans replaced east Germans as minister-presidents in Saxony-Anhalt and Thuringia.

28. *Generalanzeiger* (Bonn), February 6, 1992, translated in *German Tribune,* February 14, 1992, 3.

29. Ibid.

30. Wilfried Herz, "Vom Traum zum Trauma, *Die Zeit* (N. Am. ed.), September 18, 1992, 5.

31. Of this sum, about two-thirds was expected to support consumption, often of West German products; thus, in the words of one writer, it amounted to an expensive job-creation program for the West. Peter Christ, "Der Fortschritt ist eine Schnecke," *Die Zeit,* July 5, 1991.

32. See Thomas A. Baylis, "Transforming the East German Economy: Shock without Therapy," in Michael G. Huelshoff, Andrei S. Markovits, and Simon Reich, eds., *The New Germany in the New Europe* (Ann Arbor: University of Michigan Press, forthcoming 1993).

33. Ben Slay, "The East European Economies," *RFE/RL Research Report,* January 1, 1993, 114; Anna Sabbat-Swidlicka, "Poland: A Year of Three Governments," ibid., 106–7.

34. See David McQuaid, "The Parliamentary Elections: A Postmortem," *Report on Eastern Europe,* November 8, 1991, 15–21.

35. See *New York Times* (N.Y. ed.), January 2, 1991, 6.

36. Karoly Okolicsanyi, "The Economic Program for National Renewal," *Report on Eastern Europe,* December 14, 1990, 9.

37. *RFE/RL News Briefs,* January 11–15, 1993, 17.

38. *RFE/RL Research Report,* April 24, 1992, 25; Slay, 114–15.

39. Karoly Okolicsanyi, "The Hungarian Budget Deficit," *RFE/RL Research Report,* July 17, 1992, 53–55.

40. See Marvin Jackson, "The Privatization Scorecard for Eastern Europe," *Report on Eastern Europe,* December 14, 1990, 25; Michael Marrese, "Hungary Emphasizes Foreign Partners," *RFE/RL Research Report,* April 24, 1992, 25–33.

41. Stephen Engelberg, "Czech Conversion to a Free Market Brings the Expected Pain, and More," *New York Times,* January 4, 1991, 3.

42. Kjell Engelbrekt, "Technocrats Dominate New Bulgarian Government," *RFE/RL Research Report,* January 22, 1993, 1–5.

43. *RFE/RL Research Report,* August 21, 1992, 40.

44. Ben Slay, "Economic Reformers Face High Hurdles," *RFE/RL Research Report,* January 3, 1992, 104; Duncan M. Perry, "Bulgaria: A New Constitution and Free Elections," ibid., 79–80; Slay, "The East," 114, 117.

45. Cited in Steven Greenhouse, "Reformers in Romania Fight Ceauşescu Legacy," *New York Times,* August 6, 1990, 4.

46. Slay, "The East," 114, 116; *Economist,* March 13, 1993, 9. According to one Romanian study, 42 percent of Romanian families were destitute in 1992. Michael Shafir and Dan Ionescu, "Romania: Political Change and Economic Malaise," *RFE/RL Research Report,* January 1, 1993, 110.

47. See Gabriel Topor, "The National Salvation Front in a Crisis," *Report on Eastern Europe,* August 16, 1991, 24–29.

PART I

THE LEGACY OF THE COMMUNIST ERA

3

Postwar Western Economic Policies toward Eastern Europe: A Brief History

> We must arm ourselves with more flexible economic tools. We must be willing to recognize growing divisions in the Communist camp, and be willing to encourage those divisions.
>
> John F. Kennedy, 1960[1]

> Trade policy can never be a substitute for foreign policy. Rather, the task of politics should be to regulate interstate relations . . . so as to allow trade relations to develop as freely as possible.
>
> Wolf von Amerongen, German industrialist, 1970[2]

Western economic policies toward Eastern Europe even in the years of the cold war never constituted anything like a seamless whole. The leading Western powers, while ostensibly in agreement on their goals, often differed as to appropriate means. In fact, their objectives also suffered from ambiguity: to what extent, for example, was the West seeking to contain, and to what extent did it want to roll back, Soviet influence? As Europe recovered economically from World War II and the preeminence of the United States correspondingly receded, disagreements over policy became more open. These disagreements stemmed in part from conflicting economic interests and perceptions, but also reflected differences in the domestic policy-making environment.

Consistency in economic policy was also inhibited by the fact that officials other than those laying down the more general lines of policy often formulated individual decisions, and diverse, more particularistic interests were likely to shape them. Thus specific economic policies could sometimes take on a life of their own. We shall observe in this chapter a certain tension between the announced principles of "grand" foreign policy and the usually incremental and sometimes opportunistic development of foreign economic relations.

This book is concerned with economic policies directed specifically toward Eastern Europe, and not with those aimed at the Soviet Union. Especially during the cold war, however, the two could not readily be separated from one another, given the military alliance and close economic ties between the Soviet Union and its East European partners. Any decision to favor or to discriminate against one could be expected to have at least some influence on the other. The United States, especially, viewed its policies toward Eastern Europe almost entirely as a function of its policies toward the Soviet Union. This is not to assert that American policies toward the two were identical. On the contrary, the United States was sometimes embarrassingly candid in suggesting that an economic opening to selected East European states, for example, Romania, might serve the same end as the denial of economic benefits to the Soviet Union, that of reducing Soviet influence. Nevertheless, while the ebb and flow of the cold war influenced American policies toward Eastern Europe, it affected them less dramatically than it did U.S. policies toward the Soviet Union.

A satisfactory treatment of the development of Western economic policy must address the emergence of U.S.–West European differences over goals and strategies and their evolution in the years after the outbreak of the cold war. Such differences were in part prefigured by the divergent historical patterns of West European economic relations with Eastern Europe and the distinctive economic profiles and geopolitical interests of the West European states, but they became fully visible only in the course of the 1950s. The United States justified its policies largely in terms of cold war strategies, while the Europeans saw theirs as expressions of greater realism and pragmatism. These differences have left their mark even in the post-Communist era. In particular, the divergent approaches of the United States and West Germany command our attention.

Two characteristics of the policy of the United States have especially distinguished it from those of its allies. First, as early as the late 1940s the United States began to pursue and gradually to refine a policy of what was later termed "differentiation": the according of differentiated economic treatment to the Soviet Union on the one hand and certain East European states on the other, and also among the East European states themselves, depending on their presumed divergence from Soviet foreign policy or from the Soviet model of domestic rule. Western Europeans were less inclined to modulate their policies on such a basis. Second, American policy can not reasonably be understood without reference to the influence of Congressional intervention, or the threat of it, in the policy-making process, a phenomenon that has no real parallel in Western Europe, and whose result has been to reduce the consistency and thus, on the whole, the effectiveness of U.S. policy.

Thus at times Congress attacked administration policies as insufficiently vigilant toward the Communist threat, and at other times as showing too little concern for East-West bridge building and trade. It responded both to grass-roots anti-Communism (as reflected in the 1960s' boycotts of Polish hams and Czech crystal) and to the pleas of American exporters. The ongoing battlefields of executive-Congressional disagreement included the questions of export controls, Most Favored Nation status, and trade credits and subsidies. In general, the greater independent power enjoyed by Congress relative to European parliaments, combined with the easy access of ethnic interest groups, businesses, trade unions, and ideological groups to Congressmen, tended to give such interests greater influence over policy. Moreover, the inevitable conflicts over policy among governmental agencies and departments often were not resolved within the executive itself, but were transported into the Congressional arena.

A final caution is in order. Except at times of crisis in the region, Eastern Europe has not been a high priority area for either American or Western European foreign policy. Perhaps the most notable exception was the partial one of the Federal Republic of Germany in the period of *Ostpolitik*. Here, however, the Federal Republic's underlying priority was not Eastern Europe per se but rather the "German question" in its various guises. This comparatively low standing meant that a good deal of significant day-to-day policy toward Eastern Europe was made in both Europe and America not by elected politicians but by officials, but it also meant that such policies could on short notice be overridden by the more politically sensitive concerns (often domestic) of each state. The same is likely to be true in the future as Eastern European events recede from the front pages. The implementation of policy, to put the same point rather differently, could be, and probably in the future will often continue to be, substantially at variance with the government's professed ideals precisely because of their lower priority.

THE PREWAR BACKGROUND

The United States, Britain, and France redrew the map of Eastern Europe at the Versailles peace conference in 1919, but it was the defeated German state that was to play the most active economic role in the region during the interwar years. The new Bolshevik regime in the Soviet Union, diplomatically ostracized and economically isolated, carried on very little trade with the countries that were later to become its economic dependencies, and trade among the East European states themselves was modest. The region's foreign economic relations were dominated by the West, and with some exceptions, notably that of Czechoslovakia, followed a classic neocolonial pattern: the East Europeans sent agricultural products, raw materials, and semifinished goods to the West in exchange for industrial products.[3]

The United States ranked third among Eastern Europe's trading partners during this period, just behind Great Britain. But it had no conscious and consistent policy toward the region, economic or otherwise, in keeping with its post–World War I isolationism and in spite of Wilson's role at Versailles and the interest of the many recent immigrants from the area in the fate of the region's fledgling democracies.[4] Britain's "island mentality" toward Europe as a whole was reflected in a similar disinterest in pursuing an active policy toward Eastern Europe, in spite of its substantial trade with the region. France sought to build ties with several Eastern European countries as part of a vain effort to balance German influence, but, as Joseph Rothschild has noted, persistently refused to "support its alliances in the area with adequate trade relations." The West's "politico-economic myopia" was also illustrated by its withdrawal of capital credits to Eastern Europe during the depression of the 1930s, contributing to a catastrophic drop in production and employment.[5]

Into this breach rushed Nazi Germany. Even in the early 1920s Germany had been by far Eastern Europe's largest trading partner. Hitler pursued a conscious policy of expanding German economic influence in the region, particularly in Hungary and the Balkans, in service of his military and territorial ambitions. Germany bought East European agricultural surpluses and supplied capital for the spurt of state-sponsored industrialization that took place in the late 1930s. By the eve of World War II, Rothschild says, "Germany's economic hegemony over East Central Europe was more categorical than it had been in 1913."[6]

ECONOMIC COLD WAR

That hegemony ended, at least for the time being, with German defeat. In the early postwar period, Eastern Europe's economic relationships were shaped by the mounting hostility between the United States and its allies and the Soviet Union. The United States extended its policy of containment of the Soviet Union more or less automatically to the Eastern European states, which it viewed, by and large accurately, as the satellites of the Soviet Union. The Truman administration put sharp restrictions on trade with Communist countries into effect in early 1948, shortly after the Communist coup in Czechoslovakia; these were formalized in the Export Control Act of 1949. American trade with Eastern Europe as well as with the Soviet Union dwindled to virtually nothing; in 1952 the United States exported just $67 million worth of goods to the entire region and imported goods valued at only $1 million. Trade between Western and Eastern Europe did not end entirely, but stagnated at a low level (in spite of Western Europe's economic recovery) until after the death of Stalin in 1953.[7]

The promulgation in 1947 of the Marshall Plan to assist European recovery, and the Soviet and East European response to it, simultaneously signalled the breaking of most economic ties between the two emerging blocs. In his famous June 5 address at Harvard University, Secretary of State George C. Marshall had invited all the European nations, including those in the East, to enter a bold cooperative venture with the United States to help bring about economic recovery, but the American proposals were formulated in such a way—probably intentionally—that the USSR was highly unlikely to accept them. Indeed, had the Soviet leaders been astute enough to do so, the United States Congress would almost certainly not have approved the plan.[8] At a preliminary meeting with his French and British counterparts in Paris, the Soviet foreign minister, Molotov, showed a surprising degree of interest in the scheme, but finally did what he was expected to: he rejected proposals for the preparation of a coordinated European response to the United States that would have outlined the continent's needs and presented a joint plan for dealing with them. Molotov attacked such an approach as interference in the internal affairs of the individual states and condemned the inclusion of Germany in the proposal. The USSR withdrew from the conference on July 2, and pressured its East European allies to decline invitations to a follow-up conference on July 12. These states had shown some initial interest in the proposal, and the then still ostensibly independent Czech government, including its Communist ministers, officially accepted the invitation. Stalin, however, informed the Czech foreign minister, Jan Masaryk, that the Soviet Union would view participation as an "unfriendly act," and the Czechs reversed their decision and withdrew. This seemed, as Kovrig puts it, "incontrovertible proof that the East Europeans were no longer masters in their own houses," and confirmed that the two halves of Europe would go their own, separate economic ways.[9]

Subsequent American policy sought to assure that outcome. The 1948 legislation implementing the Marshall Plan contained provisions using aid under the program as a lever to force recipients to deny strategic exports to "nonparticipating," that is, Communist, European countries.[10] The Export Control Act of 1949 authorized the president to prohibit or curtail exports "from the standpoint of their significance to the national security" to Communist-ruled states and directed him to develop a system of controls jointly with the U. S. allies.[11] On August 12, 1949, the United States published a list of goods whose export to Communist states would require a specific license from the Department of Commerce. In November, the United States and Britain, France, Italy, the Netherlands, Belgium, and Luxemburg created the Coordinating Committee on East-West Trade Policy (COCOM); West Germany, Canada, Japan, and the other European

NATO members (except Iceland) joined later. COCOM's function was to prepare, on the basis of consensus, joint lists of goods whose shipment to Communist states was to be prohibited on strategic grounds.[12] It survives over forty years later, and even in 1991 was still the central forum in which the United States and Western Europe compromised their disagreements over strategic trade with the East. Even when first adopted, however, strategic export controls came under fire from European critics who felt that such measures were of dubious worth and would require much more economic sacrifice by Europeans than by Americans. Others, including Americans, argued that controls would tighten the hold of the USSR over its East European clients. "The trouble with the embargo," Nicolas Spulber noted, "is simply that the more effective it becomes with respect to the small countries of the Soviet orbit, the greater becomes the bargaining position of the U.S.S.R. in its intrabloc relations."[13]

The outbreak of the Korean War in June 1950 nevertheless led to an intensification of American export controls. The Battle Act of 1951 included provisions barring any American assistance to countries shipping strategic goods to the Soviet Union or countries "under its domination."[14] The United States maintained its own extra-COCOM list of goods embargoed for U.S. export, and also sought to prevent the transshipment of such goods through third countries. Imports from Communist states were also restricted by the Trade Agreement Extension Act of 1951, which directed the president to deny Most Favored Nation (MFN) treatment to the USSR and countries dominated by it;[15] the Truman administration's warnings that such actions would violate existing treaties and provisions of the General Agreement on Tariffs and Trade (GATT) fell on deaf Congressional ears. Private capital exports to Communist states, except Yugoslavia, Albania, and Bulgaria, were effectively prohibited under the 1934 Johnson Act, although certain transactions were exempted by Justice Department interpretation.[16]

The initial decision of the United States to differentiate in its economic treatment of the East European states was thrust upon it by the unexpected expulsion of Yugoslavia from the Cominform (the Communist Information Bureau, then the instrument of Soviet domination over the world Communist movement) in June 1948. Stalin's casting out of the Yugoslav party was the culmination of a series of disputes between Tito's independently inclined leadership and the insistence of the Soviet leader on bloc conformity. The significance of this portentous split was "not immediately grasped in Washington," but by 1949 the United States had adopted a policy designed to support the perpetuation of the division. Tito, for his part, was initially reluctant to turn to the West, but as Soviet pressure, including an economic boycott, increased, he sought to repair his relationships with nearby Western countries, improve trade relationships with Great Britain, and elicit a loan from the U.S. Export-Import Bank. The first American loan, for $20 million, was announced in September 1949.[17] Other forms of U.S. assistance followed.

By mid-1956, American grants, loans, and sales for local currency to Yugoslavia totalled $598.5 million; military assistance during the same period amounted to nearly an equal figure. Clearly, the United States did not view aid to Yugoslavia as aid to a Communist state—Truman, in advocating emergency relief for the country in 1950, studiously avoided any reference to Yugoslavia's political system—but as an investment in the struggle *against* Communism, at that point equated with Soviet Communism.[18] The effect of large-scale Western aid and the continuing Soviet boycott, however, was to reorient Yugoslavia's economy from East to West and to help enable the Yugoslavs to undertake bold experiments in reshaping their ideology and their domestic political and economic institutions and thus embark on a separate "Yugoslav road" to socialism.[19]

A rather different exception to the all but total severing of Western economic relations with Eastern Europe was formalized in the Berlin Agreement of September 1951 providing for substantial "interzonal" (later "intra-German") trade between East and West Germany. This agreement, made at the height of the cold war, was justified as an instrument for keeping alive the question of German reunification; it also served de facto as a means of protecting Western access to Berlin, a fact that helps explain allied acquiescence in it. Theoretically, intra-German trade was not viewed as foreign trade at all but as trade between two different currency areas of "Germany." From a low of 287 million West German marks (expressed as artifical "clearing units of account") in 1951, turnover in inter-German trade rose to over a billion marks by 1955 and continued to grow steadily thereafter.[20] This special arrangement gave the Federal Republic a lever with which it could subtly influence East German policy (even though its one attempt to do so overtly, in 1960, was repulsed)[21] and foreshadowed the distinctive role it was to play in the future in East-West economic relations.

A "DIFFERENTIATED" POLICY TOWARD POLAND

The return of Wladyslaw Gomulka to the leadership of the ruling Polish United Workers' Party in October 1956, only a few months after he had been released from prison, highlighted a change in character of the Polish regime that seemed only slightly less dramatic than Yugoslavia's expulsion from the bloc eight years earlier. The death of Stalin and the beginning of the process of de-Stalinization in the Soviet Union had brought with them a political and cultural thaw in Eastern Europe that was most pronounced in Hungary and Poland. In Hungary the process was brought to an abrupt, if only temporary, end with the crushing of the Hungarian Revolution by Soviet troops. In Poland, however, the Soviet leadership reluctantly accepted the change in leadership and a degree of domestic liberalization unmatched (at the time) elsewhere in the bloc. It included the de facto abandonment of agricultural collectivization, a measure of reconciliation with the Roman Catholic Church, an expansion of cultural freedom, the introduction of competition for some parliamentary seats, and the establishment of workers' councils.

Although Poland thus acquired an impressive degree of independence from Soviet tutelage in domestic affairs, it never broke with the Soviet Union in foreign or defense policy, avoiding the errors of the Hungarians. But it did undertake foreign policy initiatives, notably the Rapacki plan for a nuclear-free Central Europe, which suggested a small measure of autonomy. It also openly solicited economic assistance from the West, as in early 1957 when a Polish delegation went to Washington to request $300 million in credits.

Viewed in retrospect, the American response was halting and modest. Negotiations dragged on, partly because of opposition in Congress, which included the influential Senate Minority Leader William Knowland. These discussions finally led to the granting of a $30 million credit, primarily for the purchase of capital goods, and agreement to sell American agricultural surpluses amounting to $65 million, to be repaid in Polish zlotys. In subsequent years similar amounts were granted, again primarily for the purchase of farm surpluses. Beginning in 1957, the United States loosened its restrictions on exports to Poland, removing the requirement for special licenses for many goods on the extra-COCOM list. In 1960 President Eisenhower granted MFN status to Poland, formally determining in the process that the country was not Soviet-dominated as understood under the Trade Agreement Extension Act. All these measures taken together were insufficient to offset the economic influence of the Soviet Union and the other CMEA states (even if the Polish regime had desired that). Nevertheless, the special treatment accorded to Poland (and to no other East European CMEA state until Romania in 1964) established a special American economic relationship with that country that continues to the present.[22] It also implanted in the minds of many American policymakers the understanding that Eastern Europe could no longer be viewed as "a monolithic bloc dominated and controlled from one country."[23]

A comparison of American with West German policy may be instructive here. The Poles had raised the question of opening formal diplomatic relations with the Federal Republic in 1955; three years later, the proposal won the support of the Social Democratic and Free Democratic *Bundestag* delegations (and apparently the United States), but the Adenauer government rejected the idea. It did so in part because of the Hallstein Doctrine, which barred the Federal Republic from recognizing any country (except the Soviet Union) that had recognized the East German regime, and in part because of the strong resistance of the organizations of expellees from the "lost territories" of the formerly German East. Nevertheless, the West Germans, with the assistance of a modest revolving credit facility, quadrupled their exports to Poland between 1954 and 1958, while imports rose still more quickly.[24] As hopes for the continued improvement of relationships with the East faded with the Berlin crisis of 1958, however, Polish–West German trade stagnated.

TOWARD "BUILDING BRIDGES"

The discrepancy between the volume of German trade with Poland and that of the United States reflected the growing divergence of American and Western European perspectives on policy toward East-West economic exchange. From the end of the Korean War, Western European pressures to reduce the coverage of COCOM embargo lists became "quite intense."[25] Marshall Plan aid ended in 1953 and could no longer be used as a lever to enforce harmony between the American and West European approaches. The United States agreed to substantially shorten the COCOM list in 1953–1954 and 1955–1958, extracting in exchange the condition that the remaining controls be more strictly enforced, a compromise ("higher fences around fewer items") that was to be repeated several times in subsequent years.[26] The costs of the embargo policy were becoming more apparent to West Europeans, whose economies had recovered their production capacities but who now faced a widespread Western recession. At the same time the Soviet Union and Eastern Europe were showing an increased interest in foreign trade and beginning their slow movement away from Stalin's policies of economic autarky. The United States, still in the thrall of an intense anti-Communism, felt obliged to compensate for COCOM list reductions by increasing its own, unilateral restrictions, even though these could not be as effective as multilateral ones. On the import side, the United States continued to deny MFN treatment to Communist states (except Poland and Yugoslavia) even as Britain and France moved to reduce their quantitative limits on imports from the East.

Under the impact of the Polish events, however, other American voices began to make themselves heard; one such voice was that of then-Senator John F. Kennedy who, beginning in 1957, sought unsuccessfully to amend the Battle Act to give the president greater discretion in trade policy toward Eastern Europe. As he put it in a 1960 campaign speech, the United States needed to arm itself with "more flexible economic tools" in order to take advantage of the "growing divisions in the Communist camp."[27] American business interests became increasingly restive over the trade advantages they perceived that their West European competitors enjoyed, including fewer export controls and the possibility of offering long-term credits.[28] But conservative forces opposed to any trade liberalization retained a powerful foothold in Congress, a position symbolized by the passage of the "captive nations" resolution in 1959 and reinforced by the Berlin Wall and the Cuban crises of 1961 and 1962. These rival forces produced something of a counterpoint between liberalizing initiatives undertaken by the executive and restrictive legislation interposed by the Congress.

Both President Kennedy and President Johnson sought to create a more favorable atmosphere for loosening the inhibitions on East-West economic exchange and took specific measures to promote that end. Under Kennedy, a $140 million wheat deal between the United States and the USSR graphically suggested the possibilities and the potential profitability of expanded East-West trade. Johnson delivered a speech at Virginia Military Institute in mid-1964 advocating "building bridges" to Eastern Europe,[29] and appointed a special committee on U.S. trade relations with the region. The Miller Committee's report, recommending the expansion of trade to encourage favorable "internal evolution and external behavior," along with hearings of the Senate Foreign Relations Committee held in 1964, were designed to mobilize a constitutency on behalf of expanded East-West economic relations.[30] Zbigniew Brzezinski, later a member of the State Department's Policy Planning Council under Johnson, provided some of the intellectual justification for such a course in a 1961 article (written with William Griffith) and in subsequent publications.[31] Brzezinski argued explicitly that a policy of "peaceful engagement" toward Eastern Europe might serve to loosen the ties of those countries to the Soviet Union.

In 1964, the Johnson administration relaxed export controls toward Romania on all goods and technology without an immediate military potential; the Romanians, in return, "gave assurances" that they would not reexport such goods. Romania, which had initiated the negotiations leading to the relaxation, had drawn the favorable attention of American policymakers through its sometimes ostentatious departure from the Soviet leadership on such foreign policy questions as the Sino-Soviet dispute and the division of labor within the CMEA.[32] After Yugoslavia and Poland, it thus became the third beneficiary of the policy of differentiation. The Johnson administration also sought to move on a wider front; in 1966 it removed some 400 items from its commodity control list for the Soviet Union and all the Communist countries of Eastern Europe and supported the sending of trade missions to and from Eastern Europe.[33] On the other hand, it declined a Czech request in early 1968, as the ferment of the "Prague Spring" was building, for a $500 million loan, although it relaxed export licensing procedures to that country. Bolder forms of assistance, it apparently feared, might jeopardize the position of the Dubček leadership. Indeed, at about the same time, consultations between the Czechs and the West German government over possible private credits aroused deep distrust in Moscow and East Berlin.[34]

Congress, for its part, imposed a series of restrictions on East-West trade that became more severe as U.S. involvement in the Vietnam War grew deeper. Even in 1962, it inserted provisions in Kennedy's Trade Expansion Act removing the president's discretion in granting MFN status to any Communist nation; energetic administration efforts won exceptions for Poland and Yugoslavia, on the condition that the president ascertain that granting them MFN was important to the national interest of the United States and would promote their independence. The Johnson administration's attempt in 1966 to have the president's MFN discretion restored was defeated.[35] In 1964, 1967, and 1968 Congress progressively narrowed the possibility of granting Eximbank loans and guarantees to Communist states. In 1964 and 1965 Johnson was still able to—and did—make a finding of "national interest" to justify such financing. By 1968, however, the Fine amendment had prohibited all Eximbank financing for Communist states aiding North Vietnam, which in practice meant all but Yugoslavia. Similar restrictive legislation prohibited the signing of PL-480 agreements with countries trading with or transporting goods to North Vietnam.[36]

DETENTE AND WESTERN ECONOMIC POLICIES

By the time the Nixon administration took office in 1969, East-West trade statistics painted an unambiguous picture of the results of the divergence between American and Western European policies. American trade with the Soviet Union's East European allies amounted only to about 5 percent of total Western trade with the same countries. Congress, however, was now prepared to support some measure of trade liberalization. In 1968 the Johnson administration had launched a new drive to ease restrictions on trade with Eastern Europe, but it had been derailed by the Soviet invasion of Czechoslovakia. In 1969, however, Congress passed a new Export Administration Act; it acted "under the pressure of business interests" concerned over their disadvantages in competition with the West Europeans in East European markets. The new legislation actively urged the expansion of trade with the East and sought to limit export controls to goods making a "significant contribution to the military potential" (not, as before, the military and *economic* strength) of states that might threaten American security.[37] Further relaxation of American controls and licensing procedures followed; gradual reductions in the COCOM list also continued. In 1971 Congress again permitted Eximbank financing for Eastern European countries, albeit on presidential determination. President Nixon issued such determinations for Romania in late 1971 and for the Soviet Union and Poland in 1972.

In short, American policy had shifted from a presumption that trade with the East was to be fundamentally distrusted unless proven innocuous to an activist drive to expand such trade. The motivations for this change were both economic and political. On the one hand, sectors of American business had become increasingly conscious of the previously unrealized opportunities offered by Soviet bloc trade, and concern had risen over the deteriorating American balance of payments. On the other hand, the argument now was widely accepted that trade could help build bridges to the East European states and might increase their autonomy; somewhat inconsistently, the warming of detente with the Soviet Union also became a justification for expanding economic ties to the region. The result was a flurry of activity designed to promote trade: visits by the secretary of commerce, the secretary of state, and the president himself to Eastern Europe; the dispatching of trade survey missions; the establishment of trade offices, joint economic commissions, and the like with individual countries; and the creation of the Bureau of East-West Trade in the Department of Commerce. In 1973 President Nixon created a cabinet-level East-West Trade Policy Committee, chaired by Treasury Secretary George Shultz.[38]

While pursuing a broad expansion of trade with Eastern Europe and simultaneously with the Soviet Union within the framework of detente, the Nixon administration and the Congress did not abandon the policy of differentiation; indeed, the policy was formalized in a 1973 National Security Decision Memorandum which even established a rank ordering of the East European states for the granting of American favor.[39] Romania was the chief beneficiary of special American treatment in this period. In 1971 the administration further shortened the commodity control list for that country and made it the first bloc nation permitted to receive the newly reauthorized Eximbank financing. The administration supported Romanian membership in GATT and in 1972 sought Congressional approval for MFN treatment for the country; this status was granted only in 1975, however, after Nixon had left office.

This turn in American policy roughly paralleled the success of West Germany's *Ostpolitik,* which produced treaties with the Soviet Union and Poland in 1970 and culminated in the signing of the East German–West German basic agreement of 1972; a treaty with Czechoslovakia was signed the following year. *Ostpolitik* in effect brought Bonn's diplomatic and political relations with the East into somewhat greater harmony with its already vigorous economic relations and laid the basis for the further expansion of the latter—now still more highly valued by the West Germans because of its purported contribution to the stability of political ties.[40] Germany policy under *Ostpolitik* continued to depart from United States policy toward Eastern Europe, however, in avoiding overt differentiation among the states of the region on the basis of their divergence from the Soviet Union. The rationale for German policy, expressed in the phrase "change through *rapprochement,*" was subtly but significantly different from the divide-and-weaken philosophy underlying "peaceful engagement."

These developments coincided with a greatly increased interest on the part of the Soviet Union and most of the Eastern European states in importing Western goods and in utilizing Western credits, which in turn were available in almost unlimited measure from both private banks and Western public lenders, a consequence of the high levels of liquidity of the former (produced largely by recycled petrodollars) as well as of the conscious policy decisions of the latter. Under these circumstances Western exports to Eastern Europe in 1975 reached 361 percent of the level of 1970; imports were 274 percent of the 1970 figure.[41] Although these figures are somewhat exaggerated by inflation and the fall in the value of the dollar that began in 1972, they still represent a flowering of East-West trade that exceeded the hopes of the advocates of liberalized exchange.

Intruding upon these economic fruits of detente was the Jackson-Vanik amendment passed by the U.S. Congress in 1974. The amendment required that the granting of MFN status to Communist states be conditioned on free emigration from them or a presidential finding of substantial progress toward that goal. It passed in spite of the efforts of Secretary of State Kissinger to block it by obtaining substantial concessions on Jewish emigration from the Soviet Union. The amendment's approval suggested some waning of enthusiasm for detente, but it also reflected the precipitous decline in influence and the distraction of the Nixon administration as the Watergate scandal unfolded, as well as the political ambitions of Senator Jackson and the influence of his devoutly anti-Communist aide Richard Perle.[42] Although directed at the Soviet Union, Jackson-Vanik also applied to Eastern Europe, and was to constitute a formidable obstacle to the future expansion of American economic relations with those states.

The emphasis of the Carter administration on the observance of human rights as a central criterion in the foreign policy treatment of other nations might have been expected to reinforce Jackson-Vanik in linking economic relations with Eastern European countries more closely with domestic liberalization. The growing use by Soviet and East European dissidents of "basket III" (the human rights provisions) of the 1975 Helsinki accords in their efforts to wrest better treatment from their country's regimes encouraged a similar linkage. But in fact the new administration initially sought to continue the loosening of restrictions on East-West trade, while linking it more explicitly to other policy goals.[43]

The administration's human rights commitments undoubtedly reinforced its efforts to extend especially favorable treatment to Hungary, by general agreement now the most "open" country of the bloc domestically (and the one with the most generous policy on foreign travel by its citizens). The United States granted Hungary MFN status in 1978 as well as more symbolic signs of favor, for example, the return of the crown of St. Stephan in the same year. U.S.-Hungarian trade remained small in comparison with that with the other two bloc countries enjoying MFN, however. Overall, American trade with Eastern Europe more than doubled between 1975 and 1980, but it continued to be dwarfed by that of Western Europe.

Eastern Europe enjoyed somewhat greater attention under the Carter administration than under its predecessors primarily because of the presence of Zbigniew Brzezinski as the president's national security advisor. Brzezinski and Carter retained the essence of the policy of differentiation, modifying it (in Presidential Directive 21 of September 1977) to replace the rigid rank ordering with a more general division of the East European states into two groups—one including Romania, Poland, and Hungary, the other, Bulgaria, Czechoslovakia, and the GDR. Reportedly, some in the Departments of State and Commerce would have gone further and moved away from the categorization altogether, but the issue was never really joined.[44] Deteriorating relations with the Soviet Union in the late 1970s did not immediately affect American economic ties with Eastern Europe, but shortly before leaving office the administration found itself confronted with a request from Poland's (pre–martial law) government for $8 billion in Western assistance, $3 billion of it from the United States. After discussions with European allies, Carter decided that a defeated administration could not appropriately make such a commitment. In 1979, however, the administration had granted Poland $500 million worth of agricultural guarantees and credits, and in 1980, immediately after the signing of the Gdansk agreement between the Solidarity trade union and the government, it announced the extension of $670 million more in credit guarantees, a record amount, through the Commodity Credit Corporation (CCC).

CONTROVERSIES OF THE REAGAN YEARS

The Reagan administration came to power sounding an anti-Communist rhetoric unmatched in the American executive since the early years of the cold war, but among its officials no clear consensus emerged over the practical implications of this rhetoric for policy toward Eastern Europe. As in other policy areas, the administration was divided between ideologically uncompromising hard-liners and more pragmatic conservatives having a stronger sense of continuity with the policy of previous administrations and of the need to coordinate policy with the United States's European allies. The hard-line faction believed the Soviet Union's economic system to have proven a massive failure that only Western trade and credit and Eastern technological espionage had managed to keep afloat. In order to protect Western security interests—and to make the failure of Communism manifest to all—the West, this view continued, should deny the Soviet Union all forms of assistance (including most trade) and should add to the economic pressures on it where possible, for example, by forcing it to compete in an expensive new arms race. From this perspective, the more the Soviet Union could be forced to use its own resources to bail out its economically troubled allies, the better. Accordingly, the United States should offer no credits or other trade advantages to Eastern Europe—and of course no goods of conceivable strategic value.[45] Such a policy, which implied the subordination of any effort to loosen East European ties to the Soviet Union through economic blandishments to the larger purpose of weakening the Soviet Union directly, was resisted in the more traditional corners of the administration and was never authoritatively adopted by it.

From the moment it took office, the Reagan administration found itself confronted with a major East European crisis, one for which it had no settled policy. Prior to the December 13, 1981, imposition of martial law, the administration after prolonged internal debate had approved modest amounts of food aid to Poland and agreed to defer most of the official loan repayments due that year.[46] After martial law, however, the administration reversed course and imposed economic sanctions against both the Soviet Union and Poland itself. In the latter case these included the termination of CCC credits for agricultural exports, the suspension of MFN treatment, and the denial of American agreement to Poland's membership in the IMF; the last two came only after the official banning of Solidarity in October 1982. Proposals were widely mooted in Congress and the press as well as the administration to force Poland into formal default, in the hope of increasing the financial pressure on the Soviet Union. These were unsuccessful, in part because of the understandable opposition of American and European bankers.[47] Western Europe gave little support to the Polish sanctions, and the major American anti-Soviet sanction, directed at the Urengoi pipeline deal, erupted into a bitter American–West European controversy.

The effectiveness of the sanctions in influencing subsequent Polish and Soviet behavior remains uncertain; the Polish regime complained bitterly about them and used (vastly overstated) estimates of their cost to explain the country's continuing economic difficulties. But the regime also ended martial law (substituting for it, however, legislation codifying most of its repressive regulations), and granted amnesty to most political prisoners, thus meeting two of the three U.S. announced criteria for lifting sanctions. These concessions, together with pressures from the allies and later from Polish-Americans, the Polish church, and even some Polish dissidents themselves, finally persuaded the administration to remove the sanctions. The initiative in restoring the Jaruzelski regime to some international respectability, however, was taken by the French and the Germans.

After some initial uncertainty, the Reagan administration continued the policy of differentiation. Administration officials discussed a proposal to make favored economic treatment of any East European country dependent on both its deviation from Soviet foreign policy and domestic liberalization;[48] had it been approved, it would for the moment have ended differentiation, except in the case of nonaligned Yugoslavia. The proposal did not prevail, but the administration enunciated the differentiation principle more openly and bluntly than had its predecessors, most notably in statements by (then) Vice President Bush after his 1983 visit to Yugoslavia, Romania, and Hungary.[49]

Under Reagan, the State Department modestly increased the level of its contacts with the German Democratic Republic, traditionally at the bottom of the differentiation hierarchy. This slight movement reflected the obvious economic importance of the GDR in the bloc and probably also responded to the open divergence of Soviet and East German views on East-West relations that surfaced in 1984. However, a State Department proposal to liberalize trade with the GDR foundered on the unanimous opposition of other executive agencies.[50] Hungary kept its favored position (and its MFN status) in the eyes of the American administration, but the annual requirement under Jackson-Vanik of waiver renewal for MFN status for Romania provided an opportunity for critics of the harsh domestic repression of the Ceauşescu regime to voice their objections before Congress.[51] In 1983, the Romanians were persuaded to rescind their special tax (based on supposed state expenditures for education) on would-be emigrants, presumably because of the threat of loss of MFN status and also because of "stronger financial inducements" from the Federal Republic.[52] Five years later, however, Romania quietly informed the United States that it was no longer interested in MFN status, perhaps in order to avoid still another painful set of hearings.

The attempt of the Reagan administration to tighten controls over strategic exports met strong resistance not only from the West European allies but also from factions within the U.S. government, particularly the Commerce Department. The highly publicized dispute over the Soviet pipeline project acquired its particular explosiveness through the American attempt to apply its sanctions extraterritorially, to branches of U.S. companies in Western Europe and to European subcontractors of American firms. Europeans openly expressed their suspicions that the United States was using the pretense of strategic controls to secure its own competitive advantage. The controversy was resolved essentially by the United States yielding, although it saved face in the customary way by winning an agreement to establish study commissions on various aspects of the problem and to undertake stricter enforcement of COCOM regulations.

By the final months of the Reagan administration, the confrontational elements of its policies toward the Soviet Union and Eastern Europe had disappeared almost entirely under the halo of the INF (Intermediate-range Nuclear Force) agreement and successive Reagan-Gorbachev summit meetings. Enthusiastic talk of expanded U.S. trade with bloc countries became respectable inside as well as outside the administration. Under the extension of the Export Administration Act, passed in 1985 after a two-year struggle, the administration was able to support the decontrol of obsolescent items on the COCOM and domestic lists and accelerate licensing procedures even while the influence of the Defense Department in determining militarily "critical technologies" was expanded, enforcement procedures were strengthened, and penalties for violations increased.[53] In 1987 the government restored MFN status to Poland. An administration that had begun by insisting that it would stop "selling the rope" with which the Communist enemy was seeking to hang the West ended by having to defend itself against the same charge directed at it from conservative circles.

THE RESPONSE TO THE EAST EUROPEAN REVOLUTIONS

The unexpected turn of the East European states toward democracy in 1989 and 1990 fundamentally altered the premises on which over forty years of Western economic policy had been based. By riveting the attention of Western publics on the region, it also altered the environment of policy making, just as earlier East European crises had. Western governments, responding to the enthusiasm of their own populations, undertook significant economic initiatives toward the region, but the legacy of the old policies did not immediately disappear. The United States continued to pursue its policy of differentiation, Congress and the president continued to disagree on important points, and in some respects the actual and potential divergence of American and European policies seemed to grow.

The Bush administration had barely taken office when the Polish Roundtable talks produced dramatic agreements to relegalize Solidarity and to hold competitive elections for seats in parliament. Seeking to seize the public relations moment, the administration quickly developed plans for new economic assistance, and in July the president made well-publicized visits to both Poland and Hungary and announced modest programs emphasizing aid to private enterprise in the two countries and support for multilateral (especially IMF) loans to them. Congressional Democrats, seeking to outbid the president, and Polish-American groups pressed for substantially larger amounts and won grudging administration consent for an increase. At the economic summit in Paris that followed his trips to Warsaw and Budapest, Bush agreed to permit the European Community to coordinate emergency assistance to both countries—a portentous decision little noticed at the time that quietly ceded to Western Europe the leadership role in a program that was shortly to encompass the entire region.

The drama of the opening of the Berlin Wall brought the changes in Eastern Europe to the top of the front pages, and riveted the attention of the leading West European actor, the German Federal Republic, on the economic needs of East Germany, the rising tide of GDR migrants to the West, and, shortly, the prospect of unification. The United States and its allies welcomed the peaceful revolution in East Germany and the "velvet revolution" that quickly followed in Czechoslovakia, as well as the more cautious changes in Bulgaria and the end of the Ceauşescu dictatorship in

Romania. The "end of Communism" in the region, now visible to all, brought a wave of proposals for new economic assistance and changes in trade policy to undergird the emerging democratic governments.

But even at this stage the United States gave signs of moving to the economic sidelines. Confronted with the savings and loan crisis and mounting deficits, Congress and the president shunned expensive new initiatives. In February 1990, the United States found itself isolated in resisting proposals by its allies to ease COCOM restrictions; it subsequently agreed to a partial relaxation. Negotiations over President Mitterrand's proposal for a European Bank for Reconstruction and Development, designed to make substantial loans available to Eastern Europe, were slowed by American insistence that the money go only for private undertakings and that none go to the Soviet Union. Then, the crisis unleashed by Iraq's invasion of Kuwait in August all but entirely erased the region from the American consciousness.

The Europeans, in these months, proceeded to extend the EC-administered PHARE program from Poland and Hungary to the other East European states. Following a compromise that limited Soviet participation and permitted some funding of public projects, the new European Bank began operations in London, with its first loans extended in 1991. The Germans, now facing an unstoppable momentum toward unification, found themselves committing sums to the maintenance and reconstruction of the East German economy in amounts that seemed to grow more massive by the day; at the same time, they sought to assure the other East European states (and the Soviet Union) that their willingness to assist them, too, was not flagging. Although the Bush administration sought to demonstrate at least a continuing symbolic interest in the region, for example, in President Bush's visit in November 1990 to Czechoslovakia, and American business and nonprofit groups continued to be active there, it was apparent that economic policy toward Eastern Europe was becoming increasingly an affair of Western Europe and the multilateral World Bank and IMF.

The disintegration of the Soviet Union in the wake of the failed coup of August 1991 prompted a debate between the United States and its allies, notably Germany, and within the United States itself over the advisability of providing massive aid in support of economic reform in Russia. Eastern Europe appeared to be nearly forgotten in this discussion. European Community assistance to and involvement in Eastern Europe, however, had already become well established, while the comparatively weak commitment of the United States to the region seemed likely to be diluted still more.

CONCLUSIONS

The United States sought to use economic statecraft to influence events in Eastern Europe from the early years of the cold war. It did so not because it had an exaggerated faith in the potential results of such measures, but because no better alternatives were available. The use, or threat of the use, of force was exposed as hollow with the inability of the West to challenge the invasion of Hungary in 1956, if not before. No one expected other means—symbolic gestures such as state visits, the return of the crown of St. Stephan, or the use of broadcast propaganda—to have more than a marginal impact. Given the economic weaknesses of the East European states and the economic power of the United States (and, after postwar recovery, of Western Europe), recourse to economic instruments of influence seemed only logical.

Experience proved the economic leverage of the United States to be limited, however. It was limited, first, by the low level of conventional trade between the United States and Eastern Europe. The economic ability of the United States (at least until the 1980s) to provide aid or credits in large amounts, its technological resources, the attractiveness of its large domestic market, its influence in multinational financial agencies, and the strength of U.S.-based multinational corporations and banks all nevertheless encouraged the Eastern European states to deal with the United States, but these advantages were offset by its inability to act quickly or decisively, even in a period of East European crisis. That inability reflected in part the low priority assigned to Eastern Europe by most administrations, and still more the executive's need to win approval for most major measures from the Congress. Congress, in turn, was (and is) generally more responsive to short-term electoral pressures than to long-term foreign policy considerations. The unwillingness of Congress to grant the executive much discretion in East-West trade matters also reflected the now firmly institutionalized distrust between the two branches, deepened by the experiences of Vietnam, Watergate, and the Iran-Contra affair.

Over the years American administrations became increasingly explicit in identifying differentiation as the guiding beacon of their policies toward Eastern Europe. Since the decision to apply a differentiated policy depended upon American recognition of a pattern of demonstrated deviation from the Soviet model, its usefulness in encouraging *new* tendencies of change in Eastern Europe was always questionable. Moreover, the slogan of "differentiation" offered little concrete guidance as to the appropriate measures to be taken in specific cases, for example, in response to the rise of Solidarity in Poland.

It is not clear that differentiation was really an effective instrument for promoting change in Eastern Europe. Its initial use in Yugoslavia (well before the term itself was coined) probably did help sustain the independence of that country; it is less certain that it had similar effects in Poland, where the regime drifted back in the direction of orthodoxy in spite of American aid until a new crisis erupted in 1970.[54] As Kovrig points out, Hungary acquired the most relaxed and open political system in the bloc and became the most adventurous in pursuing economic reform well before the United States singled it out for special treatment under the rules of differentiation.[55] The special economic treatment accorded to Romania, on the other hand, did nothing to divert the Ceauşescu regime from its increasingly repressive path. Yet elements of the policy of differentiation have persisted in the post-Communist period.

If we compare American policy with that of the German Federal Republic, the most active of the European states in the pursuit of policy toward Eastern Europe, we find that the latter, too, sought to use economic means in the hope of achieving political and social results, particularly for the benefit of the citizens of the GDR.[56] Unlike the United States, however, the West German government avoided any clear-cut differentiation in its policies toward Eastern Europe, apart from the obvious priority it gave to relations with the GDR.[57] It avoided overt suggestions that its purpose was to weaken the ties of Eastern Europe with the Soviet Union (although for many years it could not allay Soviet suspicions on this score). On the contrary, it sought to strengthen its own economic and political links to the Soviet Union as a prerequisite for improving its East European relations. The West Germans also gave greater emphasis to "carrots" than "sticks" in their foreign economic policies, and to building long-term stable economic relations; thus they resisted American attempts to impose economic sanctions in response to specific instances of perceived Soviet or East European misbehavior. The Federal Republic built a far broader basis of trade with Eastern Europe and, like its Western neighbors, placed much more emphasis on the domestic economic benefits of trade while also assuming that the political effects would be positive; it was far less fearful that trade and economic assistance would strengthen its "enemies" or increase its dependence on them.

The West German approach was viewed with varying degrees of distrust by American officials; conservatives charged that the Federal Republic was pursuing its selfish economic interests at the expense of Western security. But in many ways the German approach was vindicated by the East European revolutions of 1989, although the magnitude and speed of the changes surprised the Germans as much as anyone else. In the post-Communist era, Germany is well positioned once again to assert a dominant influence in the region. Financial limitations imposed by the escalating costs of unification, German aid to the former USSR, the German commitment to the European Community, and the interest especially of the French in limiting the German role will probably mean that German influence will be shared in some measure with the EC, other West European states, and multinational lending agencies. The United States, however, partly as a consequence of its past policies, finds itself pushed to the margins of the East European scene. It is not inevitable that this country remain there, but if its role is to be enlarged, the nation must undertake a serious rethinking of its economic policies.

NOTES

1. John F. Kennedy, October 1960 campaign speech, quoted in Thomas A. Wolf, *U.S. East-West Trade Policy* (Lexington, Mass.: Lexington Books, 1973), 71.

2. Wolf von Amerongen, cited in Claudia Wörmann, *Der Osthandel der Bundesrepublik Deutschland* (Frankfurt: Campus Verlag, 1982), 114.

3. For interwar trade data, see Z. Drabek, "Foreign Trade Performance and Policy," in M. C. Kaser and E. A. Radice, *The Economic History of Eastern Europe 1919–1975*, vol. 1 (Oxford: Clarendon Press, 1985), 379–531, especially the extensive statistical appendix.

4. See Lincoln Gordon, "The View from Washington," in Lincoln Gordon et al., *Eroding Empire: Western Relations with Eastern Europe* (Washington, D.C.: Brookings Institution, 1987), 68–70.

5. Joseph Rothschild, *Return to Diversity* (New York: Oxford University Press, 1989), 22.

6. Ibid., 22–23.

7. See the table in Hanns-Dieter Jacobsen, *Die Ost-West Wirtschaftsbeziehungen als deutsch-amerikanisches Problem* (Baden-Baden: Nomos Verlagsgesellschaft, 1986), 306. Total West European trade with the East amounted to about $1 billion in 1952.

8. Theodore H. White, *Fire in the Ashes: Europe in Mid-Century* (New York: William Sloan Associates, 1953), 40; Walter LaFeber, *America, Russia, and the Cold War 1945–1980*, 4th ed. (New York: Alfred A. Knopf, 1980), 60–61.

9. Bennett Kovrig, *The Myth of Liberation* (Baltimore: Johns Hopkins University Press, 1973), 79.

10. Jacobsen, 61.

11. See Wolf, 49–52.

12. See Bonnie M. Pounds and Mona F. Levine, "Legislative, Institutional, and Negotiating Aspects of United States–East European Trade Relations," in Joint Economic Committee, *Reorientation and Commercial Relations of the Economies of Eastern Europe*, 93rd Cong., 2d sess. (Washington: U.S. Government Printing Office, 1974), 533.

13. Cited in Wolf, 53; see also Jacobsen, 64–66.

14. Wolf, 53.

15. Most Favored Nation status guarantees the partner country tariffs or other restrictions no more severe than those imposed on the granting nation's other "most favored" partners. For manufactured goods, this means that the United States imposes on non-MFN partners the high Smoot-Hawley tariffs of 1930; for raw materials and other nonmanufactured imports, however, MFN status makes little or no difference. The potential impact of MFN thus varies widely depending on the export structure of the country in question. See Wolf, 59–61.

16. See Jacobsen, 62–63; Wolf, 53–64.

17. John C. Campbell, *Tito's Separate Road* (New York: Harper & Row, 1967), 15–16.

18. Ibid., 22–29; Dennison Rusinow, *The Yugoslav Experiment 1948–1974* (Berkeley: University of California Press, 1977), 44–46.

19. Rusinow, 46ff.

20. See Jacobsen, 71–73, 305. I will henceforth use the term "inter-German trade," which seems to me better to express the reality of the arrangement.

21. See Robert W. Dean, *West German Trade with the East: The Political Dimension* (New York: Praeger, 1974), 56–64.

22. Piotr S. Wandycz, *The United States and Poland* (Cambridge, Mass.: Harvard University Press, 1980), 363–73; Wolf, 70–73; Pounds and Levine, 534–35; Kovrig, 234.

23. Pounds and Levine, 534.

24. See Hans-Adolf Jacobsen, "Bundesrepublik Deutschland-Volksrepublik Polen: Bestimmungsfaktoren ihrer Beziehungen 1949–1970," in Hans-Adolf Jacobsen, Carl-Christoph Schweitzer, Jerzy Sutek, and Lech Trzeciakowski, eds., *Bundesrepublik Deutschland, Volksrepublik Polen* (Frankfurt A. M.: Metzner; Warszawa: Polski Instityt Spraw Micdzynarodowych, 1979), 50–51; Eberhard Schulz, "Handel zwischen Politik und Profit," ibid., 193.

25. Wolf, 67.

26. Jacobsen, *Die Ost-West,* 74–75; the "higher fences" quote, from a European diplomat, is cited by Bennett Kovrig, *Of Walls and Bridges* (New York: New York University Press, 1991), 239.

27. Cited in Jacobsen, *Die Ost-West,* 71; see also Kovrig, *Myth,* 236ff.

28. Pounds and Levine, 535.

29. Kovrig, *Myth*, 252–53.

30. Wolf, 83–84, 86; Kovrig, *Myth*, 254–55.

31. See Zbigniew Brzezinski and William E. Griffith, "Peaceful Engagement in Eastern Europe," *Foreign Affairs* 39 (July 1961), 642–54; Brzezinski, *Alternative to Partition* (New York: McGraw-Hill, 1965). Gordon, on page 73, notes that the latter study "made a lasting impact on American policymakers."

32. Pounds and Levine, 536.

33. Ibid., 536; Wolf, 94.

34. Kovrig, *Myth,* 270–71, 274.

35. Pounds and Levine, 536.

36. Pounds and Levine, 537–38.

37. Kovrig, *Myth*, 291–92; Jacobsen, *Die Ost-West,* 98.

38. For details, see Pounds and Levine, 538–43.

39. See Raymond L. Garthoff, "Eastern Europe in the Context of U.S.-Soviet Relations," in Sarah Meiklejohn Terry, ed., *Soviet Policy in Eastern Europe* (New Haven: Yale University Press, 1984), 322.

40. See Jacobsen, *Die Ost-West,* 111.

41. Calculated from table in Gordon, 332–33.

42. See Raymond T. Garthoff, *Détente and Confrontation* (Washington, D.C.: Brookings Institution, 1985), 325–27; Joseph F. Harrington and Bruce J. Courtney, *Tweaking the Nose of the Russians* (New York: Columbia University Press, 1991), 330–80 *passim*.

43. See Garthoff, *Détente,* 575; Jacobsen, 150–52. Samuel Huntington, then a National Security Council advisor, developed a complex strategy of "economic diplomacy" to this end; it does not seem to have been fully implemented by the administration, however. See his "Trade, Technology, and Leverage: Economic Diplomacy," *Foreign Policy* no. 32 (1978), 63–80.

44. Garthoff, "Eastern Europe," 325–29.

45. See Gordon, 123.

46. Ibid., 124.

47. Ibid., 126; Nicholas G. Andrews, "The Effectiveness of U.S. Sanctions against Poland," in Paul Marer and Włodzimierz Siwiński, *Creditworthiness and Reform in Poland* (Bloomington: Indiana University Press, 1988), 325; Beverly Crawford, "Western Control of East-West Trade Finance," in Gary K. Bertsch, ed., *Controlling East-West Trade and Technology Transfer* (Durham, N.C.: Duke University Press, 1988), 302–03.

48. Gordon, 82; Garthoff, "Eastern Europe," 338.

49. Gordon, 83.

50. Interviews with State Department officials, January and November 1989.

51. See Harrington and Courtney, *passim*. The annual hearings were regularly preceded by a sharp upsurge in the number of Romanians permitted to emigrate.

52. Brown, in Gordon, 50; Ronald H. Linden, "The United States and Romania: MFN and Human Rights" (Paper presented at November 1986 meetings of the American Association for the Advancement of Slavic Studies), 11–17.

53. Gordon, 113; Jacobsen, *Die Ost-West*, 272–74; Bertsch, "Introduction," in Bertsch, 9–13.

54. Nikita Khrushchev is supposed to have told East European leaders in 1961: "Comrade Gomulka is wise. He takes the wheat from the Americans without giving anything in exchange. Follow his example." *Le Monde*, September 19, 1962, cited in Kovrig, *Myth*, 328.

55. See Kovrig, *Myth*, 266.

56. In contrast, the French generally have placed the interests of the French economy ahead of political considerations, in spite of occasional rhetoric to the contrary. See Pierre Hassner, "The View from Paris," in Gordon, 225–27.

57. Kovrig argues that German policy "undermined" the United States' "differentiation" strategy, a rather pejorative characterization of the fact that the failure of Germany and other European countries to follow the American lead undoubtedly limited the effectiveness of the policy. Kovrig, *Of Walls*, 332–34.

4

Soviet–East European Economic Relations: A Brief History

> Each side in the Soviet-East European divide is convinced the one is exploiting the other. Such is the nature of the fraternal socialist alliance.
>
> J. F. Brown (1988)[1]

> The Soviets are unwilling or unable to pay—that is the crux.
>
> Hungarian economist (1991)[2]

The new governments of Eastern Europe inherited a structure of economic relationships between their countries and the now-dissolved Soviet Union that has seriously constrained their efforts to reshape their economies and to strengthen their trade and technological links with the West. Even before the political cataclysm of 1989 and 1990, many East European economists and officials were restive over the level and character of the dependence of their countries on economic bonds with the Soviet Union, and Soviet leaders themselves had come to doubt the utility of the existing arrangements for their own nation. By the end of 1990 the disarray of the Soviet economy and the strains of reform in Eastern Europe had become so severe that both sides had good reason to view many aspects of their mutual ties as a serious liability. But these ties were rooted in a relationship of more than forty years that had shaped the economic institutions of the participants and established patterns of exchange and cooperation that did not lend themselves to easy alteration.

Nevertheless, both parties now sought to accomplish just such a change: one that would dramatically reduce their previous interdependence and shift their trade to the developed West. The process of separation has proven to be a painful one. East European leaders, having proclaimed their intention of becoming full participants in the West's economic system, now find themselves searching for ways to salvage some of their previous economic ties to Russia and the other former Soviet republics.

From the point of view of Western policymakers, the legacy of past Soviet–East European interdependence, coupled with the acute crisis of the post-Soviet economy, poses a number of dilemmas. However attractive the prospect of opening up Western economic opportunities in both the former Soviet republics and Eastern Europe in the short run, neither the economic health nor the political stability of either is likely to be served by the wholesale abandonment of their former ties. Rather, the West needs to find a strategy that balances a recognition of the legacy of such ties with the need for restructuring East European trading patterns so as to allow both East and West to benefit from the East's integration into the international economic system. Such a strategy must also take account of the West's interest in rebuilding the economies of Russia and the other republics and promoting some measure of political order there.

In this chapter I will begin by examining the historical development of the Soviet–East European relationship, an essential exercise if we are to understand the obstacles it has placed in the way of a reorientation of the East European economies. The more immediate background to many of the present difficulties, however, is to be found in the shifting and ultimately futile efforts of the Soviet leadership under Mikhail Gorbachev to remake Soviet–East European economic ties in response to the demands of *perestroika* and the changing international economic environment. With the breakup of the USSR, the relationship has fundamentally changed, but remains fluid as both sides seek to find a new basis for it.

STALINIST ECONOMICS: EASTERN EUROPE AS AN ADJUNCT TO THE SOVIET ECONOMY

The legacy of Soviet economic policies in the years of Stalinist domination of the East European states after World War II still weighs heavily on the economies of those countries. The Soviet dictator's initial priority, once the Red Army had established the Soviet Union's dominance in the region, was to exploit the East European economies for the benefit of his own war-ravaged nation. The primary, although not exclusive, targets of this policy were the countries that had belonged to the defeated Axis. A concomitant purpose, however, was to insist that each Eastern European country adopt a model of economic development and administration that had in his mind proven its worth in the Soviet Union and that would shape their economies so as to complement the Soviet economy in important respects.

Thus the Soviet Union exacted a heavy toll in war reparations, above all from the Soviet zone of Germany—later the GDR—but also from Romania and Hungary. In East Germany, entire factories were dismantled and shipped to the Soviet Union; other enterprises remained in Germany but were converted into Soviet stock companies. A proportion of East German production was delivered either to the Soviet Union directly or to the Red Army or Soviet trade organizations, and thousands of German specialists were sent to work in the Soviet Union (along with prisoners of war already there) and did not return until the 1950s, if at all. Reparations from Hungary and Romania took the form of Soviet appropriation of "German assets" in these countries; the same policy was pursued in lesser measure in Bulgaria. Some of these assets subsequently formed the basis for joint Soviet–East European companies, which, under de facto Soviet management, continued to benefit the Soviet economy until their dissolution in 1954. The Soviet Union also extracted goods from current production, especially metallurgical and petroleum products.[3] An estimated 90 percent of the production of Hungarian heavy industry went to the Soviet Union in 1945–1946, and 60 percent in 1947. Moreover, some 600,000 Hungarians were sent to the Soviet Union, one-third of whom never returned.[4] Even the economies of countries that had not belonged to the Axis were exploited, particularly through the Soviet practice of setting prices below the world market level for East European exports to itself. Poland, for example, lost some of its newly acquired industrial plants in the formerly German western territories to Soviet removals, and was forced to export coal to the Soviet Union at prices that were below the cost of production.[5] Yugoslavia also had to tolerate the exploitative presence of Soviet joint companies until its expulsion from the Cominform in 1948. Paul Marer estimates the total value of "the unrequited flow of resources from Eastern Europe to the Soviet Union" between 1945 and 1955 at some $14 billion; as he notes, this figure is of the same order of magnitude as U.S. Marshall Plan aid to Western Europe.[6] Other estimates are still higher.[7]

However painful these massive Soviet extractions, the long-term effects of the imposition of the Stalinist model on the economic arrangements of the East European countries, most of which had been predominantly agrarian before the war (the exceptions are East Germany and Czechoslovakia), were undoubtedly more profound. In all countries the state quickly took major industry into its own hands; it redistributed land to small peasants and then began the process of farm collectivization, which, however, was not completed for some years in most countries, and in the case of Poland not at all. Each country undertook a crash program of industrialization, with an emphasis on heavy industry. Particularly after the outbreak of the Korean War, each pushed its investment rate to close to 40 percent of national income, largely at the expense of consumption; in the prewar period investment rates had averaged 4–6 percent.[8] Military spending also increased sharply. Each country, regardless of its natural resource base, undertook the development of an iron and steel producing capacity; huge (and largely inefficient) monuments to this policy were built at such places as Nowa Huta (Poland) and Eisenhüttenstadt (the former GDR). Czechoslovakia had to import two-thirds of its iron ore in spite of a crash program to develop domestic supplies undertaken after Stalin's optimistic 1951 declaration that the country was really rich in this and other resources.[9] Bloc members were also required to produce such items as ships, chemicals, railroad equipment, and drilling equipment for export to the Soviet Union, whether or not they had previously manufactured them in significant quantities. Production decisions and the coordination of planning remained for some years the province of the Soviet Union itself, exercised through what has been called the "Russian embassy system of coordination."[10]

The result is perhaps best described as a "modified form of autarky,"[11] in which each country produced a broader range of industrial goods than its size and resource base could justify and often duplicated the efforts of its neighbors. Most were dependent on the Soviet Union for raw materials and, as they increased their use of cheap Soviet oil and gas, energy, while the USSR became the principal market for their products. The relationship thus established was in each case essentially a bilateral one between the Soviet Union and the particular East European state; there was virtually no division of labor or coordination of planning among the smaller East European countries, in spite of the establishment of the Council for Mutual Economic Assistance (CMEA) in the bloc in 1949, in response to the Marshall Plan. Stalin found it useful, presumably for political reasons, to isolate his East European dependencies from one another economically.[12] Even today, the volume of trade and economic cooperation among the smaller states remains surprisingly small.

Given the economic backwardness of most of the East European states, and against the background of the economic isolation of the USSR and the other bloc countries during the cold war, both the general commitment to industrialization and the efforts to achieve economic autarky for the bloc as a whole were understandable, and undoubtedly enjoyed the genuine support of the leaders of each country. But the specific Stalinist implementation of these principles, undertaken with little regard for the resource bases and other distinctive economic endowments of the individual countries, or for traditional trading patterns, produced "a grossly inefficient allocation of resources."[13] Once the impressive nominal growth rates brought about by the high rate of investment during the first postwar decades had begun to decline, the costs of this policy became clear.

The organization of East European industry on the basis of the Soviet model had additional negative consequences. The very large size of enterprises compared to their Western counterparts,[14] viewed as necessary for producing economies of scale, contributed to bureaucratic sluggishness and tended (and still tends) seriously to impede the introduction of domestic competition under subsequent and current reforms. The low value placed on entrepreneurial abilities and the rewards offered those who proved agile at following the twists and turns of bureaucratic directives nurtured a set of skills on the part of managers that were not easily adaptable to later attempts at devolving decision-making responsibilities. The emphasis on crude quantitative measures as indicators of economic success brought about an inattention to quality and assortment in production that still burdens East European economic systems as they seek to adapt to market conditions. The stress upon fulfilling steadily increasing annual plan targets inhibited serious efforts at technological innovation, which required a measure of risk taking inimical to consistent plan fulfillment. It also encouraged the notorious overmanning of East European firms, as managers sought to maintain ample "reserves" of labor for meeting such targets; countervailing incentives to streamline the work force were few.

Finally, the pattern of foreign trade imposed on Eastern Europe because of its subordination to the Soviet Union undoubtedly retarded economic growth and technological modernization in the region. The overall level of trade relative to national income in the Eastern European countries was substantially lower in the 1950s and 1960s than it was for comparable capitalist nations, and the economic benefits presumed to flow from the principle of comparative advantage in such trade were thus sacrificed. Much of the trade that did take place was with the Soviet Union, a country in most fields at a similar or inferior technological level to that of the northern-tier CMEA countries; thus the potential technology gains from trade with (and investment from) more advanced countries were lost.[15] The long-term trade agreements that the Soviet Union forged with its CMEA partners provided a measure of predictability and reliability to East European producers and consumers, but robbed them of flexibility and particularly of the ability to shift easily to Western suppliers or customers. More fundamentally, they tended to lock in industrial structures that were becoming progressively less compatible with international economic trends.[16] East European trade with the West often was itself oriented to a policy of import substitution—using Western imports to strengthen industries producing for the CMEA—designed to make future Western imports unnecessary. Elements of this approach, and the psychology underlying it, persisted into the 1980s even in the most reform-oriented economy, Hungary's.[17]

TOWARD ECONOMIC PARTNERSHIP

The death of Stalin, and fears of popular unrest in its wake, brought a partial reversal of some of his economic policies. Emulating the new Soviet leadership, East European regimes diverted more resources to light industry and the production of consumer goods, and the Soviet Union cancelled remaining reparations obligations and dissolved most of the joint companies. But the influence of the Soviet Union's heavy industry "lobby" remained strong under Khrushchev, and in any case the basic configuration of the East European economies had already been fixed.

This configuration also remained unaffected by the major wave of economic reforms that came in the 1960s. Broadly, these reforms sought not to reduce the role of central planning but to heighten its efficacy by delegating greater responsibility to individual enterprises and enterprise associations, utilizing material incentives more effectively as economic "levers," and emphasizing profit and cost efficiency rather than sheer quantitative output as the principal indicators of economic success. Economists had discussed such reforms in the Soviet Union and a number of East European countries in the 1950s, and several were actually introduced in Poland in 1956 but then were quickly curtailed.[18] The more widespread adoption of reforms was legitimated by the publication in *Pravda* in September 1962 of an article advocating them by the Soviet economist Yevsei Liberman.[19] The first Liberman-style reform program, the "New Economic System," was initiated in 1963 in the conservative GDR with evident Soviet encouragement.[20] Most of the other states of the bloc, including the Soviet Union, undertook similar and in some cases bolder reforms in the following years. By 1970, however, the reforms had already been largely abandoned everywhere but in Hungary, where the Kadar regime, acting under Soviet pressure, effectively put them on hold until late in the decade. The cautionary example of Czechoslovakia, where reform proposals had gone furthest and were most clearly linked with political upheaval, the mixed short-term economic results of the reforms elsewhere, and perhaps the eclipse of the reform-minded Soviet premier Alexei Kosygin in the CPSU (Communist Party of the Soviet Union) leadership, all help to explain this reversal.

Nevertheless, the fact that individual bloc countries took diverse paths to and away from reform, and, perhaps even more, the leverage that they achieved as a result of the efforts of the Soviet Union to persuade them to accept a greater measure of genuine economic integration in the CMEA, suggest that by the 1960s the asymmetry of Soviet–East European economic ties had already begun to moderate.[21] Rather than simply reflecting the dominance of Soviet interests, the relationship began to take on some of the characteristics of a genuine partnership, in which the smaller states were able to bargain on behalf of their own interests. The Brezhnev doctrine of "socialist internationalism" used to justify the invasion of Czechoslovakia sought to make the limits of East European deviation clear, but it could not conceal from the Soviet leadership the fragility of the legitimacy of most of the region's regimes and their corresponding need to build their credibility through improved economic performance.

THE 1970s: THE BURDENS OF EMPIRE?

The Soviet Union thus found itself required to be increasingly attentive to both the political and economic needs of its allies. At the same time it became convinced that its own economic development and that of the bloc required that it jettison its earlier emphasis on economic autarky. With the flowering of detente at the beginning of the 1970s, Soviet leaders began to emphasize international economic interdependence and sought to increase the Soviet Union's own importation of Western technology.[22] It thereby encouraged its allies to do likewise and, in so doing, to take advantage of Western credits. The effect was to persuade several East European countries to use such credits as a substitute for the economic reforms that both the Brezhnev leadership and many of their own officials distrusted. Even when Soviet desires to expand its American trade were frustrated by the passage of the Jackson-Vanik and Stevenson amendments, there was no reversal of this imprudent policy.

In the meantime, a number of Western scholars argued, the exploitative character of the Soviet–East European relationship had been effectively reversed. In a particularly influential study, the economists Michael Marrese and Jan Vanous argued that the Soviet Union was now subsidizing its partners at a considerable economic cost to itself.[23] In the interest of maintaining political loyalty and stability in Eastern Europe, Marrese and Vanous contended, the Soviet Union was selling fuel and raw materials to its allies for soft currency and at prices well below world market levels, while paying higher than world market prices for East European manufactured goods. The East European states had become an economic burden rather than a benefit; subsidizing them had become one of the "costs of empire."[24]

Other economists vigorously contested the Marrese-Vanous argument,[25] and a few East European scholars continued to argue that the Soviet Union still was exploiting its allies, principally by insisting that the long-term costs of the industrial structures and trading patterns imposed on them by Soviet control far outweighed any temporary benefits from price fluctuations.[26] There is no doubt, however, that the upward leap in oil prices dictated by the OPEC cartel in 1973–1974 and again in 1979 and the parallel increase in the prices of other fuels and raw materials, in combination with the CMEA's Bucharest pricing formula (which fixed internal bloc prices on the basis of the average world price for the preceding five years), meant that the Soviet Union for some years received less for its oil and other hard exports than it could have obtained in the West. Concomitantly, the sharp deterioration in the terms of trade of other countries heavily dependent on imported oil was somewhat cushioned for the East Europeans. The case with respect to the "overpricing" of East European manufactures was based on sketchier evidence; bilateral bargaining essentially determined intra-CMEA pricing of such goods. These prices were rarely available in the West, and their prices in Western markets may not have in any case corresponded to their "real" value to customers in the East in the context of the CMEA system.[27] Still, the Soviet Union, in enjoying the windfall benefits from the leap in world prices of its major exports, clearly elected not to subject its allies immediately to the full negative impact of the higher prices, and thereby granted them a de facto subsidy worth some tens of billions of dollars. The Soviet leadership no doubt calculated that it could not risk aggravating further the already severe deterioration in its allies' terms of trade without endangering their political stability. Once world fuel prices began their sharp decline in 1982, however, the CMEA formula worked to the disadvantage of Eastern Europe, which found itself paying prices for Soviet oil and gas nominally above world market levels, albeit largely in nonconvertible currencies.

ECONOMIC RELATIONS UNDER GORBACHEV

During Mikhail Gorbachev's six and one-half years as Soviet leader, his views of Soviet–East European economic relations went through a marked evolution. On taking office in 1985, at a time when Soviet-American relations were close to their nadir, Gorbachev appeared determined to utilize the East European economies more effectively in the service of his designs for reviving the Soviet economy.[28] Seeking initially to limit the dependence of the bloc on Western trade and technology, he sought to strengthen the CMEA's scientific and technological capacities by providing for their more effective integration in a Comprehensive Program adopted by the CMEA Council in December 1985.[29] As he and his advisors became aware of the depth of the Soviet Union's economic problems and its need for radical reform and not just reorganization, they aligned themselves more overtly with the bloc's most reformist states, Hungary and Poland. Within the CMEA, the Soviet Union began to push for marketizing reforms, including the development of an internally convertible medium of exchange. Increasingly persuaded that advanced Western technology was indispensable for the modernization of the Soviet economy, it sought to utilize Eastern Europe as a conduit for such technology, pressing for Western or Western-licensed components in its CMEA imports. By late in the decade the Soviet leadership decided that the USSR, and also the bloc, had to open itself up still more to the international—capitalist—economy to be successful; having earlier approved the membership of some of its Eastern European allies in GATT and the International Monetary Fund, the Soviet Union now sought to join GATT itself and indicated interest in entering the IMF.[30] It also sought, successfully, to participate in the formation of the new European Bank for Reconstruction and Development, although on the insistence of the United States its ability to borrow from the Bank was sharply restricted.

By the end of the 1980s, good relations with the West had come to the top of Gorbachev's priority list. Reversing the Soviet Union's earlier reluctance to expand its Western indebtedness, the Soviet leader came to view Western credits as vital to his country's revival. By contrast, although he did not say so publicly, he must have concluded that Eastern Europe had become an insupportable economic burden and a political liability. The Soviet Union's willingness to see the East European states slip, one by one, out from under Communist and thus Soviet control must be understood in part as a consequence of this altered perspective.

Even before Gorbachev became CPSU General Secretary, the Soviet Union, possibly persuaded by Western "subsidization" arguments, had made it clear that it was hardening the terms of economic exchange with its allies. The 1984 CMEA summit approved a concluding document declaring that in order to ensure "the implementation and continuation of deliveries from the USSR of a number of types of raw materials and energy carriers," other member states would have to orient production and investment to "the aim of supplying the Soviet Union with the products it needs," including "machines and equipment of a high quality and of the world technical level."[31] With the easing of the Polish crisis that had preoccupied it at the beginning of the decade, the Soviet Union pressed its allies to reduce or eliminate their deficits in its bilateral trade with them.[32] Soviet officials repeatedly demanded that the East European states improve the quality of their exports to the Soviet Union, which in a number of cases refused to accept shipments it regarded as substandard.[33]

The Soviet Union also demanded that its allies continue to contribute generously to "joint" investment projects, most of them involving the exploitation of raw materials and fuels located in the Soviet Union. An example was the construction of a 4,650-kilometer-long natural gas pipeline from Yamburg in Western Siberia to the Western borders of the Soviet Union, the major CMEA joint project for the 1986–1990 period, estimated to cost some 20 billion transferable rubles.[34] The East European states did not share ownership in these ventures; their contributions, including substantial hard-currency components, were to be compensated by deliveries of the resource in question. While the Soviet insistence that the East Europeans share in the costs of producing the additional energy and raw materials they badly needed had some justice, the expensive joint projects competed for scarce investment funds with critical domestic needs. Thus Soviet pressures met increasing resistance; in 1987 Hungary announced its withdrawal from further participation in the Yamburg project.[35]

The Soviet Union also pressed its allies to agree to "direct relations" between their own firms and Soviet enterprises, in the hope that such microlevel ties might stimulate innovation and costsaving from below. By

1988 a large number of such agreements had been reached on paper, but the scope of actual cooperation in research and development, joint production, marketing, and other areas under these agreements appeared to vary widely and to be unimpressive overall. An obvious obstacle was the differing levels of firm autonomy in countries at different stages of reform. Response to another Soviet initiative, the creation of intra-CMEA joint ventures, also was unenthusiastic.

Confronting the daunting tasks of implementing *perestroika* in its own sluggish economy, the Soviet Union sought to end any lingering subsidization of its allies. That goal did not prove easy to accomplish. As of 1986, five of the six East European CMEA countries were still running deficits in their trade with the USSR; only the fall in world oil prices and the resulting shift in the terms of trade converted these into nominal surpluses in 1987 (in three cases) and 1988 (in five cases).[36] These, however, reflected the relatively high prices set for East European manufactured goods compared to what they might bring in international markets. Soviet complaints testified to continuing resistance to the pressures for direct relations, joint ventures, and higher-quality exports.[37] The East European partner states all recognized that the price of readily agreeing to such Soviet designs would be a reduction of their flexibility in their dealings with the West, as well as a likely burden on the realization of domestic economic goals.

Another dimension of the economic relations between the Soviet Union and Eastern Europe under Gorbachev was the interest of both in economic reform. In the first years of his rule, Gorbachev frequently cited, and his economic advisors appeared to have carefully studied, the variety of economic experiments in Eastern Europe, especially the market-oriented reforms of Hungary and the efficiency-oriented measures of economic reorganization in the GDR.[38] As the Soviet leaders' own conception of the extent and boldness of the changes required to revive the Soviet economy expanded, the attraction in their eyes of the more radical Hungarian experiments grew, as did their interest in seeing them succeed.[39] The Soviet alliance with General Jaruzelski in Poland came to include a strong verbal commitment to economic reform (though little effective implementation) in both countries. Less enthusiastically, but with apparent Soviet encouragement, the conservative Bulgarian and Czech regimes promised to undertake their own cautious versions of Soviet *perestroika.* No similar pressures appear to have been applied to the GDR, perhaps in recognition of what then still appeared to be the relative success of its centralized economic model.[40] Soviet officials denied any intention of imposing their own reform plans on their neighbors, and were unable or unwilling to commit any significant resources to their allies' reform efforts. But they appeared to be convinced of *perestroika*'s broader applicability,[41] and to recognize that the multilateralization of cooperation within the CMEA would be eased if similar reforms were undertaken in all member states.

Like the Hungarians and the Poles, the Soviets under Gorbachev came to agree that economic reform could not succeed unless it was accompanied by political reform. But there was little effort at coordination of either economic policies or of political changes even among the reform-oriented countries; in each case, the domestic configuration of forces inside and outside the ruling party determined the character and pace of reform. The Soviet Union's effort to achieve reform within the framework of the CMEA soon proved fruitless, and it turned to a series of bilateral clearing agreements that sought to free intrabloc trade from some of its traditional constraints.

Economic deterioration in the Soviet Union and most of the East European states began mutually to reinforce each other, and contributed to the growing political crisis. For example, a study by a Hungarian scholar of Soviet-Hungarian economic relations in the metallurgical industry revealed, on the one hand, hardening Soviet terms and, on the other, serious problems in the quality and reliability of Soviet deliveries.[42] The 10 percent cut in Soviet oil deliveries to Eastern Europe in 1982, at a time when the intra-CMEA price was still rising, and the insistence of the Soviet Union that deliveries above a certain level be paid for in hard currency added to the difficulties of bloc states at that time. With little warning, promised oil and gasoline deliveries to the former bloc states were again cut in 1989 and 1990, presumably because of Soviet production problems, due in part to reduced investment and pipeline failures[43] and to the higher priority given to Western sales. On the other side, the East European crisis of 1989–1990 and the subsequent political changes threatened the delivery of manufactured goods and food needed by the Soviet Union. The absorption of the GDR into the West German currency area in particular endangered the fulfillment of East German trade obligations under the old quasi-barter system of the CMEA. East German plants, whose very existence was jeopardized by the currency changeover, could not afford to supply Soviet customers without payment in hard currency or new subsidies from the Federal Republic.

THE FUTURE OF ECONOMIC RELATIONS

Today, the states of the former Soviet Union and those of Eastern Europe find themselves still linked together economically, in part because of the history I have recounted and in part because of the absence of easy alternatives for either party, but the degree and nature of their mutual dependence has radically changed. In 1988, the (officially reported) proportion of trade of the East European countries with the Soviet Union had ranged from 24 percent (Poland) to 58 percent (Bulgaria); with some national variation, the basic pattern was the exchange of Soviet energy and raw materials for East European manufactured goods and foodstuffs (see Table 4.1). Under this arrangement, Eastern Europe met its needs for fuel and raw materials for much of its industrial production with only a limited expenditure of hard currency. In exchange, its factories sold goods to Soviet customers that often could not have been successfully marketed elsewhere; the Soviet market was voracious and largely undemanding. For its part, the Soviet Union obtained manufactured goods that would have been either more expensive if bought from the West or unobtainable because of COCOM restrictions. Both sides were aware of the costs of the arrangement: firms producing for the Soviet market sometimes had to be heavily subsidized, and had little incentive to innovate, improve quality, or increase their efficiency, while the Soviet Union had to forgo potential hard currency sales and accept manufactured products inferior to Western ones. Still, the advantages seemed clearly to outweigh the perils of seeking alternatives.

Now the rules have changed, and the obligations of political loyalty no longer bind the parties to one another. Beginning on January 1, 1991, trade between the Soviet Union and its former allies was to be conducted on the basis of hard currency, an arrangement widely expected to favor the former. But the Soviet Union proved to have little hard currency to spare; it fell into arrears in payments to its East European partners, and proved unable or unwilling to maintain energy supplies at their previous levels. Between 1985 and 1989, Soviet–East European trade figures roughly stagnated, but what had been a sizeable Soviet surplus changed into growing deficits. Trade declined sharply in 1990, as Soviet fuel deliveries fell and the East Europeans sought to reduce their useless ruble surpluses; then, in the first few months of 1991, trade plummeted. The East European countries, unable to expand their Western trade rapidly enough to compensate, scrambled to reach new trade agreements with individual Soviet republics, especially Russia and Ukraine.[44] The Soviet central government, after initially proscribing all barter trade, shifted course and agreed to resume some trade with Hungary and Czechoslovakia in local currencies—that is, a return to barter.[45] The growing turmoil and ultimate collapse of the Soviet Union made a restoration of anything like the previous levels of exchange improbable, however, at least in the short term.

Nevertheless, much of the inheritance of the past forty years remains. CMEA pipelines and electricity grids are still in place, and factories in Russia and the other republics remain accustomed to and partially dependent on East European machinery and spare parts, while many East European producers are hard-pressed to find alternatives to traditional Soviet markets. Many considerations favoring trade between the post-Soviet states and Eastern Europe, such as geographical proximity, similar technological

Table 4.1
East European Trade with the Soviet Union and Other CMEA Members (1989)
(as percentage of total foreign trade)

country	trading partner	imports	exports
Bulgaria	USSR	52.9%	65.2%
	other CMEA	20.8	18.8
Czecho-slovakia	USSR	29.7	30.5
	other CMEA	26.4	24.4
GDR	USSR	22.0	23.8
	other CMEA	17.4	19.4
Hungary	USSR	22.1	25.1
	other CMEA	17.6	16.7
Poland	USSR	18.0	20.8
	other CMEA	14.6	14.3
Romania	USSR	31.5	22.6
	European CMEA*	21.7	15.9
USSR	CMEA	61.2	58.2

Note: Figures for Bulgaria probably undervalue Western trade relative to Soviet trade and thus overstate the proportion of the latter.
*GDR, Czechoslovakia, Hungary, Bulgaria, Poland.
Source: Calculated from Vienna Institute for Comparative Economic Studies, *COMECON Data 1990* (Westport, Conn.: Greenwood, 1991), 177–79.

levels, and the complementarity of many needs, remain unchanged, as do the limited prospects for the rapid expansion of East European sales in Western markets. Even under anti-Communist governments determined on political grounds to shift their countries' economic orientation Westward, therefore, Eastern Europe's ability to alter entirely its trading patterns and other economic relationships is constrained, and the desirability of its doing so is at least questionable.

We need to underscore the pivotal role played by energy supplies in Soviet–East European economic relations in the past, and their likely importance in the future. As of 1987, the Soviet Union supplied around one-third of the energy requirements of the five East European CMEA countries, excluding Romania (see Table 4.2). This figure had doubled since 1965, and reflected a growing hunger for energy coupled with its highly inefficient use and the absence of serious measures of conservation. The

Table 4.2
Energy Use in Eastern Europe (1987)

country	use per capita	coal	oil	gas	nucl.	other	self-reliance
	tons of oil equivalent		% of total use				
Bulgaria	**3.8**	**31.1**	**43.9**	**14.2**	**8.1**	**2.9**	**29**
Czecho-slovakia	**4.9**	**58.6**	**20.9**	**11.9**	**6.7**	**1.8**	**68**
GDR	**5.9**	**70.2**	**17.3**	**9.1**	**2.6**	**0.8**	**74**
Hungary	**2.9**	**28.0**	**31.3**	**30.6**	**8.1**	**2.9**	**56**
Poland	**3.5**	**78.9**	**12.8**	**7.4**	—	**0.8**	**97**
Romania	**3.1**	**23.7**	**23.1**	**47.9**	—	**5.4**	**81**

Source: Calculated from Vienna Institute for Comparative Economic Studies, *COMECON Data 1989* (Westport, Conn.: Greenwood, 1990), 396, 399–401.

heavy dependence of all the East European states except Poland and Romania on Soviet oil is familiar—not only for domestic use but, especially in the 1980s, as the basis for a lucrative reexport trade. With the development of the Urengoi and new Yamburg pipelines some of this dependence was in the last years of the CMEA being shifted to Soviet natural gas. In addition, the Eastern European states were also tied into the CMEA electricity grid, in which the Soviet Union was the dominant supplier, permitting them to maintain lower emergency reserves. The CMEA's "united energy system," however, was not easily made compatible with Western grids because of its greater tolerance for large drops in frequency.[46]

East European nuclear reactors are nearly all of Soviet design (the exception is a Canadian plant under construction in Romania) and dependent on suppliers in the former Soviet Union (and, in the past, on Soviet-controlled uranium). Even after the Chernobyl accident, the East European states appeared determined to press on with the development of nuclear power in order to reduce their dependence on fossil fuels. But it is now evident that many nuclear plants will—or ought to—be closed down for safety reasons, as the four East German reactors at Greifswald already have been. Czech and Bulgarian reactors have aroused the particular concerns of Western experts, but the governments of the two countries insist that they cannot afford to give up the power they generate. Western nuclear companies have sought to rush into this breach, offering to renovate old Soviet plants and build new ones.[47]

Apart from nuclear power, the principal domestic alternative to Russian or other external fuel supplies in eastern Germany, Czechoslovakia, Bulgaria, and Hungary is brown coal (lignite). It is highly polluting, and mining it scars the landscape and is increasingly expensive. Hungary and Czechoslovakia expected substantial quantities of hydroelectric power to be generated by the construction of the Gabčikovo-Nagymaros dam complex on the Danube. The Hungarians, however, pulled out of the project in 1989 after years of environmental protests. Since Czechoslovakia had nearly completed its part of the project, bitter disputes between the two governments ensued; they continued after the end of Communist rule.[48]

The near-collapse of the exchange of Soviet energy for East European manufactured goods and other products in 1991 was a devastating blow to countries already afflicted by the high short-term costs of economic reform: declining production and living standards, rising inflation and unemployment, growing social unrest. Efforts of the new regimes to rebuild such trade, at least for a transitional period, arose out of necessity, and in spite of their new political orientation. With good reason, they protested forms of Western aid to the Soviet Union that replaced East European exports to that country, and called instead for Western support of East European–Soviet trade—in effect, asking that the West grant the Soviet Union credits for the purchase of East European goods. Some in the West showed interest in such a trilateral arrangement, but talks between the European Bank for Reconstruction and Development and representatives of East European countries and the Soviet Union revealed difficulties in finding an appropriate mechanism and a lack of Soviet enthusiasm for the undertaking.[49] The Germans, however, were able to revive some former GDR exports to the Soviet Union by offering East German firms export guarantees.[50]

The replacement of the Soviet Union by a "commonwealth" of sovereign states leaves the future of East European economic relations with them particularly difficult to forecast. The old Soviet Union owed substantial sums to most East European countries—in the case of Poland, $7 billion, according to the country's foreign minister.[51] The ability and willingness of the new commonwealth to pay these debts is at least uncertain. The material basis for mutually beneficial trade remains, however. "The Soviet Union," the Hungarian finance minister has remarked, "will always be here in our neighborhood."[52] Eastern Europe still needs the fuels and raw materials it once imported from the Soviet Union, and, as Charles Gati has put it, the technological level of East European manufacturing "is well-suited to Soviet circumstances."[53] Setting up new and workable trade arrangements, however, will depend heavily on the evolution of the new republics' institutions and the development of mechanisms of economic coordination among them, as well as their emergence from economic crisis. Another critical factor will be whether the former Soviet Union is able to continue as a net exporter of its most tradable product, oil; some Western specialists doubt it.[54]

THE POLITICS OF ECONOMIC RELATIONS

In the past, the economic relationship between the Soviet Union and Eastern Europe was always hostage to political considerations. So long as Eastern Europe appeared indispensable to its hegemon as a defensive glacis, as validation of the universal applicability of the Soviet model, and as a source of influence over Western Europe,[55] the Soviet Union had a strong interest in tieing the Eastern European economies as closely as possible to its own. As noted, its interest even extended to subsidizing the East European economies if necessary in order to assure their political loyalty and stability.

The political interests of the Soviet successor states in Eastern Europe remain substantial, but with the dramatic changes in international circumstances they now must be redefined. It is doubtful whether Russia or any of the other components of the former Soviet Union have worked through the process of redefinition, but there can be no doubt that many of them have a strong interest in retaining strong political ties in the East European region. The relationship can no longer be based on ideological claims, political control, or a military alliance; thus economic links have increased in relative importance. The post-Soviet states will continue to have an interest in minimizing political instability and ethnic turmoil in Eastern Europe, even as they seek to contain their own political and ethnic conflicts. More important, Eastern Europe has acquired a still more compelling bridge function to the "European house" on which Gorbachev once placed so much emphasis—and specifically to the European Community and to Western credits, investments, and technology.

However, how much weight the post-Soviet states will in fact continue to have in Eastern Europe, and thus how great their ability to influence events there will be, remains an open question. Both the potential capacity to exert influence and the concrete interests of Russia, Ukraine, Moldova, and the other states vary significantly. The Soviet nuclear arsenal remains, but the reality of political disintegration and the increasing desperateness of the economic situation is likely to reduce the republics' direct influence in Eastern Europe, as elsewhere. In an odd reversal, the behavior of East European governments, once largely dictated by Soviet strength, is now likely to be profoundly affected by fears of post-Soviet weakness. Any Russian desires to play an active role in Eastern Europe may be overwhelmed by the country's continuing internal crisis and its inability to meet its economic commitments.

Eastern Europe's new leaders have many reasons, even apart from recent history, to feel ambivalent over their countries' future economic relations with the post-Soviet states. Initially sensitive to Soviet wishes and feelings, their sympathies sharply diminished when the Soviet Union cut its deliveries of oil and then stopped paying for most of its East European imports.[56] The hard bargaining over East European ruble surpluses, the shift to trade in convertible currencies, and costs related to the withdrawal of Soviet forces further strained relationships. But the mounting problems of reorienting their countries' economies to the West have led most East European officials to grudgingly acknowledge the future importance of trade with the post-Soviet states. What kind of new political relationships that will imply is at present difficult for anyone to say.

Under these circumstances, what should the posture of the West be? Curiously, and contrary to the logic of the forty years of the cold war, it may be in the interest of the West to support the reconstruction of East European ties to the Soviet successor states, and even to finance a revival of their East European trade. Perhaps the most compelling reason is the need to prevent a Russian (or Ukrainian, etc.) sense of isolation in the world, which could still frustrate internal reform and strengthen Russian and other nationalisms, the possibility of civil war, and the prospect of some form of dictatorship. The second reason is that it would not be to the economic advantage of Eastern Europe to sever its economic ties to the former Soviet Union. As already noted, the lack of competitiveness of much of what Eastern Europe produces in the West and the many rivals seeking entrance into Western markets makes retention of significant Eastern trade imperative. Moreover, as the Hungarian finance minister has acknowledged, the interest of potential Western investors in Eastern Europe will depend in part on the special access it offers them to the post-Soviet market.[57] More broadly, a high level of trade with the new commonwealth would help offset the very considerable danger that Eastern Europe might become a group of poor dependencies of the West, and especially of Germany, thus returning it to something like its unhappy interwar economic position. Such a level of trade might also contribute to the ability of the post-Soviet states to stave off economic collapse, an event that would be to the benefit of no one.

NOTES

1. J. F. Brown, *Eastern Europe and Communist Rule* (Durham, N.C.: Duke University Press, 1988), 139.

2. Quoted in Stephen Engelberg, "Eastern Europe's Hardships Grow as Trade with Soviets Dries Up," *New York Times*, May 6, 1991, 1.

3. Nicolas Spulber, *The Economics of Communist Eastern Europe* (Cambridge, Mass.: Technology Press, 1957; reprinted Westport, Conn.: Greenwood Press, 1976), 35–40, 167–76, 187–205.

4. Bennett Kovrig, *Communism in Hungary* (Stanford: Hoover Institution Press, 1979), 196, 162.

5. E. A. Radice, "The Collapse of German Hegemony and its Economic Consequences," in M. C. Kaser, ed., *The Economic History of Eastern Europe 1919–1975*, vol. 2 (Oxford: Clarendon Press, 1986), 516–17; W. Brus, "Postwar Reconstruction and Socio-Economic Transformation," ibid., 603, n. 52; John P. Hardt, "Soviet Energy Policy in Eastern Europe," in Sarah Meiklejohn Terry, ed., *Soviet Policy in Eastern Europe* (New Haven: Yale University Press, 1984), 191.

6. Paul Marer, "Soviet Economic Relations with Eastern Europe," in Terry, 156.

7. See Hardt, 191, who estimates $15–20 billion, and "Reparationen," *DDR Handbuch*, 3rd ed., vol. 2 (Cologne: Verlag Wissenschaft und Politik, 1985), 1121–22, which gives the figure of $15.8 billion for East Germany alone.

8. Spulber, 297, 342; Robin Okey, *Eastern Europe 1740–1985*, 2nd ed. (Minneapolis: University of Minnesota Press, 1986), 206; George Kolankiewicz and Paul G. Lewis, *Poland: Politics, Economics and Society* (London: Pinter, 1988), 177.

9. Martin Myant, *The Czechoslovak Economy 1948–1988* (Cambridge: Cambridge University Press, 1989), 17, 85. The GDR produced only 3 percent of the iron ore it consumed, and, from 1977, no hard coal. *DDR Handbuch*, vol. 2, 162.

10. Frederic L. Pryor, *The Communist Foreign Trade System* (Cambridge, Mass.: MIT Press, 1963), 200–01.

11. Hardt, 191.

12. Zbigniew Brzezinski has noted that one "peculiarity of Stalinism as an interstate system" was the political as well as the economic isolation of the East European states from one another that it imposed. *The Soviet Bloc: Unity and Conflict* (Cambridge Mass.: Harvard University Press, 1960), 122–24.

13. Marer, 159.

14. See Frederic Pryor, "Industrial Organization," in Carmelo Mesa-Lago and Carl Beck, eds., *Comparative Socialist Systems: Essays on Politics and Economics* (Pittsburgh: University of Pittsburgh Center for International Studies, 1975), 347–66. Their size continued to grow even after the reforms of the 1960s. See Alan H. Smith, *The Planned Economies of Eastern Europe* (New York: Holmes & Meier, 1983), 77–80.

15. Philip Hanson, "Soviet Trade with Eastern Europe," in Karen Dawisha and Philip Hanson, eds., *Soviet–East European Dilemmas* (New York: Holmes & Meier, 1981), 93.

16. See Margit Racza and Sandor Richter, "The Mechanism of Hungarian-Soviet Economic Relations," in Michael Friedländer, ed., *Foreign Trade in Eastern Europe and the Soviet Union* (Boulder, Colo.: Westview Press, 1990), 86–87.

17. A. Nagy, "Why Does It Not Work?" *Acta Oeconomica* 39, nos. 1–2 (1988), 29, citing András Köves.

18. W. Brus, "1953 to 1956: The 'Thaw' and the 'New Course,' " in Kaser, vol. 3 (1986), 53–55; Brus, "1957 to 1965: In Search of Balanced Development," ibid., 97–104.

19. See Smith, 72ff.; Brus, "1957 to 1965," 109.

20. See my *The Technical Intelligentsia and the East German Elite* (Berkeley: University of California Press, 1974), chap. 10.

21. See Brus, "1957 to 1965," 70–73.

22. Eugene Zaleski and Helgard Wienert, *Technology Transfer between East and West* (Paris: Organisation for Economic Cooperation and Development, 1980), 54–55.

23. Michael Marrese and Jan Vanous, *Soviet Subsidization of Trade with Eastern Europe* (Berkeley: University of California Institute of International Studies, 1983).

24. Valerie Bunce, "The Empire Strikes Back: The Transformation of the Eastern Bloc from a Soviet Asset to a Soviet Liability," *International Organization* 39 (Winter 1985), 1–46.

25. See Marer, 171–80; Raimund Dietz, "Advantages and Disadvantages in Soviet Trade with Eastern Europe," in Joint Economic Committee, *East European Economies: Slow Growth in the 1980s*, vol. 2 (Washington, D.C.: U.S. Government Printing Office, 1986), 263–301; Kazimierz Z. Poznanski, "Opportunity Cost in Soviet Trade: Discussion of Methodology and New Evidence," *Soviet Studies* XL (April 1988), 290–307.

26. See the comments of Jadwiga Staniszkis, cited in Sarah Meiklejohn Terry, "The Future of Poland: *Perestroika* or Perpetual Crises," in William E. Griffith, ed., *Central and Eastern Europe: The Opening Curtain* (Boulder, Colo.: Westview Press, 1989), 186–87.

27. See Marer, 166–67, 176–79; Poznanski, 295–97.

28. Gorbachev's first moves along these lines helped lead even so astute an observer of the Soviet scene as Seweryn Bialer to characterize (in 1986) Gorbachev's approach to Eastern Europe as an "all-out hard-line policy" whose "main thrust" was "to strengthen the Soviet hold on its empire and to control the satellite party leaders more tightly." *The Soviet Paradox* (New York: Vintage, 1986), 206.

29. See Carl H. McMillan, "Soviet Efforts to Restructure CMEA," in Aurel Braun, ed., *The Soviet–East European Relationship in the Gorbachev Era* (Boulder, Colo.: Westview Press, 1990), 26–46.

30. See Jerry F. Hough, *Opening Up the Soviet Economy* (Washington, D.C.: Brookings Institution, 1988).

31. As quoted in Brown, 154–55.

32. For the case of Hungary, see Brown, 219.

33. For the case of Bulgaria, see Wolfgang Höpken, "Perestrojka auf bulgarisch," *Südosteuropa* (1987/10), 619–24; on the GDR, see Maria Haendke-Hoppe, "Aussenwirtschaft und Aussenwirtschaftsreform," in Forschungsstelle für gesamtdeutsche wirtschaftliche und soziale Fragen, *Glasnost und Perestroika auch in der DDR?* (Berlin: Berlin Verlag Arno Spitz, 1988), 68.

34. See Heinrich Machowski, "Der Rat für gegenseitige Wirtschaftshilfe," in *Rat für gegenseitige Wirtschaftshilfe: Strukturen und Probleme* (Bonn: Ostkolleg der Bundeszentrale für politische Bildung, 1987), 29.

35. See Keith Crane, *The Soviet Economic Dilemma of Eastern Europe* (Santa Monica: Rand Corporation, 1986), 60–61; McMillan, 35–36, 35; *Radio Free Europe Research (RFER)*, September 29, 1989, 3–4.

36. See *PlanEcon Report*, April 8, 1988, 8 and January 6, 1989, 4.

37. See the report of Gorbachev's speech at a dinner for the visiting GDR party chief Erich Honecker in *Pravda*, September 29, 1988, 2nd ed., 2, translated in Foreign Broadcast Information Service (FBIS) *Daily Report—Eastern Europe*, September 29, 1988, 38.

38. See Ed A. Hewett, *Reforming the Soviet Economy* (Washington, D.C.: Brookings Institution, 1988), 300–2. The Soviet Institute on the Economics of the World Socialist System, directed by Oleg Bogomolow, was a particularly influential source of such studies.

39. Ed Hewett, however, concluded that overall the East European (and Chinese) experience had "only limited influence on Soviet thinking." Ibid., 302.

40. The Soviet Foreign Minister Eduard Shevardnadze, commenting in February 1990 on the GDR's failure to reform, asked: "But what should we have done? After all, we could not impose our position on Honecker. One of the basic principles of our new thinking is the rejection of *diktat*." Cited in J. F. Brown, *Surge to Freedom* (Durham, N.C.: Duke University Press, 1991), 58.

41. See, e.g., Oleg Bogomolow, "Mir Sotsialisma na puti Perestroiki," *Kommunist* no. 16 (November 1987), 92–102.

42. Tamas Reti, "Hungarian Metallurgical Enterprises: Two Case Studies," *East European Politics and Societies* 2 (Fall 1988), 510–21.

43. D. J. Peterson, "Bleeding Arteries: Pipelines in the Soviet Union," in Radio Liberty, *Report on the USSR*, June 15, 1990, 1–3.

44. This process began well before the scheduled change to hard-currency trade on January 1, and had the approval of the central government.

45. See *Report on Eastern Europe*, March 5, 1991, 38; ibid., May 31, 1991, 32; *BBC Monitor, Weekly Economic Report*, Pt. 2, Eastern Europe, August 1, 1990, A/1. See also Marie Lavigne, "The CMEA's Transition from the Transferable Ruble," *Report on Eastern Europe*, November 2, 1990, 36–38.

46. *Süddeutsche Zeitung*, July 20, 1990, 25.

47. See R. Denis Hayes, "Eastern Europe's Nuclear Window," *The Nation* 253 (August 26/September 2, 1991), 222–25.

48. See Peter Martin, "The Gabcikovo-Nagymaros Dam Dilemma," *Report on Eastern Europe*, August 6, 1991, 6–11.

49. "Financing of Joint Soviet Trade to Be Discussed," *Budapest MTI* in English, May 29, 1991, FBIS-EE, May 30, 1991, 12; interview with official of European Bank for Reconstruction and Development, August 1991.

50. "Gesamtwirtschaftliche und unternehmerische Anpassungsprozesse in Ostdeutschland: Zweiter Bericht," DIW *Wochenbericht* 58 (June 13, 1991), 328.

51. *Report on Eastern Europe*, August 16, 1991, 39.

52. Mihaily Kupa, interview in *Magyar Hirlap*, May 15, 1991, pp. 1, 8, translated in FBIS-EE, May 15, 1991, 18.

53. See Charles Gati, *The Bloc that Failed* (Bloomington: Indiana University Press, 1990), 118.

54. See *New York Times*, March 20, 1991, 29.

55. See Brown, *Eastern Europe*, 30–31; John van Oudenaren, "The Soviet Union and Eastern Europe: New Prospects and Old Dilemmas," in Griffith, 104–6.

56. See, e.g., the discussion of the deterioration in the economic relationship between the Soviet Union and its once most loyal ally, Bulgaria, in Wolfgang Höpken, "Aussen- und Sicherheitspolitische Optionen Bulgariens seit der 'Wende' 1989," *Südosteuropa* 41 (January 1992), 34–36.

57. See Kupa interview, 18.

PART II

DIMENSIONS OF ECONOMIC POLICY

5

Eastern Europe and Economic Integration

> We tend to believe that under the given conditions all [CMEA members], including the USSR, are incurring losses from mutual trade.
>
> Friedrich Levcik and Jan Stankovsky, 1988[1]

> For Giscard and his fellow deepeners, the European project loses much of its meaning if more and more countries with less and less in common join the club.
>
> Walter Russell Mead[2]

An overriding reality of the East European economies, taken individually, is their small size. Ranging in population from Slovakia's five million to Poland's 38 million and in Gross Domestic Product from $15.6 to $68.3 billion (1989),[3] and endowed only modestly with natural resources, the East European states would seem to be natural candidates for close economic cooperation with their neighbors, including a high degree of product specialization and a high intensity of international trade. The autarkic bias in their initial economic development under Soviet auspices thus put them at a marked disadvantage in comparison with countries of comparable size in Western Europe, especially as the latter joined the European Community (EC) or the European Free Trade Association (EFTA) and also participated in the de facto integration implicit in the spread of multinational enterprises and financial institutions. The East bloc's answer to Western economic integration and to the more general triumph in the West of liberal trade principles was the Council for Mutual Economic Assistance (CMEA). The CMEA, founded in 1949 but activated only a decade later, was designed to facilitate economic cooperation among the state socialist countries and to bring about a mutually profitable "international socialist division of labor."

For many years, East bloc leaders promoted CMEA integration as a substitute for greater involvement in the global economy and thus for a dangerous dependence on the West.[4] As late as 1985, when the hostility between the two superpowers that characterized the late Brezhnev and early Reagan eras was only beginning to abate, Mikhail Gorbachev justified the adoption of the CMEA program for scientific and technical progress by the need to maintain technological independence and "invulnerability to pressures and blackmail" from the capitalist states.[5] Subsequent Soviet and East European rhetoric, however, denied any intention of pursuing autarky, and insisted on the contrary that as CMEA integration intensified, the bloc would have to participate more fully in the international economic system in order to keep up the technological pace with the advanced capitalist countries.[6] "It is time," wrote a Soviet economist in 1988, "to reorient the deepening integration within the CMEA framework toward the external world."[7]

The CMEA, we now know, failed. Consistently falling short of its professed goals, it came under increasingly open and bitter criticism in its last years from the more reform-minded Communist elites in Eastern Europe and the Soviet Union. It thus could not survive the election of democratic governments in Eastern Europe's northern tier. The organization's formal demise came in 1991; plans for a successor organization, serving consultative and informational purposes, were dropped.[8] Instead, the new regimes looked to the West, especially the European Community, for the benefits of economic integration. "Returning to Europe," so they hoped, would mean formal association with and in a short time full membership in the EC, and thus participation in the rich prospects of the market without internal barriers that the Community officially completed at the beginning of 1993. Less enthusiastically, discussions began concerning the possibilities of economic cooperation among some of the former CMEA states (notably Hungary, Poland, and Czechoslovakia) or other configurations such as one linking the Alpine-Adria or Pentagonal (later Hexagonal) states—Hungary, Czechoslovakia, Yugoslavia, Austria, and Italy (with Poland subsequently added).

The question of East European economic integration is complicated by the European Community's virtual completion of its drive for a single internal market, a goal formulated prior to the upheavals in the East; its longer-term pursuit of monetary and political union, embodied in the Maastricht treaty; and the uncertainties created by the controversy over that treaty's ratification. There is as yet no genuine consensus within the EC over the ultimate treatment of Eastern Europe, although sentiment is strong, most notably among the French, for "deepening" the existing Community before "widening" it to include new members. EC members do agree on the need to assist the reconstruction of Eastern Europe, and by late 1992 the organization had signed association agreements with Poland, Hungary, and Czechoslovakia and initialled agreements with Bulgaria and Romania.

For the United States, the potential development of closer links between the Eastern European states and the EC raises a different set of questions. Along with other Western countries outside the Community, it might be left with a substantially diminished economic role in Eastern Europe, which in turn could reduce its political influence throughout the continent. The likelihood of such an outcome will depend, in part, on the development of the United States' own relations with the post-1992 EC.

The European Community and the United States, nevertheless, share an interest in facilitating East European integration on two fronts: first, new forms of integration of the East European states with each other, and second, integration with the Community itself, but with appropriate safeguards and on much more generous terms than have thus far been offered. The former, ideally, should be a precondition for the latter. Making the case for such an integrationist strategy requires, however, that we address the legacy of Eastern Europe's past efforts at integration for its present economic condition and for the development of its future economic relationships, and that we then examine the prospects and pitfalls residing in alternative scenarios for integration in the near and more distant future. East and West together must find answers to the critical questions surrounding integration: with whom?, in what respects?, and according to what timetable? The choices of the West concerning these issues will be a critical component of any broader economic strategy toward the region.

THE CMEA AND ITS LEGACY

Contrary to the celebratory rhetoric devoted to the CMEA in its heyday by Soviet and East European officials, Western analysts of Eastern Europe for the most part viewed the organization with great skepticism, arguing that it failed to bring about much genuine economic integration and instead served primarily as a multilateral cover for a set of bilateral economic arrangements still dominated by the Soviet Union. Many East Europeans quietly agreed. One critic argued that the CMEA was not an "international trading system" designed to maximize efficiency at all but rather an "international protection system" intended to assure the provision of the resources necessary for the "protection and expansion of production" in each member state.[9] While this view conflicted with CMEA rhetoric and probably with the conscious intentions at least of the Soviet leadership, there was some truth in it as a description of how the organization actually operated for most of its existence.

The popular view of the CMEA as an Eastern analogue to the EC, albeit an unsuccessful one, was always somewhat inappropriate. The CMEA never had a supranational component whose decisions were binding on the member states, in spite of its formidable array of common institutions.[10] Nikita Khrushchev sought to establish a supranational planning authority in 1962, but the scheme foundered on Romanian resistance.[11] The CMEA did not establish common policies toward imports from nonmember states, nor did it eliminate internal barriers to trade. Under Communist rule, Eastern European trade was almost always based upon contractual agreements made by the region's governments and state foreign trade organizations with one another and with partners outside the CMEA. To be sure, during the reform experiments of the 1960s and again in the 1980s some decentralization of trading authority to an expanded number of specialized foreign trade organizations and even to individual enterprises took place.[12] Even then, however, East European foreign trade agreements remained almost entirely bilateral, and within the CMEA itself sought to achieve a rough trade balance between each pair of partners; because of the nontransferability of the "transferable ruble," the CMEA's nominal accounting unit, the organization never really became effective as a mechanism for the multilateralization of trade.

The CMEA's official documents invoked the goal of "socialist economic integration" without defining it, and also promised the gradual equalization of the levels of development of the member states. In practice, however, the CMEA placed its emphasis on the coordination of planning and the promotion of "specialization and cooperation" agreements in production, intended to minimize duplication while assuring that most needed goods and their components were produced somewhere in the bloc and thus did not have to be imported for hard currency. The coordination of planning was limited for the most part to linking the sections on intra-CMEA trade of the individual national plans, that is, making them consistent with bilateral trade agreements.[13] It did not mean the coordination of most production decisions or of major investments, with the important exception of the CMEA's large joint projects, most of them for energy development in the Soviet Union. Nor did it bring about the integration of research and development efforts, in spite of the CMEA's long-standing efforts to foster cooperation in this sphere, highlighted by the adoption of a Comprehensive Program for Scientific-Technical Progress in 1985.[14] Plan coordination also did not greatly affect the bilateral character of dealings by the CMEA states with capitalist firms and governments, although East European commitments for exports to the USSR and participation in joint CMEA investment projects did influence the content of their imports from the West.

However, the specialization agreements, numbering over one thousand by 1986, had some significance in such areas as the engineering and metal fabricating industries and in energy.[15] Hungary's production of *Ikarus* buses, the GDR's of numerically controlled machine tools, and Poland's of ships were examples in the former category.[16] Vladimir Sobell observes that members actually discontinued only a few lines of production because of specialization agreements, but they were probably inhibited from moving indiscriminately into new fields.[17] It is noteworthy that one area in which the CMEA was said—for a time—to have successfully divided its labor was in the computer industry; "in terms of real progress in international specialization, computing is a CMEA showcase," wrote one expert.[18] Specialization in computer production had its limits, however, and did not allow the CMEA to overcome its technological lag in this industry—in part because of Western strategic trade restrictions.[19] In general, members were inhibited from relying too heavily on CMEA specialization agreements because of their concern over the reliability and quality of deliveries from their partners and the fear of some that they would be inadequately compensated for their contributions. Available statistical evidence does not indicate that specialization agreements contributed much to the integration of the CMEA economies.[20]

The volume of intra-CMEA trade as a proportion of total East European trade suggests considerable mutual dependence, however. Apart from the high level of trade between each East European state and the Soviet Union, the six smaller CMEA members in the region traded extensively with one another, although less than one might have expected, given their proximity. About 30 percent of Czechoslovakia's trade (according to official figures) was with the other five East European CMEA states (excluding the Soviet Union), as was some 26 percent of the GDR's (see Table 5.1).[21] These two states, the most advanced industrially of the bloc, traded most heavily with each other and with Poland. Trade between Czechoslovakia, the GDR, and Poland, on the one side, and Bulgaria and Romania, on the other, was relatively unimportant for the first three countries, with trade with Hungary occupying something of a middle position. With the partial exception of Romania, trade among all six was dominated by capital goods. This market was captive in both directions: sellers could not easily have found alternative customers and buyers would have been hard-pressed to find suppliers who did not demand hard currencies in payment. The relationship was thus a relatively stable one, but it was not favorable to either quality or innovation.

THE FUTILE QUEST FOR REFORM

Some 70 percent of the gross domestic product of the CMEA as a whole (including its three non-European members, Cuba, Vietnam, and Mongolia) was produced by the Soviet Union.[22] The economic predominance of the Soviet Union, coupled with its political and military weight and the ultimate dependence of most of the East European regimes on its support,

Table 5.1
Intra-CMEA Imports and Exports (1987)
(as percentage of total trade)

country	trading partner	imports	exports
Bulgaria	**USSR**	**57.3**	**61.1**
	Czechoslovakia	**5.0**	**4.9**
	GDR	**5.7**	**5.5**
	Hungary	**2.0**	**1.8**
	Poland	**4.7**	**4.3**
	Romania	**2.2**	**2.1**
	Total East Europe	**19.6**	**18.6**
Czecho-slovakia	**USSR**	**43.6**	**43.3**
	Bulgaria	**3.2**	**3.6**
	GDR	**10.2**	**9.2**
	Hungary	**5.2**	**5.6**
	Poland	**9.8**	**9.5**
	Romania	**2.0**	**2.1**
	Total East Europe	**30.4**	**30.0**
GDR	**USSR**	**38.8**	
	Bulgaria	**3.2**	
	Czechoslovakia	**8.1**	
	Hungary	**5.2**	
	Poland	**6.5**	
	Romania	**2.9**	
	Total East Europe	**25.9**	
Hungary	**USSR**	**28.5**	**32.7**
	Bulgaria (1986)	**1.4**	**1.5**
	Czechoslovakia	**5.4**	**5.0**
	GDR	**5.4**	**5.6**
	Poland	**4.0**	**3.4**
	Romania	**1.8**	**1.8**
	Total East Europe	**19.0**	**17.3**
Poland	**USSR**	**27.3**	**24.8**
	Bulgaria	**2.0**	**2.2**
	Czechoslovakia	**6.2**	**6.0**
	GDR	**5.5**	**4.2**
	Hungary	**2.5**	**2.4**
	Romania	**1.9**	**1.5**
	Total East Europe	**18.1**	**16.3**
Romania (1985)	**USSR**	**22.4**	**21.4**
	Bulgaria	**3.0**	**1.7**
	Czechoslovakia	**3.3**	**2.6**
	GDR	**5.8**	**4.2**
	Hungary	**2.8**	**2.4**
	Poland	**5.5**	**3.5**
	Total East Europe	**20.4**	**14.4**

Note: Figures for the GDR are for trade turnover (imports + exports).
Source: Calculated from Vienna Institute for Comparative Economic Studies, *COMECON Data 1988* (Westport, Conn.: Greenwood, 1989), 175–96.

could have led one to believe that it would have no difficulty in imposing its own vision of socialist economic integration on its allies. In fact, from almost the beginning of Khrushchev's efforts in the late 1950s to revive the CMEA as an active instrument of economic cooperation, the Soviet Union met strong resistance to its designs for the organization, and proved either unwilling or unable to insist upon them.

As noted earlier, the attempt of Khrushchev in 1962 to create a supranational planning authority was frustrated by the unwillingness of Romania to accept it. The Romanian deviation was rooted in that country's refusal to accept the role contemplated for the less developed states as producers of raw materials, food, and consumer goods for the more industrialized ones, a position favored by the East Germans, Czechs, and Russians.[23] After Khrushchev's removal, continuing Romanian opposition led to the adoption in 1967 of the "interested party" principle, which provided that a country declaring its disinterest in a CMEA project could not be obliged to participate in it, but also could not impose a veto.[24] The interested party principle became an enduring part of CMEA operations.

The annual meetings of the CMEA Council, usually attended by the bloc's prime ministers, or the rarer CMEA summits of the general secretaries of the ruling parties were far from harmonious sessions devoted to the uncritical ratification of Soviet wishes. Instead, they seem to have been characterized by the energetic assertion of the national interests of member states.[25] The evidence for these conflicts could be found in the often carefully balanced wording of closing communiqués and other documents[26]; the repeated difficulty the CMEA experienced in moving from broad declarations of principle to concrete economic decisions and then to their implementation[27]; the leaks, especially by disgruntled parties, that became more frequent in the Gorbachev era; commentaries on CMEA problems published in various member states; and even the delays in holding CMEA meetings, most notably the CMEA summit first publicly requested by Romania in 1980 but held only in 1984.[28] As a Hungarian expert noted, national interests within the CMEA came to be "articulated more openly, differences of approaches [were] published more directly."[29] Increasingly, these differences led to policy stalemates.

The sources of conflicting interests varied, but several remain relevant in the post-Communist era. As the Romanian deviation suggests, one important source dating from the early years of the CMEA's activity was the differing levels of economic development of the member countries, with the more advanced countries unwilling to give more than lip service to the goal of reducing the gap separating them from the more backward ones. The specific configuration of export strengths and import needs also strongly influenced the positions taken by the member states. Thus Hungary and Romania, as net agricultural exporters, pressed for investment contributions to that sector by their partners, analogous to those being provided for Soviet energy projects; agricultural importers like Czechoslovakia opposed them. The GDR sought similar investment contributions in competitive manufacturing sectors, and the Poles demanded them for coal and sulphur.[30] When the member states adopted divergent positions toward domestic reform, the character of their economic institutions affected their positions. As early as the late 1960s Hungarian advocacy of currency convertibility and other "marketizing" reforms within the CMEA reflected its role as the bloc leader in domestic reform; Romanian and East German resistance to similar measures, and to the full-scale direct relations between enterprises promoted by the Soviet Union, expressed their continuing devotion to a highly centralized system of economic planning and management.[31]

Under Gorbachev, the Soviet position in these disputes underwent a marked shift. Joining the criticisms of the Hungarians and others, the Soviet Union attacked the poor quality and minimal competitiveness of goods produced in the CMEA, the lack of progress in restructuring the organization, and the inflexibility of its monetary arrangements and price system.[32] At its October 1987 extraordinary meeting, the council agreed to streamline the CMEA bureaucracy, reducing the size of its staff and the number of central bodies.[33] More dramatically, the Soviet Union began to advocate "marketizing" reforms for the organization; it called for the creation of a convertible ruble and the construction of a "unified socialist market." It also pressed for direct interfirm relationships across national boundaries that would encourage microeconomic initiatives based on market incentives and would presumably bypass the central planning level.

Implementing the proposal for a convertible ruble would have required the establishment of comparable, realistic prices in all participating CMEA states, and thus would have all but forced them to adopt market reforms domestically. Both Romania and the GDR rejected the proposal at the 1987 meeting; in July 1988 the GDR (but not Romania) did accept a loosely worded commitment to work toward a "unified market in the long term."[34] No further progress had been made by the time of the upheavals of fall 1989; both a CMEA summit planned for early that year and a session of the CMEA Council scheduled for June had to be postponed.

When the council finally did meet in January 1990, it was essentially to negotiate the terms of the demise of the organization in its previous form. The participants discussed plans for replacing old trading patterns with "normal" ones based on world market prices and hard currencies, and appointed a commission to study basic changes in CMEA institutions and statutes.[35] A year later even these plans had been overtaken by events, and the members of the organization decided to disband it. It could be argued that the breakup came with entirely too much haste, since negotiations with the East Europeans' preferred alternative, the EC, were still in their early stages.[36] Each country suddenly found itself obliged to rebuild economic relations with its neighbors on an individual, bilateral basis.

EASTERN EUROPE AND THE EUROPEAN COMMUNITY

For most of the cold war, the East European members of the CMEA and the European Community officially ignored each other's existence, although nonaligned Yugoslavia signed extensive trade and cooperation agreements with the EC beginning in 1970. In the last years of Communist rule in the region, however, the two sets of states cautiously opened formal relations, and when the process of democratic transformation in Hungary and Poland was threatened by growing economic difficulties in the two countries, the EC was charged with administering an extensive program of aid on behalf of the G-24 group of Western nations.[37] After the revolutions of late 1989, new East European leaders proclaimed their intention of "returning to Europe" and, as part of the process, seeking full membership in the Community for their countries. The European Commission, and the present member states of the EC, already caught up in the historic effort to achieve a fully unified internal market by the end of 1992, found themselves puzzling over the proper mode of their future relations with their newly emancipated Eastern neighbors.

After some thirty years of mutual nonrecognition, in June 1988 the CMEA signed an agreement with the EC establishing formal relations between the two. The agreement, essentially one of political intent, created a framework within which individual CMEA countries could negotiate their own trade agreements with the EC.[38] The first of these, with Hungary, was in fact negotiated simultaneously with the overall EC–CMEA accord, and was signed only a few days later. While it provided for the reduction of EC quotas on some two thousand different items by 1995, and additional ones by 1998, Hungarian steel products were excluded, and the Hungarians failed to win any immediate concessions on their important agricultural exports. Hungarian officials expressed disappointment with some of the agreement's terms, and calculated their potential increase in exports at only between 0.5 and 1 percent of the country's total convertible currency trade.[39]

In 1989, the EC signed additional trade agreements with Poland, the USSR, and Czechoslovakia. (Romania, the bloc pioneer in establishing formal relationships with Western economic groupings, had already signed general trade agreements with the EC, and indeed won generalized trade preferences from the Community in 1974 by having itself categorized as a "developing country."[40]) Diplomatic relations were established between the Community and the individual East European states and, after the upheavals of late 1989, the Commission proposed new trade and cooperation agreements with East Germany, Czechoslovakia, Bulgaria, and Romania. The last of these, with Romania, was signed on October 22, 1990, after having been delayed because of the attack by Romanian miners on opposition demonstrators in Bucharest.[41] On October 3, the former GDR entered the EC as part of a reunited Germany; it was granted special transitional provisions with respect to EC environmental requirements, agricultural subsidies, and existing trade commitments to the Soviet Union and other CMEA members.

The July 1989 Western economic summit charged the EC Commission with administering an extensive program of aid to Poland and Hungary. The resulting PHARE program (Poland/Hungary: Assistance to the Restructuring of the Economy) was designed to coordinate bilateral aid from the G-24 (Paris Club) countries and to provide some Ecu 300 million (about $390 million) directly for such purposes as food assistance, the establishment of joint ventures, training in managerial skills, opening up access to West European markets, and environmental cooperation. In addition, the Generalized System of Preferences was extended to many Polish and Hungarian industrial products and some agricultural ones, and provision was made for the European Investment Bank to loan Ecu 1 billion ($1.3 billion) to the two countries over a three-year period. The success of the PHARE program led by mid-1990 to its being extended to the other East European countries.[42]

This level of assistance, while substantial, paled beside the massive needs of the region. With German resources strained by unification and other EC members facing budgetary stringency in the wake of the Persian Gulf crisis, the growing recession, and pressures to assist the former Soviet republics, the likelihood of a large-scale expansion of EC aid was diminished. There was also the question of competing claims from the southern EC states, and the uncertainty over how efficiently the East European states could absorb what aid they received.

The more fundamental, longer-term issue was that of EC membership for the East European countries. That all five were interested in joining was clear; the Hungarian premier Jozsef Antall called for full Hungarian membership by as early as 1995.[43] The EC, confronted by these "gatecrashers" at the European 1992 "dinner party,"[44] and already in receipt of membership applications from Turkey, Austria, and Sweden as well as prospective ones from other EFTA countries, found itself forced to wrestle with the fundamental issue of its future character as an organization. The twelve EC member states seemed to agree on a number of points. No new applicants were to be considered for membership before the completion of the internal market by the end of 1992, and then the EFTA applicants were to be given priority. The next stage for Eastern Europe after the implementation of the new trade and cooperation agreements would be some form of association. Association agreements, unlike full membership, could be asymmetrical, allowing for greater access of East European goods to EC markets while protecting the Eastern economies from the full impact of Western competition.

But the European Community's association agreements with Poland, Hungary, and Czechoslovakia, signed in late 1991 after difficult negotiations, frustrated the more optimistic expectations of the Eastern Europeans. While opening EC markets for some manufactured goods, the Community still denied greater immediate access for pivotal East European exports—agricultural products, steel, and textiles—since these were already in surplus in the West and their Western producers energetically resisted the removal of import barriers.[45] A French government veto of increased meat quotas, stimulated by domestic protests, at one point threatened to derail the talks. Small concessions by the EC finally made it possible to conclude the agreements, but the liberalization of terms for the entry of agricultural goods, steel, and textiles was scheduled to take place only later in the decade, and the terms were subject to possible renegotiation.[46] As it stands, some 40 percent of the three countries' exports remain subject to trade restraints.[47] Moreover, as of the end of 1992 the association agreements, dependent upon ratification by all member states, had not yet gone into effect, and the breakup of Czechoslovakia required that new negotiations be opened between the EC and the two successor governments. Additional agreements were initialled with Romania and Bulgaria, however.

The final stage, full EC membership, remains controversial, and appears to be receding into a rather distant future. As framed, perhaps somewhat simplistically, in the media, the Community faces a choice between "widening" and "deepening." "Wideners," favoring the relatively rapid extension of membership to the East European states and other applicants, often have in mind an implied corollary: that the degree of integration in (and the sacrifice of sovereignty to) the Community as a whole should remain limited. The Thatcher government in Britain was the clearest advocate of such a course.[48] "Deepeners," most notably the French, argue for the intensification of cooperation, and its extension to foreign, defense, and monetary policy, with the expansion of membership put off until much later, if not indefinitely. Some, like the Germans, affect to favor simultaneous "widening" and "deepening," although skeptics tend to view the two as difficult to reconcile. Nervous outsiders, especially the United States and the successor states of the Soviet Union, have some reason to wonder what simultaneous widening and deepening might mean for them. Eastern Europeans, sobered by their experience in the negotiations over association, also face predictions that they will not be economically ready for EC membership until after the year 2000,[49] while recognizing that such a delay might make it still harder to join a Community deepened and perhaps widened by several EFTA countries in the interim.

ALTERNATIVE CONFIGURATIONS

There is a strong case to be made in the abstract for creating a new East European economic organization, without the former Soviet Union, fostering the close cooperation of the region's states with one another. Such a grouping could take advantage of the fact that all have now begun to create market economies and have moved toward currency convertibility, which should make possible a level of genuine integration and multilateral cooperation never achieved by the CMEA. A regional free trade agreement, for example, would make possible expanded competition, which in turn should produce higher quality and greater efficiency in production. The larger market thus created and—assuming they could be quickly put into force—uniform business regulations, similar taxation principles, and common monetary policies would prove attractive for potential foreign and domestic investors. If successful, such a grouping could be a stepping stone to membership in the EC.[50]

In fact, trade among the East European states fell precipitously after the collapse of the CMEA, for example, by 60 percent between 1990 and 1991 in the case of Hungary's trade with Poland and Czechoslovakia.[51] As early as January 1990, however, the (then) Hungarian deputy prime minister, Peter Medgyessy, proposed a new, trilateral organization for economic cooperation, confined to Hungary, Poland, and Czechoslovakia, on the grounds of their similar levels of development.[52] Czechoslovak President Václav Havel offered similar proposals on visits to Hungary and Poland, and in February 1991 Havel, Polish President Wałęsa, and Hungarian Prime Minister Antall signed a cooperation agreement at their Visegrád (Hungary) summit. But subsequent summits in Cracow (October 1991) and Prague (May 1992) and active cooperation among the three in negotiations with the EC brought little concrete progress toward economic integration. In December 1992, after several postponements, the three (soon to be four) states signed an agreement to establish a free-trade zone (but not a customs or monetary union) over a period of eight years; in the short term it reduced duties only to the level already negotiated with the EC.[53]

The division of Czechoslovakia is particularly threatening to prospects for regional integration, since the governments of the two successor states are likely to pursue divergent economic and monetary policies, even though they have agreed to maintain free trade between them. The independence of Slovakia also threatens to deepen Slovak-Hungarian tensions. Feuding over Slovak determination to complete the Gabcikovo-Nagymaros dam project on the Danube, and in so doing to divert the river's flow, was already intense prior to the separation, and the nationalist Hungarian government is profoundly concerned over the treatment of the 600,000 Hungarians living in Slovakia.[54]

Even apart from the Czechoslovak separation, there are a number of inhibitions on regional economic cooperation. Prior to World War II, the level of economic cooperation and exchange among the East European states was low.[55] Under Communist rule, Eastern Europeans acquired a deep distrust of the economic reliability of their neighbors, in some cases reinforced by the national stereotypes so prevalent in the region. Complaints, for example, over the failure of the Poles to deliver promised coal or television tubes, or over the East Germans' unwillingness or inability to provide parts and service for their tractors, were a staple of the old order.[56] Moreover, the domestic political preoccupations of the new regimes, responding to the strong Western orientation of their citizenries, has made efforts at building closer links to the EC seem more pressing than the reconstruction of Eastern ties. Antall, for example, has resisted the institutionalization of Visegrád Triangle cooperation on these grounds,[57] and Václav Klaus, now the Czech prime minister, has expressed his preference for bilateral agreements and characterized Visegrád as an artificial process created by the West.[58]

The Visegrád grouping also suffers from the absence of the former GDR, which was a pivotal participant in earlier intra-CMEA relations. After the economic unification of Germany on July 1, 1990, GDR producers cancelled many of their agreements with their former CMEA partners or demanded hard-currency payment for their goods; overall, eastern Germany's trade with Eastern Europe fell precipitously, and producers on both sides suffered.[59] Only special concessions by the German government, approved by the EC and a corresponding German industrial strategy, could even partially restore this missing link to schemes for integration of the northern tier. On the other hand, the exclusion of Bulgaria and Romania from tripartite integration plans probably eases cooperation among the northern-tier states; it is likely, however, to worsen still further the two Balkan countries' desperate problems by increasing their isolation.[60]

EAST EUROPEAN INTEGRATION AND WESTERN POLICY

The ultimate outcome of Eastern European aspirations to join the European Community will, of course, depend on the decisions of the Community itself. The case is persuasive that a headlong rush of East European states into full Community membership would be economically perilous for them, if politically and psychologically attractive in the short run. Movement toward more generous terms in the treaties of association, however, would be both practicable and desirable, although hardly uncontested, given the determination of the poorer EC states and of all the Community's agricultural and steel producers to defend their interests. The United States will have the secondary, but still important, role it once played with respect to Western Europe: encouraging integration from afar. It may well be in this country's best economic interest, however, to support the "wideners" rather than the "deepeners."

Both the EC and the United States (and other Western countries) have every reason to encourage the economic integration of an East European core at least as a transitional measure. EC officials, including Jacques Delors, have recognized this need, and suggested linking Western aid to progress along such lines.[61] The former Czech dissident and present editorial writer for *Lidove Noviny* Jan Urban has indeed proposed that Western aid be provided *only* to joint, integrative projects, and not to individual governments.[62] His recommendation is worth taking seriously, even if, as a practical matter, not all individual country assistance can be proscribed.[63] Poland, Hungary, and Czechoslovakia learned the advantages of forging a common front in negotiating the terms of the EC association agreements; the logic of that cooperation needs to be extended to form the basis for a much broader strategy of integration.

NOTES

1. Friedrich Levcik and Jan Stankovsky,"Eastern Europe's Trade Problems: Between the USSR and the West," in John P. Hardt and Carl H. McMillan, *Planned Economies Confronting the Challenges of the Eighties* (Cambridge: Cambridge University Press, 1988), 150.

2. Walter Russell Mead, "The Once and Future Reich," *World Policy Journal* 7 (Fall 1990), 618.

3. World Bank, *World Development Report 1991* (Oxford: Oxford University Press, 1991), 209.

4. See András Köves, *The CMEA Countries in the World Economy: Turning Inwards or Turning Outwards* (Budapest: Akademiai Kiado, 1985), 51–54.

5. Quoted in J. F. Brown, *Eastern Europe and Communist Rule* (Durham, N.C.: Duke University Press, 1988), 155–56.

6. See "East-West Relations and Eastern Europe," *Problems of Communism* (September–October 1988), 65.

7. Valery Karavayev, "Foreign Economic Reserves of *Perestroika*," *International Affairs*, Moscow (December 1988), 57.

8. Vlad Sobell, "East European Integration: The Disbanding of the CMEA," *European Trends*, Economist Intelligence Unit, no. 1 (1991), 74; *Business Eastern Europe* 20 (May 20, 1991), 155.

9. Vladimir Sobell, *The Red Market: Industrial Cooperation and Specialisation in Comecon* (Aldershot, Hants, England: Gower, 1984), 5; see also the critique by Jozef M. van Brabant, *Adjustment, Structural Change, and Economic Efficiency: Aspects of Monetary Cooperation in Eastern Europe* (Cambridge: Cambridge University Press, 1987), 9–10.

10. See Heinrich Machowski, "Der Rat für gegenseitige Wirtschaftshilfe: Ziele, Formen und Probleme der Zusammenarbeit," in *Rat für gegenseitige Wirtschaftshilfe* (Bonn: Ostkolleg der Bundeszentrale für politische Bildung, 1987), 30–31; van Brabant, 54–60.

11. See Franklyn Holzman, *International Trade under Communism* (New York: Basic Books, 1976), 97–99.

12. Harriet Matejka, "The Foreign Trade System," in M. C. Kaser, ed., *The Economic History of Eastern Europe 1919–1975*, vol. 3 (Oxford: Clarendon Press, 1986), 265–69.

13. László Csaba, "Coordination of Interests in the CMEA," *Soviet and East European Foreign Trade* 24 (Spring 1988), 38–44.

14. See Lucja Ursula Swiatkowski, "*Perestroika* of the Council of Mutual Economic Assistance: The New Science and Technology Policy," in Joint Economic Committee, *Pressures for Reform in the East European Economies*, vol. 2 (Washington, D.C.: U.S. Government Printing Office, 1989), 534–49; Steven W. Popper, "Conflicts in CMEA Science and Technology Integration Policy," in ibid., 564–69.

15. See Sobell, *The Red Market*, for a detailed account of specialization and cooperation arrangements; see also Keith Crane and Deborah Skoller, "Specialization Agreements: An Effective CMEA Policy Tool?" *Pressures for Reform*, vol. 2, 570–75. Such agreements were said to cover over 20 percent of intra-CMEA trade as early as 1976. Crane and Skoller, 572.

16. See Sobell, *The Red Market*, 238–40, for a more complete list.

17. Ibid., 242–43.

18. Seymour E. Goodman, "The Partial Integration of the CMEA Computer Industries: An Overview," in Joint Economic Committee, *East European Economies: Slow Growth in the 1980s*, vol. 2 (Washington: U. S. Government Printing Office, 1986), 337.

19. See Gary L. Geipel, A. Tomasz Jarmoszko, and Seymour E. Goodman, "The Information Technologies and East European Societies," *East European Politics and Societies* (Fall 1991), 394–438. The authors note that by the late 1980s the region's most advanced producer, the GDR, had become virtually "an island unto itself," having lost faith in the advantages of CMEA cooperation, while other countries had turned to final assembly of components purchased when possible in the West. Ibid., 436–37.

20. See Crane and Skoller, 573–75.

21. Here it should again be noted that Czech and East German statistics tended to overstate the volume of CMEA trade relative to Western trade.

22. See table in *Rat*, 200.

23. See Brown, 146–48.

24. See the CMEA Statute, Article 5, as reprinted in *Rat*, 170; Machowski, "Der Rat," 31.

25. Włodzimierz Brus remarks that as early as the late 1950s the invigoration of the CMEA improved the bargaining position of the East European states by creating "an institution for pursuing (or at the very least presenting) national interests." Brus, "1957 to 1965: In Search of Balanced Development," in Kaser, vol. 3, 73.

26. See the analysis by Karen Dawisha, *Eastern Europe, Gorbachev, and Reform* (Cambridge: Cambridge University Press, 1988), 94, of the careful balance between the points of view of the USSR and the East European states in the final document of the 1984 CMEA summit.

27. See the somewhat despairing comments of the then–Czech prime minister Lubomir Štrougal quoted in Siegfried Kupper, "Absichtserklärungen—kein konkretes Programm," *Deutschland Archiv* 21 (January 1988), 62–63.

28. van Brabant, 69–70.

29. László Csaba, "CMEA and the Challenge of the 1980s," *Soviet Studies* 40 (April 1988), 276. Elsewhere, however, Csaba notes that differences on important conceptual issues "mostly do not follow national lines." Ibid., 274.

30. Csaba, "CMEA," 275–78.

31. On the GDR, see Kupper, 60–64.

32. *Süddeutsche Zeitung,* July 8, 1988, 8; *Tagesspiegel,* July 7, 1988, 6.

33. Ibid.

34. Vlad Sobell, "The CMEA's Goal of a 'Unified Market' " *RFE Research,* BR/130 (Economics), July 12, 1988, 1.

35. Vlad Sobell, "In Search of a New CMEA," *Report on Eastern Europe,* February 9, 1990, 39–42; Sobell, "East European Economies at a Turning Point," ibid., May 4, 1990, 41–43.

36. *Wall Street Journal,* July 20, 1990.

37. These include the twelve states of the Community, the six members of the European Free Trade Association, the United States, Canada, Japan, Australia, New Zealand, and Turkey.

38. *Frankfurter Allgemeine Zeitung,* June 27, 1988, 3. For the background of the EC-CMEA negotiations, see Sophie Verny, "The EEC and CMEA," *Soviet and Eastern European Foreign Trade* 24 (Summer 1988), 6–21; Christian Meier, "Die DDR und das Verhältnis zwischen RGW und EG," *DDR Report* 20 (1987/6), 321–24.

39. Karoly Okolicsanyi, "Hungary Reaches a Trade Agreement with the EEC," *RFE Research,* SR/12 (Hungary), August 12, 1988, 27–30; interview with Deputy Prime Minister Jozsef Marjai, July 5, 1988, Budapest *MTI* in English, FBIS *Daily Report—Eastern Europe,* July 7, 1988, 30–31.

40. Michael Shafir, *Romania: Politics, Economics and Society* (London: Frances Pinter, 1985), 112.

41. See *European Trends,* Background Supplement 1990–1991, 76; *Report on Eastern Europe,* November 2, 1990, 51.

42. *European Trends,* ibid.; Mark Baker, "EE Aid Now Over $20 bn; Getting a Piece of the Pie," *Business Eastern Europe* 19 (October 22, 1990), 345–46.

43. *Financial Times,* July 18, 1990, 2.

44. *Economist,* November 25, 1989, as cited in Vladimir Sobell, "Eastern Europe and the European Community," *Report on Eastern Europe,* February 23, 1990, 48.

45. Joseph C. Brada, "The European Community and Czechoslovakia, Hungary, and Poland," *Report on Eastern Europe,* December 6, 1991, 27–32. See also Jan B. de Weydenthal, "Czechoslovakia, Hungary, and Poland Gain Associate Membership in the EC," *RFE/RL Research Report,* February 7, 1992, 24–26.

46. When, nevertheless, Czechoslovak steel exports to Germany and France leapt upward in the first months of 1992, supposedly because of "dumping," the EC imposed quotas on them. *RFE/RL Research Report,* August 14, 1992, 64; August 28, 1992, 72. East European steel exports currently face a 30 percent EC tariff. Jan B. de Weydenthal, "EC Keeps Central Europe at Arms Length," *RFE/RL Research Report,* January 29, 1993, 30.

47. "Survey—Eastern Europe," *Economist,* March 13, 1993, 20.

48. See Richard Weitz, "The Expanding Role of the Council of Europe," *Report on Eastern Europe,* August 24, 1990, 56.

49. This was a conclusion of a study by Britain's National Westminster Bank, as cited in Karoly Okolicsanyi, "Relations with the European Community," *Report on Eastern Europe*, July 26, 1991, 34; it now seems to be almost universally accepted, even by the Eastern Europeans.

50. See Tibor Palankai, *The European Community and Central European Integration* (New York: Institute for East-West Security Studies, 1991), 48–58.

51. Karoly Okolicsanyi, "The Visegrad Triangle's Free-Trade Zone," *RFE/RL Research Report*, January 15, 1993, 20.

52. See Sobell, "In Search," 41.

53. Okolicsanyi, "The Visegrad Triangle's," 19–22.

54. See Jan Obrman, ed., "Roundtable: Relations with the Czech Republic and Hungary," *RFE/RL Research Report*, December 11, 1992, 33–42; Karoly Okolicsanyi, "Slovak-Hungarian Tension: Bratislava Diverts the Danube," ibid., 49–54.

55. Paul Marer, "The Economies and Trade of Eastern Europe," in William E. Griffith, ed., *Central and Eastern Europe: The Opening Curtain* (Boulder, Colo.: Westview Press, 1989), 37–38.

56. The examples of the Polish television tubes and East German tractors were provided to me by a Hungarian economist. Interview, June 24, 1988.

57. Alfred Reisch, "Hungary Sees Common Goals and Bilateral Issues," *RFE/RL Research Report*, June 5, 1992, 30.

58. *RFE/RL Research Report*, September 25, 1992, 73; *RFE/RL News Briefs*, January 11–15, 1993, 12.

59. See Marie Lavigne, "The CMEA's Transition from the Transferable Ruble," *Report on Eastern Europe*, November 2, 1990, 41; András Inotai, "Economic Implications of German Unification for Central and Eastern Europe," in Paul B. Stares, ed., *The New Germany and the New Europe* (Washington, D.C.: Brookings Institution, 1992), 279–85

60. The three Visegrad leaders rejected an overture from Romania's prime minister to join them in February, 1991. Reisch, "Hungary Sees," 30.

61. See Yuri Sinyakov, "COMECON: Time to Write an Obit?" *Business in the USSR*, July-August 1990, 47.

62. Jan Urban, "Divided it Falls," *New York Times*, November 21, 1990, 15.

63. On the same lines, see Mead, 631.

6

Patterns of East-West Trade

> Let me repeat that we do not need direct financial aid, but rather an open market for our exports—if we fail and there is destabilization, it will not be destabilization for the central Europeans alone. It will be destabilization for the whole of Europe.
>
> Vladimir Dlouhy, former Czechoslovak Minister of the Economy[1]

Prior to the upheavals of 1989, Eastern Europe's trade with Western industrial nations was highly asymmetrical. As of 1987, trade with Eastern Europe accounted for only about 1 percent of total Western trade,[2] while trade with the West amounted to at least one-third of the total trade of the East European states.[3] The composition of the commodities exchanged was also unbalanced. The largest category of East European imports from the West consisted of machinery and transportation equipment, followed by chemicals and intermediate manufactures; machinery, however, accounted for only about 11 percent of East Europe's Western exports, which were dominated by fuels, metals, intermediate manufactures, consumer goods, and in some cases agricultural products.[4] This pattern contrasted sharply with the heavy concentration of machinery in the exports of the East European states to each other, the Soviet Union, and other Communist and developing nations. The political changes of 1989 and 1990 altered many of the conditions of East-West trade, but did not remove the asymmetries.

The precipitous decline of Eastern Europe's trade with the Soviet Union, and the other former CMEA countries after 1989 forced the region's new governments to seek an even more rapid expansion of their Western trade than they otherwise might have. Their success was mixed, and most countries faced the threat of deficits in their Western trade in spite of severe domestic recessions and exchange rates designed to favor exports and limit imports.[5] Bringing trade back into balance, reducing the asymmetries in trade composition, and assuring that trade support rather than subvert economic reform and development will require that the West look beyond short-term self-interest in its trade policies. It will need to remove the remaining obstacles to imports from Eastern Europe without demanding full and immediate reciprocity. More generally, it will need to find ways to help the Eastern Europeans strengthen their export capacities.

EAST-WEST TRADE UNDER COMMUNISM

Trade between the Eastern European states and the West had grown rapidly in the 1970s, but the growth was highly unbalanced. East Europe's imports, financed by generous Western credits, greatly exceeded its exports. The strategy followed during this period, most visibly by Poland but in lesser measure by most of the other states, was to import Western machinery in order to modernize its industry, which subsequently, it was hoped, would be able to sell more finished products to hard-currency markets, as well as to supply more and higher-quality goods for domestic consumption. Attractive consumer goods were a necessary incentive, it was thought, for a more productive work force.[6] This import-led strategy was frustrated by a variety of factors: economic stagnation and recession in the West, the often indiscriminate character and reckless pace of the importation of Western technology (most notoriously in Poland),[7] its inefficient incorporation into East European industry, and the failure to accompany the import boom with needed economic reforms. By 1980 Poland, Hungary, the GDR, and Romania were all heavily in debt to Western creditors; the rising cost of Soviet fuels brought about by OPEC price increases and the Polish upheaval brought matters to a crisis point. Western banks abruptly turned off the credit spigot, and the East European states had to scramble to avoid default.

To do so, they dramatically curtailed Western imports, and sought to increase their exports with the help of price cutting and other extraordinary measures. But in all six countries exports to the West still fell or (in the GDR) stagnated, owing to the Western recession and competing demands from the Soviet Union for larger and higher-quality deliveries. In order to keep consumption from falling too drastically, the bloc states all were forced to reduce investment sharply, slowing the pace of modernization (and thus the potential for future sales to the West) still further.[8] By the late 1980s, to be sure, trade with the West had largely stabilized and in the cases of Hungary, Poland, and Czechoslovakia had again begun significantly to expand.

Trends in the composition of East European exports to the West in the last years of Communist rule were disquieting. East Europe's market share of machinery purchases by the West, already small, had declined still further, while that of the East Asian and Latin American newly industrializing countries (NICs) had dramatically risen. In 1987, when machinery and transportation equipment comprised just 11 percent of East Europe's exports to the West, the corresponding figures for the East Asian and Latin American NICs were 32 percent and 27 percent.[9] The large East European exports of refined oil products, which took on particular importance in the early 1980s, lost much of their profitability owing to the drop in world oil prices, and other leading exports—steel, textiles, other low-technology consumer goods—faced stiffer competition from the NICs and/or satiated markets. Agricultural exports had to contend with worldwide surpluses and the export subsidies of competing countries. Price movements also did not favor East European exports: the terms of trade with the West had dropped by 1985 to some 80–85 percent of the 1970 level for most countries, although they recovered somewhat between 1985 and 1989.

On the import side, the proportion of total imports from the West composed of machinery and transportation equipment rose from 31 percent in 1979 to 38 percent in 1987. This figure, however, was lower than the proportion of such goods among overall Western exports (41 percent), and substantially below the proportion imported by East Europe's competitors, the East Asian and Latin American NICs and Southern Europe.[10] What this fact suggests is that the use of Western machinery for modernization was restricted by the priority given to other critical import needs—semi-finished goods, chemicals, and in some cases agricultural products. Moreover, as we shall see in chapter 7, only a small proportion of the machinery East Europe imported from the West could be described even loosely as high tech. This fact was partly a consequence of Western strategic trade restrictions, but it also reflected the relatively underdeveloped state of many East European industries and their insulation from the international economy.

The burden of hard currency debt also impeded the development of East-West trade. For Poland and Hungary, heavy debt service obligations devoured export earnings and sharply restricted the possibility of expanding the Western technology imports badly needed for the modernization of their aging industry. Romania slashed its Western imports to a fraction of their previous level in an effort to eliminate its debt entirely. Even countries with smaller debts suffered from high interest rates and the effects of currency fluctuations. Western bankers, now somewhat more prudent than they had been during the 1970s, became leary of granting additional broad trade credits, especially to Poland, although private lending to other countries resumed later in the decade.

AFTER THE REVOLUTIONS: A NEW TRADE ENVIRONMENT

The demise of Communist rule in the region quickly brought significant improvements in the conditions of East-West trade. The European Community and, more hesitantly, the United States eased import restrictions on East European goods, and the EC began to negotiate association agreements with Poland, Hungary, and Czechoslovakia, promising still more favorable trade terms for those countries. The former GDR was incorporated into the EC (albeit with certain transitional provisions) with German unification, and it thereby automatically acquired MFN status from the United States. COCOM barriers to strategic trade were reduced (though not fully eliminated), making more high-technology goods available to the region. The prospect of Western private investment brought with it the possibility of valuable technology acquisitions and ultimately an improvement in the marketability of East European manufactures. Politically inspired East European barriers to Western imports, particularly of consumer goods, fell, and the effort to move toward currency convertibility enhanced the prospects for sales of such items to consumers long hungry for them. The great expansion of Western public credits and credit guarantees—through individual governments, the EC, the IMF, the World Bank, and the European Bank for Reconstruction and Development—supported foreign and domestic investment, including investment in the badly needed modernization of infrastructure.

Not all the new developments were positive. Private bank loans not backed by public agencies all but ground to a halt as bankers observed the parlous state of the region's economies.[11] Economic reforms dramatically reduced the purchasing power of Eastern consumers and thus their ability to buy Western imports, in turn made increasingly expensive by progressive currency devaluations. The changeover to West German currency in East Germany made many East German products unsalable in the West and unaffordable in the East. East European firms now had less incentive to sell their goods at a loss to the West (something the Communist regimes had regularly done to generate hard currency);[12] significant export items, such as East German Praktika cameras, thus lost markets that the old regime had cultivated. In some cases, market-oriented accounting, revealing actual production and marketing costs, demonstrated for the first time that many exports were in fact unprofitable.

The decline of the East European states' trade with the Soviet Union and with each other made more goods available for Western export. By early 1991, the termination of the CMEA, the inability of the Soviet Union to pay many of its debts or to deliver promised oil supplies, and the elimination of subsidies to firms producing for the Soviet market all increased the incentive for East European firms to shift their trade to the West. Unfortunately, many of the goods once produced for CMEA customers had little allure for Western buyers. Published trade data since 1989 is maddeningly inconsistent, but Poland, Hungary, and Czechoslovakia appear to have roughly balanced the dramatic decline in their Soviet and East European trade with gains in trade with the West; Romania and Bulgaria (and the former GDR) have not, especially with respect to exports, which have fallen precipitously.[13]

Most of the fundamental problems that impeded trade between the West and Eastern Europe remained. The low quality, inferior technology, and high production costs of many East European goods made them difficult to market. The glut on the world market of some of the most important East European export items limited possibilities for trade expansion. Western businessmen seeking trade agreements faced many of the same obstacles they had encountered under Communist rule, as well as some new ones: bureaucratic hurdles, difficulties in identifying those responsible for and capable of making decisions, a shortage of suitable space for sales or manufacturing facilities, uncertainty over property rights, and inadequate communications, transportation, and housing. New East European entrepreneurs (and new or restructured and restaffed government agencies) lacked experience in marketing to the West. The competition of the NICs and Southern Europe for Western markets remained unabated. Overall, the climate of great political and economic uncertainty in the region made potential investors wary of making substantial financial commitments.

INDIVIDUAL COUNTRY PROFILES

These generalizations help us to understand some of the broader dilemmas that face any effort to invigorate East Europe's trade with the West. But they also mask some significant differences among the individual East European countries in the level, composition, and conditions of their Western trade. These differences reflect their respective resource endowments, the structure of their work forces, and their levels of economic development, but they are also a legacy of the conscious policy choices of their former ruling elites.

One important difference is in the proportion of trade each country carried out with the industrialized West while still under Communist rule. By 1988 three countries conducted nearly half of their trade with members of OECD (the West's Organization for Economic Cooperation and Development), although that fact was acknowledged in only two of them. In that year Hungary sent 43 percent of its exports to and received 46.3 percent of its imports from the West; for Poland, the figures were 46.9 and 48.1 percent. After revaluation at realistic exchange rates, 45.4 percent of East German exports and 51.4 percent of imports could be assigned to the West. The figures for Czechoslovakia, even after a similar revaluation, were substantially lower: 30.9 percent and 34.0 percent. Romania's once-vigorous Western trade had declined to 35.4 percent (exports) and 14.9 percent (imports). At the bottom was Bulgaria, which, according to artificially low official figures, sent just 7.2 percent of its exports to the West and received only 16.4 percent of its imports from there.[14]

In terms of total trade volume, the GDR was easily the West's most important trading partner, followed by Poland and Czechoslovakia. Hungary, in spite of its prominence on Western financial pages, ranked just fourth in Western imports and fifth in exports, while Romania was fourth in exports and last in imports. Bulgaria was at the bottom in exports and fifth in imports. Calculated on a per capita basis, however, Hungary ranked second in both exports and imports, while Poland was only fourth in imports and fifth in exports.[15] These patterns have persisted under post-Communist rule, except for the disappearance of the GDR and the widening of the gap between Romania and Bulgaria and the rest. Newly independent Slovakia is likely to lag behind the Czech Republic but remain ahead of Poland in per capita trade (see Table 6.1).

Hungary

Hungary's reputation as the East European country most receptive to Western trade and investment goes back to the conscious policy choices of its Communist leaders. In the last years of their rule they made clear their intention of stimulating the country's modernization through the importation of Western technology and competition in international markets as well as through continuing domestic economic reforms that were already the most far-reaching in the bloc.[16] Hungary was the first CMEA country to conclude a comprehensive trade agreement with the European Community; it had been a member of GATT since 1973 and joined the IMF and World Bank in 1982. It was the only East European country to enjoy Most Favored Nation (MFN) status from the United States throughout the 1980s, owing to the regime's liberal domestic policies and the relative freedom of movement it permitted its citizens.[17] Hungary welcomed joint ventures with Western capitalist firms; 111 of them, more than in the other 5 East European countries together, were already in place at the end of 1987.[18] It also pioneered in setting up bond and stock markets. Beginning in 1989, it invited Western investors to purchase shares, or even a majority interest, in some of its most successful firms; among those responding were General Electric, which purchased a majority interest in the electric light bulb producer Tungsram. Perhaps the most striking symbol of Hungary's rapprochement with capitalist economies was the busy, giant McDonald's restaurant in Budapest's central pedestrian zone, the largest McDonald's in the world prior to the establishment of the company's Moscow outpost.

Nevertheless, Hungary remained dependent on the Soviet Union for over half its oil and 25–30 percent of its total trade. The regime devoted a significant portion of its investment resources to CMEA joint energy projects, notably the Yamburg pipeline, and subsidized enterprises producing

Table 6.1
East European Foreign Trade Data (1991)

	Bulgaria	Czecho-Slovakia	Hungary	Poland	Romania
Overall Trade (billion U.S. $)					
Exports	2.2	10.9	10.5	14.9	4.1
Imports	2.9	10.2	11.3	15.5	5.2
Trade Balance	-0.7	+0.7	-0.8	-0.6	-1.1
Exports per capita (U.S. $)					
	245	696	1012	392	177
Trade by Regions (percentage of total trade)					
Exports to:					
Western countries	23.3%	51.9	66.7	73.7	44.7
Former CMEA	54.9	32.9	19.2	16.8	28.3
Developing	17.5	8.6	9.7	7.7	19.0
Imports from:					
Western countries	31.9%	51.3	67.8	68.9	39.6
Former CMEA	48.9	37.5	22.2	19.0	24.0
Developing	17.2	7.9	8.2	10.4	30.2
Commodity Composition (percentage of total Western trade)					
Exports to West:					
primary goods	40.0%	16.8	31.5	30.7	10.2
food	(29.4)	(6.9)	(22.8)	(16.7)	(5.2)
fuels	2.3	5.2	5.0	11.9	11.1
semi-manufactures	21.9	28.7	17.1	18.9	18.2
engineering goods	12.7	21.4	18.5	13.8	9.5
consumer goods	21.9	26.6	27.0	24.0	50.1
Imports from West:					
primary goods	19.5%	11.4	7.9	13.8	23.4
food	(14.9)	(6.0)	(4.5)	(11.1)	(18.5)
fuels	4.0	0.9	1.1	6.3	9.5
semi-manufactures	19.2	18.7	24.6	17.2	18.9
engineering goods	43.5	54.4	45.3	41.4	28.5
consumer goods	12.1	13.4	20.2	19.0	17.2

Sources: International Monetary Fund, *Direction of Trade Statistics Yearbook 1992* (Washington, D.C.: International Monetary Fund, 1992); Economic Commission for Europe, *Economic Bulletin*, vol. 44, 1992 (New York: United Nations, 1992), 51–52, 140–41.

for the Soviet market. When world oil prices dropped and Hungary began to achieve substantial surpluses in its trade with the USSR, it sought to cut its subsidies, and won Soviet agreement to reduce deliveries. It also announced its intention of ending further participation in the Yamburg project. In 1989, Hungary's exports to the Soviet Union and other socialist countries fell, while exports to and imports from the developed West rose by 7 percent and nearly 11 percent respectively.[19]

The non-Communist government elected in March 1990, proclaiming its devotion to liberal economic principles, carried further the foreign trade course initiated by its predecessor. Trade figures for 1990 through 1992 showed an acceleration of the shift of Hungary's trade Westward. By 1991 two-thirds of the country's trade was with OECD members; over half of that was with Germany and Austria. Imports, however, rose faster than exports, producing a $1.1 billion trade deficit in 1991 and a $365 million one in 1992, according to Hungarian customs figures. Trade with the Soviet Union and other former CMEA partners fell to less than 25 percent of Hungary's total, and overall trade volume remained essentially stagnant. Some 70 percent of Hungary's trade, it might be noted, was still controlled by state foreign trade organizations.[20]

Domestic economic conditions continued the deterioration they had experienced under Communist rule throughout the 1980s. Hungary's inflation rate reached 29 percent in 1990 and 35.2 percent in 1991, falling to 22–25 percent in 1992. Living standards have seriously eroded, and the country's Gross Domestic Product declined by 4 percent in 1990, 10 percent in 1991, and an estimated 5–7 percent in 1992, after having virtually stagnated throughout the 1980s.[21] Unemployment had reached 12.2 percent by the end of 1992.[22] Large numbers of homeless persons take shelter in Budapest's railway stations[23]; "at least" three million of the country's 10.6 million citizens are estimated to fall below the official poverty line.[24]

Hungary's hard-currency debt as a proportion of its gross national product was even higher than Poland's (prior to the reduction of the latter by Western governments). Nevertheless, foreign governments, multilateral lending agencies, and even private lenders continue to approve substantial loans to Hungary; at the beginning of 1991, for example, the IMF agreed to provide a $1.7 billion standby credit.[25] Foreign (especially American) investors also continued to favor Hungary; by October 1992, Western investment totalled some $3.8 billion, more than that placed in all other East European countries (without eastern Germany) combined.

Nearly a quarter of Hungary's exports to the West (and to the rest of the world) are agricultural products, particularly live animals and meat products, reflecting the relative efficiency of its farmers, unparalleled elsewhere in the region. Other exports are diverse, but include items like iron and steel products (2.9 percent in 1991) and textiles and clothing (14.3 percent) often subject, like farm products, to Western trade restrictions. While sales of engineering goods to the West have expanded (18.5 percent), they have fallen sharply overall, largely because of the virtual disappearance of the CMEA market for them. Western imports are similarly diverse; in 1991 45 percent fell in the category of machinery and equipment, while 25 percent went for intermediate manufactures and chemicals.[26] Especially after the fall of the country's Communist regime, consumer goods imports rose sharply, albeit in part as an artifact of changed statistical conventions.

Poland

Poland has a longer post–World War II history of extensive economic relations with Western countries than any of its neighbors. As early as 1960, 30 percent of Poland's trade had been with the West, reflecting the special Western favor shown the country after Gomulka's return to power in 1956. Between 1972 and 1975, however, the Polish government promoted a veritable explosion of Western imports. These grew at an annual rate of 46.9 percent—58 percent for capital goods—and by 1975 amounted to half of all the country's imports. Exports to the West, while also increasing, lagged sharply behind imports, and amounted to just over 30 percent of the country's total in 1975.[27] The result was a yawning annual hard-currency deficit; Poland managed to cut the deficit in half in the second half of the decade, but its cumulative effects, coupled with the political crisis of 1980–1981, left the country with a nearly unmanageable foreign debt, negative growth rates, and the pressures of Western economic sanctions in place of the generous credits of earlier years. The unavoidable consequence of these events was a sharp drop in the overall level of Poland's trade and a shift of much of what remained of it to the East; yet the very need to service Western debt kept this shift within bounds. In 1985 one-third of Poland's trade was still with the industrialized West, and by 1987 this trade was again expanding rapidly, both in absolute terms and relative to its trade with the socialist world; by 1989, Western trade accounted for half of Poland's total, while ruble trade had gone into a sharp decline. Poland also enjoyed a substantial trade surplus, both with the West and with the Soviet Union.[28]

Nevertheless, Poland's Solidarity-led government, formed in September 1989 under Tadeusz Mazowiecki, inherited severe economic problems from its Communist predecessor. The country's hard-currency current account remained in deficit, and its $41.8 billion net debt appeared to be virtually impervious to attempts to reduce it; it remained more than four times Poland's annual export earnings, as it had throughout the 1980s.[29] The change of government and the subsequent adoption of economic reforms did serve to open Western purse strings, as the European Community, the United States, and other Western countries provided substantial food aid, credits, and a stabilization fund to shore up the zloty. The IMF and World Bank rewarded the government's policies with substantial support; the Bank agreed to grant more than $2 billion in credits, and in March 1991 the government approved an agreement with the IMF providing some

$2 billion for restructuring.[30] Payment of the latter was suspended in midyear, however, because of ballooning budget deficits.

The most dramatic Western step in support of Poland's economy also came in March 1991, when the Paris Club countries agreed to forgive at least 50 percent of that part of Poland's debt owed to Western governments ($33 billion), and to restructure the rest. The United States agreed to reduce its portion of the debt (some $3 billion) by 70 percent, and France its portion ($5.2 billion) by 60 pecent. Debt reduction was made dependent on Poland's returning to the good graces of the IMF, however. Negotiations with Poland's private creditors (principally banks that had already written off much of the debt) for similar concessions have yet to bear fruit.[31]

Poland's domestic economy and, less directly, its foreign trade, came under the discipline of the Balcerowicz Plan, a "shock therapy" approach to economic reform named for the government's liberal finance minister and considerably influenced by the advice of the Harvard economist Jeffrey Sachs. The plan entailed the decontrol of most prices, the elimination of most subsidies, and the simultaneous freezing of wages; the zloty was made internally convertible. While these policies brought down Poland's hyperinflation (the 1992 inflation rate was still 45 percent, however) and eased the chronic shortage of consumer goods, they also brought considerable hardship: a drop of some 22 percent in production figures in 1990 and 12 percent in 1991, in spite of a substantial expansion of private-sector activity, and unemployment that exceeded 13 percent by November 1992.[32]

One benefit of domestic hardship, coupled with the sharp devaluation of the zloty, was the creation of an impressive trade surplus in 1990. In 1991, however, imports soared and export volume dropped slightly, leaving a significant deficit, according to most figures. In response, the government raised customs duties, and President Wałęsa complained to Western journalists that a "flood" of Western imports was harming Polish industry. Exports grew again in 1992, but overall Polish trade remained much lower than Hungary's or Czechoslovakia's as a proportion of GNP.[33]

Privatization of large-scale enterprise has moved slowly in Poland, in part because of the shortage of domestic capital and in part because of lack of foreign interest; of five enterprises whose stock was put on sale in December 1990, the issues of three were not fully subscribed.[34] Long-debated plans for a voucher scheme of privatization were approved only in 1993 and have yet to be implemented. However, an indigenous private sector has grown rapidly, and accounted for nearly half of Poland's GDP in 1992.[35]

Poland's export and import structure is in one way more favorable than that of its neighbors, making it the only East European country whose terms of trade with the West have actually improved since 1970. It possesses a significant domestic energy source in its hard coal, which it exports to both East and West, and which diminishes its dependence on oil imported from Russia or elsewhere. It also exports refined copper and other metals, as well as significant quantities (17 percent of Western exports in 1991) of agricultural (primarily meat) products. About 18 percent of Poland's exports fall in the sensitive areas of iron and steel products and textiles. As elsewhere in Eastern Europe, capital goods exports to the West are small (12.5 percent), even though under Communism they made up over half of Poland's total exports.[36]

Eastern Germany

Prior to *die Wende,* as East Germans refer to the overturning of their country's old Communist order, the German Democratic Republic enjoyed the reputation of being the most prosperous and technologically advanced of the East European states. It was the Soviet Union's leading trading partner, and ranked behind only the Soviet Union in its trade with its Communist neighbors, supplying machine tools and other vital capital goods. Its Western trade, particularly with the Federal Republic, was vigorous; in absolute terms, the volume of East Germany's Western trade was the greatest among the East European states, and, although official statistics long concealed the fact, the Western proportion of its total trade was as great as that of Hungary and Poland. Western observers agreed that if any East European economy could weather the difficult transition to market capitalism with relative ease, it was East Germany's.

Six months after the deutsche mark became the GDR's official currency, and three months after political unification, it was apparent that the eastern German economy was in shambles—chilling testimony to the limits of "shock therapy." A protectionist set of economic structures designed for closed socialist markets and for state-controlled foreign trade, giving priority to the volume and diversity of production at the expense of efficiency, quality, technological sophistication, and the environment, was unable to adapt to a competitive Western market setting, especially when there was no possibility of manipulating exchange rates to restrain imports and encourage exports. Eastern Germans, armed with their new deutsche marks, rushed to buy Western products (even such items as eggs, whose superiority to their eastern German counterparts was not obvious), while eastern German producers lost their domestic customers and most of their East European ones (since they were now obliged to demand payment in hard currencies) and were not competitive in the West. Industrial production dropped by 1991 to one-third the level of 1989. Countless eastern German firms, now under the supervision of the government's giant trusteeship agency, the *Treuhandanstalt,* faced bankruptcy because of high production costs or inferior technology or for environmental reasons; in their desperate effort to survive, they laid off thousands of employees. The official unemployment rate stood at 15 percent in January 1993, and did not include the hundreds of thousands of East Germans who had retired early, were commuting to jobs in the West, or had been placed in temporary state-financed jobs and training programs.

This unhappy situation produced a brief bonanza for western German companies, whose rising sales in the East helped the old part of the Federal Republic escape for the moment recessionary trends elsewhere in the West. Western German firms did not, however, rush to invest in the East at the pace anticipated by the German government, in spite of low wage levels and a relatively skilled work force. Their reluctance could be attributed in part to the shortage of attractive properties to purchase, in part to the expectation that wages would quickly rise to western German levels, and in part to the uncertainty of property titles, owing to the government's decision to restore most property seized under Communist rule to its earlier owners, and the mountain of pending litigation that decision produced. When the Western recession finally reached western Germany in 1992, the firms cut back their investment plans still further.

Prior to the collapse of the old order, trade with the Federal Republic had dominated the GDR's Western transactions—according to Western figures, something like 60 percent of them. (Revised East German figures put the proportion at about 40 percent; the old regime, concerned to minimize the appearance of economic dependence, had claimed it was only 25–30 percent.[37]) "Intra-German" trade, as the West Germans called it, was favored by a number of special provisions: the GDR's exports entered the Federal Republic tariff-free, and the value-added tax on goods moving in both directions was reduced. GDR agricultural exports—primarily to West Berlin—also benefitted from high EC prices.[38]

The long-standing special relationship between the two Germanies created a dense network of economic ties and probably contributed to inhibiting the entrance of non-German Western companies into eastern Germany after the *Wende;* 95 percent of the joint ventures established in the GDR by August 1990 were said to be with western German firms,[39] and a similar proportion of *Treuhand* sales have been to Germans. This reluctance persists in spite of the several advantages the former GDR would seem to offer to Western investors by comparison with the other East European countries: the full convertibility of the deutsche mark, the familiarity of the legal terrain (East German law has largely been supplanted by West German law), the fact that eastern Germany (as part of the Federal Republic) belongs to the EC, the fact that many such firms are already established in the western part of the country, and so on. It is likely that the higher wage levels, along with the hesitancy of western German companies, in spite of their linguistic advantages, their experience, and government encouragement, to invest in the East has discouraged other potential Western investors.

Less than 2 percent of Germany's foreign trade can now be attributed to the five eastern states[40]; thus the profile of East Germany's Western trade prior to unification in October 1990 offers only limited guidance to future trade and investment possibilities. Although within the CMEA the GDR was a leading producer and exporter of computers, industrial robots, and other machine tools, the proportion of its exports to the West made up of capital goods (15.8 percent to the Federal Republic and 13.7 percent to all OECD countries in 1989) was little higher than the bloc average. Ironically, the "key technologies," such as microelectronics and industrial robots, that East Germany's former Communist rulers had emphasized to the neglect of others were ones in which it could not hope to be competitive with the West. Instead, East Germany's leading export in the 1980s was, surprisingly, oil products, refined from Soviet and some Middle Eastern imports obtained in barter deals; this once-profitable business was subsequently undermined by the fall in world oil prices.[41] Other exports included intermediate manufactures, chemicals, and, especially to the Federal Republic, consumer goods.

Among Western imports, investment goods in 1989 took up a lower proportion of the total—some 32 percent—than for any of the CMEA six except Romania. Now, eastern Germany's need to rebuild its industry, modernize its infrastructure, and curb pollution, coupled with the availability of substantial government financing for these purposes, should produce a boom in capital goods imports, although largely from western Germany (and thus technically not imports at all). Consumer goods imports, only 5.8 percent in 1989, exploded even before unification.[42]

The prospects for east German exports to the West are not cheerful, and are likely to depend in large part on the pattern of west German investment and the structural transformation it effects. Islands of relatively advanced technology, for example, the new Volkswagen and Opel (General Motors) plants, will produce high quality products for export; other, "screwdriver" enterprises will assemble less sophisticated goods for sale in German and foreign markets.[43] The unhappy environmental legacy left by East Germany's chemical industry makes it certain that its size and the importance of its exports will greatly decline. In trade as in other matters, eastern Germany is likely for years to function as a de facto colony of west German business.

Czech Republic and Slovakia

At the beginning of the 1980s, the economic course of Czechoslovakia, especially from the perspective of its own conservative Communist elite, must have looked considerably more prudent than those of its neighbors. It had restrained its appetite for Western imports and avoided a level of debt exposure to Western banks and governments comparable to that of

Poland, Hungary, Romania, or the GDR. Officially, 70 percent of its trade in 1980 was with "socialist" countries (because of price distortions, the real figure was probably closer to 55 or 60 percent). More than half of that was with the Soviet Union, while almost 30 percent was with other CMEA countries—the highest proportion in Eastern Europe.

Yet Czechoslovakia did not escape the difficulties of its allies. Like them, it had to scale back its Western imports and cut back on its investments in order to keep its citizens' standard of living from falling; growth rates virtually stagnated.[44] Heavy dependence on Soviet oil meant a sharp decline in the country's terms of trade and thus the need to expand significantly its exports, primarily of capital goods, to that country. Trade with the West shrank still further, to just over 15 percent of the country's total in 1985, according to official figures. Trade with "socialist" countries, on the other hand, rose to a proportion (officially) of nearly 80 percent.

The new Czechoslovak government that took power in the wake of the country's "velvet revolution" was slow to tackle the country's economic problems, in part because of internal disagreements over the pace of reform. While it debated, Western imports rapidly increased, as did the country's hard currency trade deficit; as elsewhere, trade with the Soviet Union and other CMEA partners (especially the GDR) fell, with exports dropping faster than imports. The country experienced only a modest decline in production (and living standards) in 1990 and virtually no unemployment.[45]

All that began to change on January 1, 1991, when the country's controversial and contentious finance minister, Václav Klaus, initiated his version of economic "shock therapy." Klaus's economic philosophy represents a uncompromising rejection not only of the former regime's approach, but of any sort of dirigistic strategy. "We want to achieve the transition from a state-dominated economy to an economy based on private sector, private initiative and private entrepreneurship. We do not want to orchestrate the economy from above and we do not want to start another vicious circle of pseudo-rationalistic engineering, based on ambitions of irresponsible intellectuals and technocrats."[46]

Accordingly, price controls on 85 percent of all goods were lifted, state subsidies (and the government's budget as a whole) were slashed, and the koruna was made internally convertible. The regime began the process of auctioning off small businesses to private individuals, and plans were launched for the rapid sale of large enterprises with the help of a voucher privatization plan. These measures were taken with the approval of the IMF, which granted the country a $1.78 billion standby loan in January.[47]

The severity of the resultant decline exceeded government projections, in part because of the country's previous heavy dependence on CMEA trade, now in disarray. Unemployment reached 6.6 percent by the end of 1991, and the inflation rate for the year was 57.9 percent, although it fell sharply after an initial spurt. Industrial production dropped by 23.1 percent in 1991 and almost 20 percent in 1992; GDP (Gross Domestic Product) dropped by some 13 percent and 5–7 percent, respectively. Klaus's reforms met especially strong resistance in Slovakia, where they hit much harder than in the Czech lands; Slovak unemployment, for example, was 10.4 percent in November 1992, as opposed to a Czech figure of 2.5 percent.[48]

Czechoslovak exports dropped by 7.5 percent in 1991; imports, however, fell by 20 percent, leaving a positive trade balance. Responding to domestic criticism, government officials announced a departure from Klausian laissez-faire to the extent of introducing modest export promotion measures.[49] Both exports and imports grew in 1992, even though foreign sales prospects were inhibited by the structural composition of previous Western exports: high on refined oil products, iron and steel, and consumer goods, low on machinery and transportation equipment, by far Czechoslovakia's most important industrial sector. Nevertheless, in 1991 Czechoslovakia led the region in exporting engineering goods to the West—and in importing them.[50]

Some two thousand Western joint ventures and wholly owned subsidiaries were operational by November 1992.[51] The most notable of these was Volkswagen's acquisition of a major share of Skoda, after a prolonged competition between the German firm and a Renault-Volvo consortium. The Volkswagen agreement represented by far the largest single Western investment in Eastern Europe to date. Other Western investments were small, however, and Czechs worried about the predominance of German capital—said officially to be 40 percent.[52] Moreover, only 7.7 percent of foreign investment in the first nine months of 1992 went to Slovakia.[53]

The Slovak economy seemed destined to suffer more than the Czech Republic's from their separation. Especially damaging were its dependence on heavy industry, particularly the arms trade, and its loss of Czech subsidies. It was not even clear in early 1993 whether the Czech-Slovak customs union would survive the divergent economic paths of the two states, a critical matter since in 1991 over 32 percent of Slovak industrial production was sent to the Czech Republic. Slovakia does, however, enjoy a higher GDP per capita and is less heavily burdened by foreign debt than either Hungary or Poland.[54]

Romania

Romania's foreign trade strategy from the beginning of the 1980s until the fall of Nicolae Ceauşescu at the end of 1989 was dominated by a furious effort to eliminate its once formidable hard-currency debt by drastically curtailing Western imports and increasing exports. This policy was largely successful—by the end of 1988 the country's gross debt was reported to about equal the amount owed it—but at the cost of extraordinary domestic privation and a fundamental shift in the orientation of the country's trade. From early in the 1960s, Romania had turned Westward for much of its trade[55]; by 1975 its imports from the advanced capitalist countries far exceeded those from the CMEA states (which did not, to be sure, include its significant trade with Yugoslavia and China). By 1987, however, Romania had cut its Western imports to just 15 percent of a substantially reduced total. Sales to the West remained at 30 percent of total exports, though. Trade with the socialist world dramatically increased. By 1988 30 percent of Romania's imports again came from the Soviet Union, and almost one-quarter of its exports went there, in spite of Ceauşescu's long-standing assertion of Romanian independence and his unconcealed distaste for Gorbachev's reforms. Perhaps another quarter of the country's trade was with other Communist nations.

Romania's relations with the West sharply deteriorated during Ceauşescu's last years in power. In 1988 Romania gave up its Most Favored Nation trading status with the United States rather than face still another Congressional hearing delving into its human rights performance—a significant sacrifice, since the United States had become an important Western export market and ranked second as a source of Romania's Western imports. In March 1989 the European Community suspended talks on a new trade agreement with Romania because of concerns over the abuse of human rights.[56] Although Romania remained a member of the IMF and World Bank, and had previously received loans from those organizations and assistance in rescheduling foreign debts,[57] Ceauşescu's course precluded any further support from them.

After Ceauşescu's removal and execution, Romania's relations with the outside world briefly improved. But Western misgivings about the new Romanian regime, heightened by the violence directed at protesting students and intellectuals in June 1990, initially kept any of the generous assistance and credits that were being extended especially to Poland and Hungary from going to the desperately impoverished Romanians. New talks between Romania and the EC were suspended after the June violence, but subsequently resumed, leading to the signing of a trade and cooperation agreement on October 22. Early in 1991 the IMF granted Romania credits, linked to economic reform measures, totalling more than $1.2 billion.[58]

In the first months of 1990, Romania's imports of Western goods skyrocketed while exports went into sharp decline. The country's deep recession—GDP fell by some 25 percent in 1990 and 1991 and 16.5 percent in 1992—slowed down the import boom, but exports continued to fall. In 1991 exports amounted to just $3.5 billion, 40 percent below the 1989 level, and the trade deficit reached $1.345 billion.[59]

As the only East European country with its own oil, Romania for many years was able to avoid dependence on Soviet energy supplies. However, its oil reserves have dwindled and are not able to supply the country's greatly expanded refining capacity. Thus, in order to maintain its high levels of exports of refined oil, Romania must import greater quantities of oil than it produces; Ceauşescu also drastically curtailed the domestic use of energy, to the point where the streets of Bucharest and other Romanian cities remained dimly lit or dark at night in order to conserve electricity.[60] The succeeding government was forced to cut hot water and heating supplies and even to close down important enterprises in similar efforts to save energy.[61] In 1991, half of Romania's exports to the West were (low-tech) consumer products, notably furniture, clothing, and footwear. After a sluggish start, the interest of foreign investors in Romania grew markedly in 1991 and 1992. Nearly 19,000 joint ventures had been registered by November 1992, most of them, however, in small service-sector industries, and only a fraction of them actually operational. Romania's imports of capital goods in 1990 and 1991 were the lowest in the region, reflecting weak investment and a shortage of convertible currency.[62]

Bulgaria

The dependence of Bulgaria on foreign trade with the Soviet Union was the highest in Eastern Europe, while the proportion of its trade carried out with the West was the smallest among the six countries. Nevertheless, in the late 1980s Bulgaria found itself with a rapidly mounting hard-currency debt; by 1990 it exceeded $10 billion. Imports from the West were roughly double exports between 1985 and 1989, while the favorable hard-currency trade balance with developing countries that earlier offset Western deficits had shrunk. In March 1990, the country's new (but still Communist) government felt obliged to stop payment on the debt.

Economic problems continued to mount in the course of the year, aggravated by political turmoil. Drought cut the grain harvest by 23 percent.[63] A sharp drop in Soviet oil supplies, coupled with the Gulf crisis (Iraq owed Bulgaria some $1.5 billion, which it had agreed to pay off over five years in oil deliveries), stoppages at the Kozloduy nuclear plant, and other factors led to an acute shortage of energy.[64] Inflation shot upward, and industrial production dropped by 13 percent during the year, as shortages of food and other goods grew. Exports to both East and West fell by a reported 28 percent in the first ten months of the year.[65] Early in 1991, in response to conditions set forth by the IMF, the government—now led by a non-Communist—raised the price of food, transportation prices, and interest rates severalfold. In return, the IMF agreed to provide as much as $1.7 billion in financial support.[66] Sizeable credits and other aid from the European Community and the G-24 nations followed.[67]

Nevertheless, the economic slump worsened in 1991 and continued in 1992. Unemployment reached 13.3 percent in September 1992, and inflation a daunting 550 percent in 1991, falling to 100 percent the next year. GDP dropped by a reported 19.5 percent in 1991 and 15–20 percent in 1992. The volume of exports fell by 60 percent and imports by 70 percent in 1991, although the rate of decline slowed late in the year and in 1992. Continuing political instability contributed to Bulgaria's economic distress; after less than one year in office, the third post-Zhivkov government, one excluding the former Communists, fell in October 1992 because of internal divisions.[68]

A large proportion of Bulgaria's exports to the West in the 1980s consisted of refined or crude oil originating in the Soviet Union and the Middle East; as in the case of the GDR, Romania, and other CMEA countries, the viability of this business has tumbled along with world oil prices and Soviet deliveries. Bulgaria is also, along with Hungary, one of the region's principal exporters of agricultural products; the future of such exports will rest in part on the success of the government's ambitious program of land restitution and privatization and perhaps even more on the EC's willingness to lower import restrictions.[69] Capital goods were the country's most important export to the East, but in 1991 constituted only 12.7 percent of its sales to the developed West.[70]

The economic disarray of the former Soviet Union, which had dominated Bulgarian trade, makes the economic prospects of the country particularly unfavorable. Not only has Bulgaria relied on Soviet oil, but it is also dependent on the post-Soviet states for all its natural gas and much of its coal and electricity. Few of its machinery exports seem likely to find Western markets; even the USSR, early in the Gorbachev era, complained pointedly about the poor quality of Bulgarian products.[71] Bulgaria appears to rank at the bottom of the former CMEA countries of Eastern Europe in numbers of Western joint ventures and other investments; although a new, liberal foreign investment law was approved in January 1992, the depressed economy and the continuing, unresolved question of foreign debt relief does not offer a very congenial investment environment.[72]

WESTERN TRADING PARTNERS

If the East European states display varying degrees of past involvement in trade with the West and varying prospects for expanding Western economic ties, there are analagous differences among the major Western nations. For years, the Federal Republic of Germany far outdistanced all other OECD countries in the level of its trade with Eastern Europe, even apart from its relationship with the former GDR. Prior to the fall of the old regimes, it was the leading Western trading partner of every Eastern European country except, on the import side, Romania, as well as of the Soviet Union. In 1987, it alone accounted for more than one-third of the industrial West's imports from Eastern Europe (including the GDR) and close to one-

Table 6.2
Western States' Trade with Eastern Europe (1991)
(value in U.S. dollars and as percentage of total trade)

country	total trade	exports (%)	imports (%)
Germany	$22,985 mill.	11,904 (3.0%)	11,081 (2.8%)
Italy	4904	2378 (1.4)	2526 (1.4)
Austria	4786	2700 (6.7)	2086 (4.1)
France	3836	2011 (0.9)	1825 (0.8)
Netherlands	2637	1532 (1.2)	1105 (0.9)
United Kingdom	2384	1244 (0.7)	1140 (0.5)
United States	2259	1185 (0.3)	1074 (0.2)
Belgium/Lux.	1650	946 (0.8)	704 (0.6)
Sweden	1451	759 (1.4)	692 (1.4)
Japan	1353	748 (0.2)	605 (0.3)
Switzerland	1291	912 (1.5)	379 (0.6)

Note: Figures include trade with Poland, Hungary, Czechoslovakia, Romania, and Bulgaria, but not the former GDR.
Source: Calculated from International Monetary Fund, *Direction of Trade Statistics Yearbook 1992* (Washington, D.C.: International Monetary Fund, 1992).

half of its exports.[73] Yet the share of East European trade (including inter-German trade) in the Federal Republic's total trade wasless than 3.5 percent, a significant drop from the high levels of the mid-1970s.

The changes of regime in Eastern Europe and German unification gave the Federal Republic still greater dominance (see Table 6.2). Apart from the near monopoly over trade and investment in the former GDR that west German business now enjoys, the new Germany has replaced the former Soviet Union as the leading trading partner of Hungary and Poland, responsible for some 25 percent of the trade turnover of each. In 1991 it became the leading customer for Czechoslovak exports, but remained behind the former Soviet Union in imports, while its trade with Romania and Bulgaria was second only to that of the Soviet Union. Germany absorbed between 40 and 50 percent of the growth of Czechoslovak, Polish, and Hungarian exports from 1988 to 1991.[74] It is clear, however, that much of the trade of

Eastern Europe with the former GDR has shifted to the western part of Germany and does not benefit the depressed east German states.[75] Germany's lead in Western investment in the region probably assures that its preeminence in trade will continue.

Other members of the European Community occupy four of the next five places behind Germany among Eastern Europe's Western trading partners. Italy ranks second among Western countries in its trade with Eastern Europe, in spite of a sharp decline in its once high volume of imports from Romania; its East European trade is less than one-fourth of west Germany's, however. Italy is closely followed by Austria, whose already high levels of trade with Hungary and Czechoslovakia expanded rapidly in 1990 and 1991. Austria leads all countries in the *proportion* of its total trade that it conducts with Eastern Europe, at 6.7 percent of exports and 4.1 percent of imports. France dropped from third to fourth in trade volume between 1989 and 1991. The Netherlands and the United Kingdom follow, with the United States ranking only seventh in both exports and imports. Japan, in spite of its role in East European lending and a growing interest in investments, sent just 0.2 percent of its exports to Eastern Europe in 1991.

How can we explain the overwhelming dominance of the Federal Republic and the relatively weak position of the United States in trade with Eastern Europe? The first goes back in part to historical patterns of economic exchange and to geographical proximity; in 1938 the German *Reich* had been responsible for 36 percent of all Western exports to and imports from Eastern Europe and the Soviet Union.[76] West German dominance also reflects its position as the world's second leading exporter, just behind the much larger United States. But German economic involvement in Eastern Europe is in many respects a matter of conscious political choice, reinforced over the years by the concrete economic interests these choices created. The Federal Republic's government encouraged and materially supported trade with Eastern Europe because of its constitutionally mandated concern for German unity, translated in practice until 1989 as an effort to maintain ties with and ease the lot of the Germans in the GDR. It sought good relations with the other East European nations in part in pursuit of these inter-German interests, but also out of a concern for ethnic Germans in several of those countries and perhaps—largely with respect to Poland—from a sense of moral obligation stemming from the crimes of the Nazi period. Now it has an added incentive: the fear of unmanageable immigration from Eastern Europe if economic conditions there continue to deteriorate.

The United States was not immune to the idea of linkage between economic relations and the advancement of its foreign policy goals in Eastern Europe, but, as we saw in chapter 2, often placed greater emphasis on economic punishment for presumed Communist misbehavior than on positive incentives. Moreover, the United States is more distant both geographically and culturally from Eastern Europe than the Federal Republic and other West European states. American businessmen tend to look first to their own vast internal market—in 1990, total exports worldwide represented only 7.3 percent of the United States GDP, as compared to 27.5 percent for West Germany[77]—and then to more familiar trading partners in Western Europe, East Asia, and the Americas. Strategic export concerns were more sensitive in the United States than in Western Europe, and the bureaucratic hurdles impeding trade with the East bloc were correspondingly more formidable. American firms that were neverthless interested in East bloc trade tended to focus on the Soviet market, whose potential size rivalled that of the United States itself, and not on the smaller East European countries. Thus, while 60.3 percent of West Germany's exports to the Soviet Union and Eastern Europe went to the latter in 1989, only 19.3 percent of United States' exports did.[78]

Austria's geography, history, and, in the past, its status as a neutral and a nonmember of COCOM help explain that country's high level of East European trade. Its trade with Hungary in 1991 was nearly half that of Germany.[79] The comparatively high level of Italian trade with Eastern Europe—twice that of the United Kingdom and some one-and-one-half times that of France, proportionate to each country's total trade—can probably be explained by the special ties of the Catholic Church and the Italian Communist party (now the party of the Democratic Left) to some of the countries in the region, by Italy's proximity to the Balkans, and by economic and political initiatives of the Italian government dating back to the 1960s.[80]

OBSTACLES TO EAST-WEST TRADE

The proportion of Western trade carried on with Eastern Europe dropped from 2.2 percent in 1975 to just 1.2 percent in 1989.[81] Prospects for improvement brightened with the fall of the region's Communist regimes, but numerous obstacles to trade, while associated with the old order, are likely to persist for years to come. Western critics long argued that Eastern Europe did not produce enough exports that were competitive in Western markets to balance its growing hunger for imports. They cited the generally low technological level of East European manufactured goods, their often poor quality (and their firms' poor quality control), and the inefficiency of East European industry in comparison with its competitors in the NICs and Southern Europe. They noted East European deficiencies in marketing, design, packaging, timely and reliable delivery, and service. East European producers, they argued, also tended to be too plan-bound to respond quickly to rapid changes in Western demand.[82] While obligatory state plans are now gone, patterns of bureaucratic sluggishness stubbornly remain, and the palette of potential export goods has changed little. The prospect that in most countries the majority of major industry will effectively remain in the hands of the state for some years to come and the fact that managers may not be changed even in "privatized" firms reinforce the presumption that old habits and practices will fade only slowly. To the extent that East European currencies do not become fully convertible, bureaucratic restrictions on their exchange, notably in Bulgaria and Romania, will continue to impede trade.

The impediments to expanding trade are underlined by the existing structure of East European exports to the West. A high percentage of East European exports is made up of iron and steel, low-technology consumer products (textiles, footwear, furniture), and agricultural products, which face stiff competition and often import barriers in Western markets. Many are produced by the "sunset" industries that Western countries frequently shield from foreign competition because their sales are not expanding and their products are in surplus worldwide.[83] Other major exports include chemicals and semimanufactured goods; refined oil products have largely lost their significance with the loss of plentiful and cheap Soviet supplies. Exports to the West of machinery and transportation equipment have increased since the fall of Communism, but only modestly.

On the import side, while 1990 brought a rise in Eastern Europe's comparatively modest level of capital goods imports from the West, prospects for rapid additional expansion are questionable. A large proportion of export earnings will need to go for energy imports that were previously obtained through barter arrangements with the Soviet Union. East European governments will have a difficult time resisting pressures from their own citizens to increase the volume of consumer goods imports, especially in so far as they remove import barriers at the urging of the IMF, the EC, or other Western partners. The continuing international shortage of capital and the level of previously existing debt will limit the possibility of importing machinery and other capital goods on credit.

Not all the obstacles to Western trade with Eastern Europe lie in the East. If the COCOM and other strategic trade restrictions, which often denied Eastern European states the very technology they needed to make their industries more competitive, have been relaxed, they have yet to be entirely eliminated, except in the case of Hungary. Western tariff barriers and quotas are being lowered, but only gradually; more subtle protectionist measures, such as antidumping rules, persist. The United States has now granted Most Favored Nation status to all the East European states except Romania,[84] but many potential exports from the region still face restrictions. The EC, Eastern Europe's most important market, has excluded or imposed special conditions on agricultural products, steel, and textiles in its association and trade agreements with individual countries of the region.

A catalogue of barriers to East-West trade like this one can be misleading if it leads the reader to conclude that the objective of strengthening economic exchange with Eastern Europe is unattainable. The relatively high level of East European imports that the German Federal Republic, one of the most advanced Western nations, is able to absorb and the success of Hungary and Czechoslovakia in shifting at least some of their capital goods exports from Soviet to Western destinations suggest that, where sufficient will and imagination exist, there is considerable room for trade expansion. It is also evident that a number of the obstacles listed above are diminishing in importance and can be lowered further through political decisions or economic reforms. Western investment itself will spur future trade.

THE PUBLIC SECTOR AND THE PRIVATE SECTOR

Unlike most other areas of foreign policy, foreign economic policy is heavily dependent on cooperation between government and the private sector; such cooperation is inhibited, however, by liberal economic ideology. The religion of free trade—which has been promoted energetically by the United States since World War II and is now endorsed with varying enthusiasm by all Western countries—clashes in principle with government's desire to use trade as an instrument of politics, and can constrain close and effective public-private cooperation. The arsenal of measures governments have used in the past to foster or inhibit East-West trade is formidable: embargoes and strategic restrictions, tariffs, quotas, antidumping rules, credit regulations and guarantees, the provision of marketing advice and information, subsidies, standardization requirements, content and safety regulations, exchange rate and interest rate manipulation, positions taken in multilateral bodies, and so on. They were invoked partly as an expression of broad policy concerns, but also in response to a variety of private pressures; the precise mix of measures in effect at any given time usually did not reflect any one actor's conscious intention. The differences between American levels of East European trade and those of its allies in Western Europe, however, can be explained in part by the emphasis, during the cold war years, in the American mix on trade-inhibiting measures and the greater attention in the European mix devoted to trade facilitation. Now, the United States and West European governments are closer to agreement on the need for trade facilitation in the interest of economic modernization, the rebuilding of the infrastructure, and environmental protection. They may find it harder to agree that some forms of trade are more helpful than others in these respects, and deserve special, preferably coordinated, political favor. The accusations of protectionism that already color U.S.-European trade relations can be expected to extend to any such arrangements. The U.S. has already complained of Polish favoritism toward the EC—a supposed 15–20 percent tariff advantage—resulting from the terms of the Polish-EC association agreement.[85]

WESTERN TRADE STRATEGIES

The issues surrounding Western trade with Eastern Europe are now considerably altered from what they were during the last years of Communist rule. The new governments in the region are all anxious to expand such trade; they are not inhibited by political fears of integration into the world (capitalist) economic system or other forms of dependence on what was earlier viewed as the class enemy. Their economic obligations to the former Soviet Union and other former CMEA members, which once limited the prospects for Western trade expansion, have now all but disappeared. The West, for its part, no longer needs to fear the strategic risks it once saw inherent in expanded East European trade.

An overriding problem that remains, however, is the threat of renewed trade imbalance. The appetite of East Europeans for some Western imports and their need for others, along with the higher cost of oil and gas supplies, exceed their present capacity to expand exports. In spite of the temporary trade surpluses that some countries have managed to achieve with the West through domestic depression and currency devaluation, there is a serious danger that a new cycle of borrowing and rapid deficit and debt growth is in the offing. Western policies of export promotion and unrestrained lending to finance the purchase of Western products will not necessarily serve the interests of the East Europeans—or, over the long run, of the West itself.[86] It may, indeed, not prove particularly helpful to increase the volume of Eastern Europe's Western trade relative to its regional and post-Soviet trade or its trade with the NICs and other Third World countries, to the extent that the former is conducted on less favorable terms or, by virtue of its composition, inhibits needed restructuring. Eastern Europe's comparative advantage, in the broadest sense, may not always be served by across-the-board Western dominance.

What this means is that the West needs to be selective in revising its trade policies. It will be especially important to remove the remaining obstacles to imports from Eastern Europe, while the impulse to demand reciprocal reductions in East European import barriers will have to be resisted. The EC has begun to move in this direction; the United States, whose trade with Eastern Europe remains desultory, will need to take similar steps. More generally, the West should view its trade policies toward the East as part of a broader framework of economic cooperation that also includes investment, technical assistance, the exchange of expertise, and other elements. Trade cannot flourish if it is separated from questions of technology transfer, international finance, and economic reform—the subjects of the next three chapters.

NOTES

1. Interview in *Financial Times,* November 5, 1991, section III, 2.

2. In this chapter "Western trade" refers to that with the Western industrial (OECD) countries only.

3. Leyla Woods, "East European Trade with the Industrial West," in Joint Economic Committee, *Pressures for Reform in the East European Economies,* vol. 2 (Washington, D.C.: U.S. Government Printing Office, 1989), 388; figures published by the United Nations Economic Commission for Europe indicate that in 1988, after Czechoslovakia and the GDR recalculated the relative value of their Eastern and Western trade, 35.8 percent of all East European imports came from the West and 33.6 percent of all exports were sent there. Economic Commission for Europe, *Economic Survey of Europe in 1989–1990* (New York: United Nations, 1990), 409–10. Cited hereafter as *Economic Survey.*

4. Woods, Table 6, 408–9.

5. Because of the numerous changes needed to compile accurate statistics during the transition from state socialist to market economies, post-Communist trade data has tended to be incomplete, often conflicting, and not readily comparable with Communist-era figures. Thus the data cited here need to be viewed with caution. For examples of gross discrepancies in Hungarian statistics, once viewed as Eastern Europe's most reliable, see Karoly Okolicsanyi, "Hungarian Foreign Trade Turns from East to West," *RFE/RL Research Report,* April 10, 1992, 34. See also Economic Commission for Europe, Economic Bulletin for Europe vol. 44, 1992 (New York: United Nations, 1992), 48–50, 54–55, 64. Cited hereafter as *Economic Bulletin.*

6. See Alan H. Smith, *The Planned Economies of Eastern Europe* (New York: Holmes & Meier, 1983), chap. 10; Zbigniew M. Fallenbuchl, "East-West Trade in Capital Goods Since 1970," *Studies in Comparative Communism* 19 (Summer 1986), 129–47.

7. See J. F. Brown, *Eastern Europe and Communist Rule* (Durham, N.C.: Duke University Press, 1988), 178–80.

8. For studies of the responses of Eastern Europe to the credit crisis of the early 1980s, see Ellen Comisso and Laura d'Andrea Tyson, eds., *Power, Purpose, and Collective Choice* (Ithaca, N.Y.: Cornell University Press, 1986).

9. Woods, 415, and Table 6, 408–9.

10. Ibid., Table 4, 404–5.

11. *Wall Street Journal,* February 27, 1991, A5.

12. However, some frantic price discounting was reported in 1991, as firms that had lost their CMEA markets sought to find customers for their products in the West. See, e.g., Okolicsanyi, "Hungarian Foreign Trade," 35.

13. See *Economic Bulletin,* vol. 44, 49.

14. *Economic Survey 1989–1990,* 409–10. These figures are based on ones reported by the East European countries themselves, and must be taken as approximations. They depend on the East-West (and East-East) exchange rates used in computing relative trade volume, the treatment of transshipped goods, and other variable factors. Although the GDR and Czechoslovakia joined Poland, Hungary, and Romania in using a relatively realistic ruble valuation to calculate the figures cited, Bulgaria's figures were unreformed and thus undervalue its Western trade. It

has often been noted that Eastern European statistics on trade with the West differed considerably from Western (OECD) data. See "East-West Trade," in *Economic Survey 1989–1990,* 195.

15. Calculated from *Economic Survey 1989–1990,* 409–10.

16. See Ellen Comisso and Paul Marer, "The Economics and Politics of Reform in Hungary," in Comisso and Tyson, 431–32.

17. Poland's MFN status was suspended between 1982 and 1986, and Romania's was terminated in 1988.

18. Vladimir Sobell, "Prospects for Shifts in East European Trade," *RFE Research,* BR/84, May 20, 1988, 3.

19. *PlanEcon Report* April 13, 1990.

20. As of early 1992. See Okolicsanyi, "Hungarian Foreign Trade," 34–36; *EIU Country Report—Hungary,* No. 2 (1992), 18–19; No. 2 (1993), 18–20.

21. *EIU Country Report—Hungary,* No. 1 (1991), 6; Michael Marrese, "Hungary Emphasizes Foreign Trade Partners, *RFE/RL Research Report,* April 24, 1992, 25; Ben Slay, "The East European Economies," *RFE/RL Research Report,* January 1, 1993, 114.

22. *RFE/RL News Briefs,* January 11–15, 1993, 17.

23. Judith Patacki, "Major Political Change and Economic Stagnation," *Report on Eastern Europe,* January 4, 1991, 23.

24. See Edith Oltay, "Poverty on the Rise," *Report on Eastern Europe,* January 25, 1991, 13.

25. *EIU Hungary,* No. 1 (1991), 5.

26. *EIU Hungary,* No. 2 (1992), 19; Economic Commission for Europe, *Economic Survey of Europe in 1991–1992* (New York: United Nations, 1992), 81; *Economic Bulletin,* vol. 44, 140–41.

27. Vienna Institute for Comparative Economic Studies, *COMECON Foreign Trade Data 1986* (Westport, Conn.: Greenwood Press, 1988), 137, 160–69.

28. "Polish Foreign Trade Performance in 1987," *PlanEcon Report,* May 20, 1988, 1–2; Roman Stefanowski, "Poland's Economic Results in 1988," *RFE Research,* Polish SR/4, March 3, 1989, 34; *EIU Poland,* No. 4 (1990), 15–16.

29. Vlad Sobell, "OECD Report on Financial Situation of CMEA Countries," *RFE Research,* BR/51, March 17, 1989, 3.

30. *EIU Poland,* No. 1 (1992), 24; *Radio Free Europe Daily Report,* March 15, 1991.

31. *EIU Poland,* No. 1 (1992), 24.

32. Ibid., 15–16; Slay, "The East," 114.

33. *RFE/RL Research Report,* April 3, 1992, 46; *EIU Poland,* No. 1 (1993), 21–22.

34. See Delia Meth-Cohn, "Poland to Adopt a More Active Privatization Plan," *Business Eastern Europe* 20 (January 28, 1991), 27; Zbigniew M. Fallenbuchl, "The New Government and Privatization," *Report on Eastern Europe,* March 22, 1991, 11–16.

35. Ben Slay, "Poland: An Overview," *RFE/RL Research Report,* April 24, 1992, 15–21; Slay, "The East," 114.

36. *Economic Bulletin,* vol. 44, 140.

37. Maria Haendcke-Hoppe, "Aussenwirtschaft und Aussenwirtschaftsreform,"

in Forschungsstelle für gesamtdeutsche wirtschaftliche und soziale Fragen, *Glasnost und Perestroika auch in der DDR?* (Berlin: Berlin Verlag Arno Spitz, 1988), 68–69; Statistisches Amt der DDR, *Statistisches Jahrbuch der Deutschen Demokratischen Republik '90* (Berlin: Rudolf Haufe Verlag, 1990), 272–73.

38. John Garland, "FRG-GDR Economic Relations," in Joint Economic Committee, *East European Economies: Slow Growth in the 1980s* (Washington: U.S. Government Printing Office, 1986), vol. 3, 169–206.

39. *Financial Times,* August 24, 1990, cited in Marvin Jackson, "The International Economic Situation and Eastern Europe," *Report on Eastern Europe,* December 28, 1990, 39.

40. *Die Zeit,* September 4, 1992, 9.

41. Haendcke-Hoppe, 66.

42. See Horst Lambrecht, "Innerdeutscher Handel im Übergang," DIW *Wochenbericht* no. 25 (1990), reprinted in *Deutschland Archiv* 23 (July 1990), 1089.

43. See Peter Christ, "Der Osten schreibt rot," *Die Zeit,* March 6, 1992, 7–8.

44. See Friedrich Levcik, "The Czechoslovak Economy in the 1980s," *East European Economies,* vol. 3, 85–93.

45. See Marvin Jackson, "The Economic Situation in Eastern Europe in 1990," *Report on Eastern Europe,* January 4, 1991, 52–53; *EIU Czechoslovakia,* No. 1 (1991), 3.

46. Cited in Martin Wolf, "The End of the Beginning," *Financial Times,* November 8, 1991, Section III, 2.

47. See Jiri Pehe, "The Agenda for 1991," *Report on Eastern Europe,* January 18, 1991, 11–13; Peter Martin, "The 1991 Budget: Hard Times Ahead," *Report on Eastern Europe,* March 1, 1991, 12–16.

48. Slay, "The East," 115; Jiri Pehe, "Czechoslovakia: Towards Dissolution," *RFE/RL Research Report,* January 1, 1993, 88.

49. See *EIU Czechoslovakia,* No. 2 (1992), 26–27.

50. *Economic Bulletin,* vol. 44, 140–41.

51. *Business Eastern Europe,* January 11, 1993, 4–5.

52. Ibid.

53. *RFE/RL Research Report,* December 18, 1992, 60.

54. Jari Kobylka, "Sandpaper Transition Follows Velvet Divorce in Czechoslovakia," *Business Eastern Europe,* January 18, 1993, 1–2.

55. Joseph Rothschild, *Return to Diversity* (New York: Oxford University Press, 1989), 163.

56. "Weekly Record of Events," *RFE Research,* March 23, 1989, 13–14.

57. See Michael Shafir, *Romania: Politics, Economics and Society* (London: Frances Pinter, 1985), 119–20.

58. *Business Eastern Europe* 20 (March 18, 1991), 81–82.

59. *Business Eastern Europe,* 21 (April 20, 1992), 196; Michael Shafir and Dan Ionescu, "Romania: Political Change and Economic Malaise," *RFE/RL Research Report,* January 1, 1993, 110.

60. Shafir, 118.

61. *Report on Eastern Europe,* February 15, 1991, 50.

62. Shafir and Ionescu, 111; *Business Eastern Europe,* January 25, 1993, 5; *Economic Bulletin,* vol. 44, 64, 140.

63. Jackson, "The Economic Situation," 52.

64. Kjell Engelbrekt, "Food and Energy Shortages," *Report on Eastern Europe*, March 8, 1991, 1–4.

65. Marvin Jackson, "The International Economic Situation," 40.

66. *Report on Eastern Europe*, February 15, 1991, 46.

67. Rob Whitfield, "Bulgarian Outlook Better—but Rescheduling Still Needed," *Business Eastern Europe* 20 (May 6, 1991), 137–39.

68. See *Business Eastern Europe* 21 (March 9, 1992), 112–13; Kjell Engelbrekt, "Bulgaria's Foreign Debt Predicament," *RFE/RL Research Report*, February 21, 1992, 38–40; Engelbrekt, "Bulgaria: The Weakening of Postcommunist Illusions," ibid., January 1, 1993, 80–81; *Economic Survey 1991–1992*, 75.

69. See Rada Nikolaev, "Bulgarian Farmland Law Seeks to Hasten Privatization," *RFE/RL Research Report*, May 22, 1992, 30–33.

70. *Economic Bulletin*, vol. 44, 140.

71. See Wolfgang Höpken, " 'Perestrojka' auf bulgarisch," *Südosteuropa* no. 10 (1987), 620–21.

72. Michael L. Wyzan, "Bulgarian Law Lowers Foreign Investment Barriers," *RFE/RL Research Report*, March 27, 1992, 41–43.

73. Woods, 388.

74 *Economic Survey 1991–1992*, 78.

75. András Inotai, "Economic Implications of German Unification for Central and Eastern Europe," in Paul B. Stares, ed., *The New Germany and the New Europe* (Washington, D.C.: Brookings Institution, 1992), 280–82.

76. Claudia Wörmann, *Der Osthandel der Bundesrepublik Deutschland* (Frankfurt: Campus Verlag, 1982), 13.

77. *OECD Economic Survey—Austria 1992–1993* (Paris: Organisation for Economic Cooperation and Development, 1993), appendix.

78. Calculated from OECD, *Monthly Statistics of Foreign Trade*, October 1990, 38–39; Statistisches Bundesamt, *Statistisches Jahrbuch für die Bundesrepublik Deutschland 1990* (Stuttgart: Metzler-Poeschel Verlag, 1990), 252. On the other hand, the distribution of imports was similar for the two countries: 65.8 percent of U.S. and 67.6 percent of West German imports from the USSR and Eastern Europe came from Eastern Europe.

79. *EIU Hungary*, No. 2 (1992), 19.

80. See J. F. Brown, "The Views from Vienna and Rome," in Lincoln Gordon et al., *Eroding Empire: Western Relations with Eastern Europe* (Washington, D.C.: Brookings Institution, 1987), 279–91.

81. Gordon, 332–33; International Monetary Fund, *Direction of Trade Statistics Yearbook 1990* (Washington, D.C.: International Monetary Fund, 1990), 8–12.

82. See, e.g., Fallenbuchl, "East-West Trade," 130–31.

83. Woods, 19.

84. Congress rejected MFN treatment for Romania following the reelection of President Iliescu in the fall of 1992.

85. *RFE/RL Research Report*, May 15, 1992, 14.

86. See Misha Glenny, *The Rebirth of History: Eastern Europe in the Age Democracy*, 2nd ed. (London: Penguin Books, 1993), 242. He argues that Western export credits amount to "subsidizing the dumping of goods" into Eastern Europe.

7

Western Investment and the Transfer of Technology

> The experience of the 1970s and 1980s is that technology has flowed, but profound economic problems remain. . . . Technology transfer itself is disruptive. It rarely resembles the simplified process portrayed in economic theory.
>
> Steven W. Popper[1]

> [There is] a deliberate German policy to subordinate Western security to the commercial interests of German exporters.
>
> Richard Perle[2]

For East European officials and economists, a significant part of the promise of expanded trade with the West lies in the technological boost they expect it to provide. The acquisition of Western technologies, they believe, will help them close the economic gap between their own countries and the West and rekindle growth by modernizing production facilities, improving the quality and attractiveness of their products, and drastically reducing the profligate use of labor, fuels, and materials. Such technologies are needed for the unavoidable restructuring of their economies and for curbing the region's daunting levels of pollution. They are seen as the key to improving living standards and fulfilling the material aspirations that played so large a role in building support among ordinary citizens for Eastern Europe's democratic revolutions.

During the long years of Communist dominance, however, the question of technology transfer from the West was a matter of intense controversy. Soviet and East European officials periodically warned that excessive dependence on Western technology could subject bloc members to political blackmail, a possibility underlined by the sanctions imposed by the United States following the invasion of Afghanistan and the imposition of martial law in Poland. East bloc scientists and economists expressed the fear that Western technological imports could come at the expense of indigenous research and development efforts.[3] For their part, Western critics of expanded East-West economic links argued that the existing and potentially expanded transfer of Western technologies to the East constituted a serious threat to Western security. Even when such technology transfer did not directly contribute to the capabilities and the sophistication of Communist armed forces, they argued, it served to rescue inefficient Communist economies from the consequences of their own systemic failings and thereby perpetuated their oppressive regimes in power, while allowing them to divert vital resources to the military. In a widely cited metaphor attributed to Lenin, Western capitalists, through international trade, were said to be selling the East the rope with which the latter planned to hang them.[4]

It now appears that the East's ambition to acquire Western technological "rope" was a precipitating element in the process that led to its own demise. The available evidence does not lend much support to the proposition that large-scale imports of Western technology were of great assistance in improving productivity or strengthening the export performance of the East European economies. On the contrary, the growth of Western technological imports in the 1970s was in large measure responsible for the mounting debt that helped unleash the ultimately fatal crisis of the 1980s. Even the degree to which legally obtained Western technology proved useful for East bloc military purposes is by no means clearly established, in spite of occasional, well-publicized horror stories.[5]

Disregarding their predecessors' experience, the new regimes have been at least as interested in the rapid acquisition of Western technology as the old ones were. They are less inhibited than the Communist regimes were about obtaining it through direct, large-scale Western investment and joint ventures. But they, and the West, need to learn from the failure of the import-led strategy of the 1970s. The indiscriminate importation of Western technology does not automatically promote balanced economic development. Western investment does not always bring the most advanced or suitable technology along with it, and even when it does there is no guarantee that the technology will be quickly diffused.

Western governments thus need to consider what kind of support for private investment and what sort of complementary public investments can best promote effective technology transfer without neglecting other important ends such as job creation and improvement in the quality of life. They need to remove the remaining legal barriers to the export of technology and give much greater attention than they have to date to helping Eastern Europe absorb, adapt, and further develop the technologies it acquires. This objective implies especially that the West concern itself with the depressed state of East European educational institutions and seek to strengthen scientific and technological communications networks.

THE TECHNOLOGY GAP

The premise of the emphasis placed on technology transfer in discussions of East-West economic exchange is that there exists a sizeable technology gap between the two. There is no single satisfactory measure of this gap, in part because "technology" itself is not, as usually defined, a concrete and measurable object, but rather a "capability" or form of knowledge that can exist in either "embodied" or "disembodied" forms.[6] The transfer of technology can accordingly take place through trade in products embodying various technologies, but also through the licensing of patent rights (usually accompanied by technical assistance); the transmission of knowledge through professional conferences, journals, and scientific and educational exchanges; and the practical transfer of "know-how" through direct investment, joint ventures and other cooperative commercial undertakings, the sale of turnkey plants, and so on.

The measures of technology transfer are all imperfect. All of them, however, as well as studies of individual industries and less quantifiable judgments, suggest a significant lag of Eastern Europe behind the West in most fields. Western businessmen surveying investment possibilities in the region sometimes compare their experience to entering an industrial museum. The gap, however, varies widely from industry to industry and country to country. Moreover, much of the disparity is not a matter of the absence of the requisite knowledge but of its efficient application in the production process.

If we ask why the East-West gap exists, we find something of a puzzle. Under Communist rule, the East European countries (and the Soviet Union) all trained an impressive number of scientists and engineers, and overall research and development expenditure was also high.[7] Comparative patent statistics also suggest a fairly high level of technological prowess, even though the level of CMEA patenting in the West was not impressive.[8] But official East European sources often complained of the organizational and motivational obstacles that impeded the application of scientific and technological innovations in production. Under Communism, Western commentators and Eastern specialists agree, there were serious systemic barriers to the introduction and especially the diffusion of innovations, barriers that tended to apply whether the innovation in question was produced indigenously or imported. Many of these barriers persist.

TECHNOLOGY TRANSFER UNDER COMMUNISM

As we saw in chapter 6, Eastern European imports of Western capital goods, as measured by the "machinery and transport equipment" category of standard international trade statistics, amounted in 1987 to about one-third of total East European imports from the West, a smaller proportion than was sent to the rest of the world, including East Europe's competitors in the East Asian and Latin American NICs and Southern Europe.[9] Attempts to identify the trade subcategories that were most likely to include "products combining world 'best practice' in critical technologies" suggested that in the early 1980s only 11–12 percent of all Western exports to Eastern Europe consisted of high-technology goods.[10] A different attempt to measure the technological sophistication of East European imports, by assessing their "R & D [research and development] intensity," indicated that in 1983 only 4.32 percent of all OECD exports of "embodied technology" to Eastern Europe were "highly" R & D intensive, while over 70 percent were "low" R & D intensive.[11] The share of the critical engineering industry in imports from the West was comparatively modest: in 1983 just 30 percent of all capital goods imports in this sector came from the West, equalling the proportion for all capital goods imports.[12] Imports for energy and energy-related projects (such as pipeline equipment) and the chemical industry appeared to enjoy an equal or higher priority.[13]

Studies that sought to measure the impact of technological imports from the West on Eastern Europe (or Soviet) economic performance showed only a modest relationship between the two. "The conclusion seems to be," noted a Trilateral Commission report, "that while the impact is certainly not negligible, it is also not particularly great."[14] An OECD study revealed little relationship between import growth rates and Western export performance in various sectors for Eastern Europe between 1970 and 1983, except for a negative one in the case of Hungary. It noted that "the greater part" of technology imports from the West went to sectors producing for the domestic or other non-Western markets, and showed a modest but positive impact of capital goods imports from both the West and elsewhere on labor productivity. "There is no hard evidence," the study concluded, "to show that the mere expansion of Western imported technology offers a short cut for 'closing the technology gap.' "[15]

THE PROBLEM OF TECHNOLOGY ASSIMILATION

This sort of evidence has not led either Eastern European or Western economists to conclude that Western technological imports are inherently valueless in bringing about economic growth and modernization. The evidence, however, does suggest that such imports by themselves are unlikely to be helpful unless they are assimilated and diffused more effectively than they were under Communist rule. Critics have frequently charged that, particularly in the 1970s, East European governments viewed imports of Western technology on credit as a substitute for domestic economic reforms that would stimulate innovation. What the experience of that decade seems to have demonstrated is that Western technology could not be employed with maximum effectiveness in the *absence* of such reforms.[16] It would be comforting to believe that with the market reforms now being undertaken the obstacles to assimilation and diffusion will quickly fall, but that seems unlikely until the new competitive mechanisms begin to function smoothly and the relationship between research and production is restructured.

What problems impeded the timely and cost-efficient assimilation of such technologies into East European systems of production, and to what extent do they persist? To begin with, the technologies sold to East Europe by Western firms often did not represent the most advanced designs, which were withheld for proprietary reasons or because of strategic export controls.[17] Their timely utilization, moreover, was likely to be delayed by the often lengthy licensing procedures required in COCOM member states and by the typically protracted negotiation and approval process preceding the signing and implementation of an agreement. Presumably because of planning failures, and especially owing to poor synchronization of license purchases with the adaptation of domestic research and development facilities, some licenses purchased by the East Europeans went entirely unused, while others were utilized only after long delays.[18] Delays in realizing investment projects were sometimes responsible for expensive imported machinery aging (and perhaps rusting) in warehouses or on railroad sidings before being put to use.[19] Once installed, the machinery might operate less efficiently than it did in the West because the work force had been poorly or inappropriately trained or because of the low level of worker discipline and motivation that burdened all East European economies.[20] Western imports were not always effectively integrated with other, non-Western machinery and equipment; the production process as a whole was often not adapted to their most efficient use. When East Europeans used "reverse engineering" to reproduce imported goods embodying high technology, the process was apt to be long and difficult.[21]

Even if successfully introduced in one enterprise, an imported technology might not readily be diffused to other enterprises in the same or related fields. The deficiencies of East European information systems—even such things as the restrictions on the use of copiers—as well as rigidities in regime investment policies, the reverse engineering problem, and other factors shared responsibility for such sluggishness.[22] Similarly, even in the heyday of the CMEA, diffusion of Western technologies from one East European country to another or to and from the Soviet Union appeared to be surprisingly slow,[23] testimony to the shortcomings of that organization as an instrument of scientific and technical cooperation.

Once introduced, Western technologies often required additional, and not always foreseen, inputs of materials and parts from the West[24]; if anticipated hard-currency sales were insufficient, the costs of these could consume any profits or other expected benefits. Moreover, for many industries a single infusion of Western technology was not sufficient, especially if the products were meant to be sold on Western markets. For example, Poland's manufacture under license of Fiat-designed automobiles, begun in the 1960s, required the purchase of additional rounds of new Fiat technology to avoid falling hopelessly behind rapidly changing Western standards of design and performance.[25]

Many of the problems resulted more or less directly from the infirmities of centrally planned economic systems, but to the extent that these became embedded in the industrial cultures of the countries concerned, they will not disappear simply because central planning and direction have been dismantled. Other problems can be attributed to economic backwardness itself, and are likely to persist. Still others may be created or intensified by the problems of transition: the new governments will often lack the resources or expertise to encourage the diffusion of technology through subsidies or other means, and newly privatized firms may still lack the competitive pressures and/or the capital to make use of new technologies. Beleaguered managers and trustees of the many firms in limbo—still state-owned but with their subsidies removed and identified as candidates for sale or liquidation—are not well positioned to purchase new technology or to demand it as they search for Western "saviors." The diffusion of technology across Eastern European borders may also be impeded by the resurgence of nationalism and the resistance of most countries to new forms of regional economic integration.

TECHNOLOGY TRANSFER THROUGH WESTERN INVESTMENT

In the last years of Communist rule, the advantages that joint ventures and other forms of cooperation agreements with Western firms seemed to offer as channels for the transfer of technology persuaded most of the East European states to liberalize substantially the terms on which they could be permitted. The new, post-Communist governments, no longer restrained by ideological misgivings, have relaxed foreign investment rules still further and in most cases are vigorously soliciting Western capital in almost any form. For them, Western investment promises not only an infusion of advanced technology but desperately needed revenues and jobs, at an apparently modest cost, although prospective investors frequently demand and are granted generous tax incentives and other forms of subsidy. Volkswagen, for example, was given a two-year, extendable "tax holiday," by the Czech government as a reward for its DM 1.2 billion investment in Skoda.[26] Western joint ventures with East European firms are expected to bring the latter a steady flow of technical assistance, including the training of local workers and management and the upgrading of production techniques and machinery. In many cases they also mean the opening up of third-country markets. In joint ventures, as opposed to Communist-era cooperation agreements, the Western partner's share in ownership and potential profits is expected to strengthen its commitment to the undertaking and its willingness to permit the use of its more advanced technologies. From the East European perspective, direct investments are also desirable on most of these counts, although they reduce the ability of each country's government, trade unions, or other interests to influence the firm's behavior in such critical matters as hiring levels, plant location, and the reinvestment of profits. (For corresponding reasons, Western firms often prefer direct investment to joint ventures.)

East European diplomats and the myriad specialized publications and consulting firms that now offer their advice to potential Western investors point to a number of advantages those firms taking the plunge can enjoy. One is gaining access to still largely untapped (albeit at present rather impecunious) East European markets; in the past, penetration of one of the region's countries often eased the path to the others and to the Soviet Union. A second attraction is reduced production costs, based primarily on low East European wage levels, for goods to be sold in the West or non-Communist developing nations. General Electric, in its joint venture with Tungsram, for example, pays its Hungarian workers $2,000 a year, as opposed to $20,000 in Western Europe[27]; overall, Hungarian wage levels are said to be below those of South Korea and Taiwan.[28] The only exception to this rule is eastern Germany, where wage levels are approaching those in the West; as a result, some west German investment has been diverted from the east German states to the countries further east.[29] East European workers are well educated in comparison with those in other low-wage countries, and unions are by and large divided and weak, if sometimes feisty (some of the old Communist unions have disintegrated, while others survive in altered form, often in competition with new ones).[30]

Nevertheless, Western investment has lagged well behind East European hopes. "Most of the stylishly clad executives who filled the best hotels of Warsaw, Prague and Budapest in the exuberant fall of 1989, came, saw and left," remarks a journalist.[31] While the number of Western joint venture agreements in eastern Germany, Hungary, Poland, and Czechoslovakia has leapt upward since the end of 1989 and now is in the thousands in each case, the number actually operational is much smaller—about 40 percent in Poland as of 1991—and all but a few are small and represent modest amounts of Western capital. In 1992, joint ventures with foreign participation were responsible for just 4 percent of Czechoslovak industrial output.[32]

The reasons for this sluggish response are several, with the region's pervasive political and economic uncertainty, much of it the unavoidable consequence of the transition process, at the top of the list. One of the major impediments to Western investment in eastern Germany, for example, has been the difficulty of establishing property ownership rights, owing to German recognition of a variety of claims to the restitution of property seized during the forty-five years of Communist rule.[33] The West German Commerzbank, considering the purchase of an office building in Leipzig, was confronted by sixteen people claiming to be the rightful owners; the bank finally took space in a hotel.[34] Somewhat similar, if less drastic, restitution/compensation laws have been passed in Hungary, Czechoslovakia, and, for farmland, Bulgaria; they can be expected to raise comparable obstacles to investment. Another inhibition is the fear of Western investors that they will be held liable for ecological damage previously committed by the enterprise they are acquiring.

Potential investors must also contend with a rapidly changing legal and bureaucratic environment. Commercial law, foreign trade law, banking law, and tax law are all being rewritten by fractious parliaments. Privatization rules frequently shift—in Hungary, for example, some sixteen times in less than a year.[35] The intention of these legal and regulatory changes is to reduce complexity and encourage investment, but the short-term effect may be to reduce economic predictability and thus to inhibit investment. Similarly, most countries are seeking to simplify the formidable gamut of bureaucratic rules and procedures that new firms must run, but the decentralizing thrust of reforms often leaves it unclear where authority to approve or disapprove a request may lie. Western businessmen sometimes profess to miss the days when they could confidently turn for a decision to a powerful central ministry.

East European governments are rapidly lifting or reducing restrictions on the repatriation of earnings in hard currency, and pressures for countertrade agreements, under which the Western exporter must agree to accept East European goods to sell in the West, are declining, except in Bulgaria and Romania. But the prospect of making any profit at all in the short term is often bleak because of a domestic market afflicted by declining real income and rising unemployment. Poor work discipline and inappropriate training of the work force remain serious problems. For many firms, the most frustrating obstacles are the inadequacies of the infrastructure—most acutely, perhaps, in telecommunications—and the difficulty in finding suitable and reasonably priced office space.[36] There are also cultural barriers and misunderstandings, reflecting the inexperience of Western (especially American) businessmen in the East, and the unfamiliarity of their East European partners with capitalist markets and business practices. A leading Czechoslovak official complained to me that Americans were excessively preoccupied with short-term profit and were reluctant to make use of small but necessary bribes.[37]

Viewed in a broader context, capitalist investment in Eastern Europe is falling short because the worldwide demand for capital has grown while the supply, notably from Japan and Germany, has, if anything, diminished. Under pressure from the IMF and leading Western powers, many Third

World countries have imbibed the free trade–free market religion and compete to open their economies to foreign investment. At the same time, commercial banks, especially in the United States, have become more cautious in their lending practices. Western business finds itself offered a wide range of foreign investment opportunities; in such a setting, the risks and drawbacks of involvement in Eastern Europe are magnified.

In these circumstances, the leverage of East European officials over the terms and particularly the type of Western investments they attract is limited. Yet, like all poor countries, they have an interest in differentiating among their capitalist suitors: encouraging investments that promise to contribute the most to their economic and technological development as well as creating jobs and enhancing the quality of life for their citizens, while resisting those that will weaken their autonomy and lead to (or reinforce) their "peripheralization" within the world economy. When they have attractive properties to offer, they can exercise influence over investment patterns by inviting competitive bids, as the Czechs did with Skoda and the Hungarians have done with their privatization program. But the number of such attractive properties is small. Many Western firms, for their part, would like to sell their products in the new markets without exposing themselves to the risks of undertaking production there.

If the problem for the moment is the reticence of outside investors, some East European officials have a different fear for the longer term: that in important industries, Western investment might overwhelm the stake of domestic owners. In Poland and the Czech Republic, where German firms have been the heaviest investors, such nervousness has been particularly pronounced.[38] But indigenous alternatives are limited by the meager supply of domestic capital. One solution already launched in several countries is the distribution at little or no cost of vouchers for stock purchase to employees of the concerned enterprise or to ordinary citizens, a problematic course that I shall return to.

STRATEGIC EXPORT CONTROLS

Western investment and other transactions transferring technology to Eastern Europe are still subject to the extensive system of controls established under the leadership of the United States and designed to prevent militarily valuable exports from reaching potential enemies. With the putative end of the cold war, the application of these controls to Eastern Europe has been softened but, except for Hungary, not eliminated. Although some remain nervous over the possibility of a conservative military resurgence in Russia or other parts of the former Soviet Union, the focus of Western concern over strategic exports shifted dramatically during the Persian Gulf crisis to the Middle East, especially with respect to nuclear, chemical, and biological weapons capabilities. Both Eastern Europe's long association with the Soviet Union and its past role in supplying arms to the Middle East makes it likely, however, that it will continue to be affected by the export-control debate.

Strategic export controls have been surrounded by controversy both among the allies and within the United States itself ever since they were introduced early in the cold war. The controversy, which reached a high level of intensity in the early 1980s following efforts of the Carter and Reagan administrations to tighten existing restrictions, reflected fundamental differences over the potential benefits of East-West trade and the dangers to Western security it might entail. The United States, with varying degrees of fervor, generally pressed for stronger controls, while its allies typically urged their relaxation. Within the United States, the Defense Department, backed by its conservative allies in the Congress and elsewhere in the administration, acquired a preeminent voice in export control policy in the early 1980s, but faced opposition from export-oriented businesses and their sympathizers in the Commerce Department and in Congress.

The controversy centered on trade with the Soviet Union, but most of the arguments deployed applied equally, or nearly equally, to Eastern Europe, since it was assumed that any technology acquired by the latter would quickly find its way to the former.[39] Nevertheless, the West sometimes applied a slightly looser control standard to exports destined for certain East European countries than for those to the Soviet Union; for example, the "no exceptions" rule applied in COCOM to the Soviet Union following the invasion of Afghanistan was not extended to Eastern Europe (except to Poland after the imposition of martial law).[40] After the fall of Communist governments in the region, Western European members of COCOM—the Coordinating Committee for Multilateral Export Control, an informal and secretive body based in Paris that has made the critical decisions in this area since 1949—pressed the United States to agree to a drastic reduction of controls. After putting up considerable resistance, the United States, which feared that the end of Communism in Eastern Europe by no means meant the end of KGB penetration, finally acceded to a compromise. The agreement cut the number of controlled dual-use items by a third, relaxing controls over vital telecommunications and computer exports, on the condition that their use be closely monitored to prevent any reexport to the Soviet Union.[41] There was no thought of abolishing COCOM itself, although in May 1991 the list was cut again, by half.[42]

There is no significant disagreement in the West over the principle that purely military technologies should be controlled. The controversy in the Reagan years centered rather on dual-use technologies: civilian technologies with potentially valuable military applications, for example, those involved in the manufacture of computers, specialized steel products, and optical equipment. Almost any technology can have military uses, of course, and the elastic character of this category allowed it to be used by those whose real objective was probably to wage full-scale economic warfare against the East bloc, on the assumption that any economic transaction the "enemy" might be willing to enter into would at least indirectly benefit its military.[43] It is also clear that broad arguments invoking the demands of security were sometimes used to justify measures undertaken essentially for foreign policy reasons, for example, to punish the Soviet Union for its alleged misbehavior in Afghanistan and Poland.

Opponents of such extended export controls generally argued that their costs far outweighed any potential benefits. The costs, they contended, were not only those of lost Western economic opportunities in the East—or the loss of potential U.S. contracts with the East to Western European or Japanese competitors. The impediments created to trade among the Western nations themselves and with third, non-Communist partners were still more expensive, the critics argued. About 40 percent of all U.S. exports of manufactures in 1988 were said to require some sort of export control license,[44] but only a small proportion of license applications to the U.S. government were for direct exports to the Communist countries. A study done for the National Academy of Sciences (NAS) in 1987, *Balancing the National Interest,* estimated direct annual losses to the United States due to strategic trade controls at over $9 billion as of 1985, and employment losses at 188,000; the total loss to GNP, including multipliers, was estimated at over $17 billion.[45] The political costs of the dissension and distrust sown among the Western allies by aggressive American control policies could not be assigned a dollar figure, but were also substantial. In the early 1980s, claims of extraterritoriality invoked by the United States in its attempts to reduce the reexport of American technology by foreign firms and to apply its rules to the foreign subsidiaries of U.S.-based firms were often viewed as breaches of sovereignty by this country's allies. Europeans and East Asians also frequently repeated the charge that the United States was using its allegedly "strategic" misgivings over their exports to win competitive advantages for U.S. firms.[46]

The costs of an overextended system of controls in impeding East-West *and* West-West trade and undermining Western comity appears to have greatly exceeded its benefits. As the NAS study pointed out, the "most significant" channel of militarily valuable technologies to the East bloc countries was unquestionably espionage, and "export controls do not represent an effective means to deter—much less prevent—espionage."[47] The very feasibility of keeping technologies that are offered commercially by competing firms in international markets out of hostile hands for very long seems in principle remote.

In a larger sense, the effectiveness of Western export controls was inevitably related to the perception of the participant governments of the threat that such controls were directed against. Their effectiveness also depended on the number of countries whose technological level would require their participation in any effective control regime. In the Gorbachev era and after, the Western perception of the Soviet threat rapidly diminished, and the newly perceived threat represented by ambitious Third World states, notably in the Middle East, has not replaced it. Meanwhile, the number of countries producing advanced technology has grown. Under these circumstances, and in spite of improved staff and technical support within COCOM and American successes in persuading its allies to strengthen their enforcement procedures, the efficacy of COCOM is likely to continue to erode. Only by narrowing its scope to the most critical dual-use items can the United States expect to maintain the consensus necessary to its successful operation.

For Eastern Europe, the benefits to be gained from a further lowering of Western strategic trade barriers are potentially significant. What once could be defended as genuinely necessary protective measures for Western security are now for the most part anachronisms that place still another layer of bureaucratic obstacles in the way of economic modernization and reconstruction. Eastern Europe will not benefit from greater access to sophisticated Western technologies unless it manages to overcome its difficulties in assimilating them, however.

CONCLUSIONS

Advanced technology now seems most likely to arrive in Eastern Europe in the form of Western investment. But experience under Communist rule suggests that such technology, when purchased by the state or domestically owned firms, does not guarantee prosperity or balanced growth. Popular expectations aroused by private Western investment may also be disappointed; the technology it brings may remain isolated and have little impact on the rest of the economy. Such undertakings could remain modern islands in a sea of economic backwardness, perhaps along Third World lines.

It is therefore essential that the East European nations construct a capacity for absorbing, adapting, and further developing Western technology. The West needs in particular to support the reform of East European educational systems, many now suffering from the penury imposed by their country's budgetary crises. It should also support the strengthening of domestic and international avenues of scientific and technological communications. Neither of these tasks have yet received the attention they deserve amid the region's many other pressing needs. The West should provide additional support for East-West scientific and technological exchange and support for East European scientific and technical libraries. It should give more support for the direct transfer of know-how rather than embodied forms of technology. For example, fledgling East European entrepreneurs in the computer field might be offered experience in small but successful Western firms.[48] But the West needs also to be attentive to the danger that, now that East European borders are open, many of the region's most able scientists and technicians will emigrate; this too speaks for the need to support East European universities and research institutes.[49]

Finally, while it is easy to be mesmerized by the world of computers, lasers, and genetic manipulation, it is useful to remember that at least in the near term Eastern Europe's economic well-being is likely to depend more heavily on domestic production and exports that require middle-range and lower-end technologies and on organizational and administrative reforms. Eastern Europe needs better roads and adequate housing and office space, electrified rail lines, greater agricultural efficiency, and food-processing and storage facilities more than it needs its own cutting-edge computer technology. It needs, quickly, to rebuild distribution networks and to set up competent taxing and regulatory authorities. Meeting most of these needs will require determined state action. The creation of a favorable climate for private investment and technology transfer, in other words, will depend heavily on public investment, which in turn will require vigorous Western support.

NOTES

1. Steven W. Popper, "East European Reliance on Technology Imports from the West," Rand Corporation Report R–3632–USDP, August 1988, 44.

2. Richard Perle, "Selling Security for Deutschmarks," *U.S. News and World Report*, July 31, 1989, 36.

3. See Gordon B. Smith, "The Politics of East-West Trade," in Gordon B. Smith, ed., *The Politics of East-West Trade* (Boulder, Colo.: Westview Press, 1984), 15–16; Eugene Zaleski and Helgard Wienert, *Technology Transfer between East and West* (Paris: OECD, 1980), 120.

4. See Smith, 1–2.

5. For a debunking of the frequently cited cases of Kama River (USSR) trucks and ball-bearing production equipment, see William A. Root, "COCOM: An Appraisal of Objectives and Needed Reforms," in Gary K. Bertsch, ed., *Controlling East-West Trade and Technology Transfer* (Durham, N.C.: Duke University Press, 1988), 423.

6. See John A. Martens, "Quantification of Western Exports of High-Technology Products to Communist Countries," in Joint Economic Committee, *East European Economies: Slow Growth in the 1980s*, vol. 2 (Washington, D.C.: U.S. Government Printing Office, 1986), 93; Smith, 22.

7. See the figures in Jan Monkiewicz and Jan Maciejewicz, *Technology Export from the Socialist Countries* (Boulder, Colo.: Westview Press, 1986), 18–22, on the proportion of research and development expenditures and employment in a number of East European and Western countries. The Czechoslovak Communist prime minister Ladislav Adamec complained in 1989 that while nearly 200,000 Czechs

and Slovaks were employed in scientific and technological research and development, "most industrial sectors are lagging 10 or more years behind the world." Cited in Peter Martin, "Prime Minister Ladislav Adamec Discusses the Economic Situation," *Radio Free Europe* [*RFE*] *Research,* Czechoslovak SR/14, July 5, 1989, 4.

8. Monkiewicz and Maciejewicz, 22–30.

9. Leyla Woods, "East European Trade with the Industrial West," in Joint Economic Committee, *Pressures for Reform in the East European Economies,* vol. 2 (Washington, D.C.: U.S. Government Printing Office, 1989), Table 4, 404–5.

10. Martens, 98.

11. Helgard Wienert and John Slater, *East-West Technology Transfer: The Trade and Economic Aspects* (Paris: OECD, 1986), 260.

12. Ibid., 25, 246–47, 263, 266.

13. Ibid., 25–26, 247–48. On the extensive (and at least moderately effective) use of Western technology in the Soviet and East European chemical industry, see Kazimierz Z. Poznanski, *Technology, Competition, and the Soviet Bloc in the World Market* (Berkeley: University of California Institute of International Studies, 1987), 72–81.

14. Cited in Robert V. Roosa, Michiya Matsukawa, and Armin Gutowski, *East-West Trade at a Crossroads* (New York: New York University Press, 1982), 59. The report cites a study by Philip Hanson estimating that the Soviet Union may have enjoyed an additional 0.5 percent growth rate per year "at the most," thanks to Western technology.

15. Wienert and Slater, 26–27, 377–404 (quote from p. 27). Another OECD study suggests that Western machinery imports contributed much more substantially to East European than to Soviet growth, but that Western technology transfer in all forms was unlikely to help the East make "much further progress in closing the present technology and productivity gaps at the aggregate level." Stanislaw Gomulka and Alec Nove, *East-West Technology Transfer: I—Econometric Evaluation of the Contribution of West-East Technology Transfer to the East's Economic Growth* (Paris: OECD, 1984), 24–25, 39–40. The economist Kazimierz Poznanski, however, has argued that the CMEA states that were the most cautious importers of Western technology showed the smallest technological improvements in their offerings to the West. Poznanski, *Technology,* 88; Poznanski, "The Competitiveness of Polish Industry and Indebtedness," in Paul Marer and Włodzimierz Siwiński, eds., *Creditworthiness and Reform in Poland* (Bloomington: Indiana University Press, 1988), 45–60.

16. See Wienert and Slater, 36.

17. See, e.g., Eric W. Hayden, *Technology Transfer to Eastern Europe: U.S. Corporate Experience* (New York: Praeger, 1976), 59–61.

18. See Zbiegniew Fallenbuchl, *East-West Technology Tranfer: Study of Poland 1971–1980* (Paris: OECD, 1983), 47–49, for the case of Poland.

19. A Soviet source notes that in the 1970s "equipment, costing billions of rubles, zlotys and korunas, ended up in storage, uninstalled, and in some cases waiting for buildings to be completed." Valery Karavayev, "Our Debts," *Literaturnaya gazeta,* October 21, 1987, translated and condensed in *Current Digest of the Soviet Press,* December 2, 1987, 12.

20. See Hayden, 48–49, 54.

21. See National Academy of Sciences, *Balancing the National Interest: U.S. Na-*

tional Security Export Controls and Global Economic Competition (Washington, D.C.: National Academy Press, 1987), 47.

22. Smith, 14–15. Poznanski, *Technology*, 162–67, 173–80, offers data on the slow diffusion of steel-making technologies in the Soviet bloc.

23. "The experience of more extensive East-West trade has tended to suggest, moreover, that in practice Eastern Europe is a poor conduit for the channelling of Western technology to the USSR." Philip Hanson, "Soviet Trade with Eastern Europe," in Karen Dawisha and Philip Hanson, eds., *Soviet–East European Dilemmas* (New York: Holmes & Meier, 1981), 103. See also Morris Bornstein, *East West Technology Transfer: The Transfer of Western Technology to the USSR* (Paris: OECD, 1985), 125.

24. See András Köves, *The CMEA Countries in the World Economy* (Budapest: Akademiai Kiado, 1985), 89–90.

25. See Wojciech Bienkowski, "CMEA Trade with the West—Present Problems and Future Prospects," *International Spectator*, April–June 1986, 15–18.

26. The government has also promised to impose protectionist measures if the Volkswagen-Skoda undertaking is threatened by foreign competitors. *Business Eastern Europe* 20 (April 15, 1991), 117.

27. *Business Eastern Europe* 20 (January 14, 1991), 12.

28. David Stark, "Privatization in Hungary: From Plan to Market or from Plan to Clan?" *East European Politics and Societies* 4 (Fall 1990), 360.

29. Arne Daniels, "Tiger im Hinterhof," *Die Zeit*, June 11, 1993, 9–10.

30. See "Unions in the New Eastern Europe," *Report on Eastern Europe*, March 29, 1991, 19–45.

31. Stephen Engelberg, "Eastern Europe Foils All but the Hardiest of Western Investors," *New York Times*, March 5, 1992, A1, C8.

32. *Business Eastern Europe* 20 (February 18, 1991), 53. A joint East-West report noted in 1989 that "the gestation period for investment projects remains very long. The resulting impact of a signed joint venture agreement upon domestic production and then trade may take several years to be realized, if the agreement proves to be effective at all." *Managing the Transition: Integrating the Reforming Socialist Countries into the World Economy* (New York: Institute for East-West Security Studies, 1989), 60.

33. German law gives explicit priority to restitution over paying compensation to the former owners, a provision that has greatly slowed economic reconstruction and proven psychologically devastating for many affected east Germans. See Thomas Kleine-Brockhoff, Marlies Menge, and Ralf Neubauer, "Der Häuserkampf," *Die Zeit*, March 27, 1992, 7–8.

34. *Christian Science Monitor*, September 18, 1990, 5.

35. Gary Humphreys, "Privatisers Get Back on Track," *Euromoney*, March 1991, 42.

36. "How can you spot an American in Hungary? Answer: He's the one who starts dialing as soon as he picks up the phone" (that is, without waiting patiently for a dial tone). "What the Brochures Don't Tell You," *Business Week*, April 14, 1991, 53.

37. Interview with Czech official, April 22,1991.

38. Stephen Engelberg, "Eager if Uneasy, East Europe Accepts German Investments," *New York Times*, January 23, 1992, 1.

39. Bennett Kovrig cites a number of cases in which East European agents, including Hungarians and Poles, covertly acquired Western technology. Bennett Kovrig, *Of Walls and Bridges* (New York: New York University Press, 1991), 240–41.

40. Roosa, Matsukawa, and Gutowski, 81; Root, 421; Michael Mastanduno, "The Management of Alliance Export Control Policies," in Bertsch, 272. The application of the "no exceptions" rule to Poland was lifted again in 1987.

41. See "The Dismantling of a Cold-War Icon," *Business Week*, June 25, 1990, 41–42; *New York Times*, February 27, 1991, C12.

42. *Wall Street Journal*, May 28, 1991, A8; *Handelsblatt*, May 27, 1991, translated in the *German Tribune*, June 9, 1991, 7.

43. The Reagan administration denied that it wished to wage economic warfare, but some outside observers have attributed that intention to it. See Philip Hanson, *Western Economic Statecraft in East-West Relations* (London: Routledge & Kegan Paul, 1988), 53–54. The term probably comes close to describing the position of the then Assistant Defense Secretary Richard Perle and his chief Caspar Weinberger.

44. Hanson, *Western*, 26.

45. National Academy of Sciences, app. D, 254–77. The response of the supporters of rigorous export controls, of course, was to cite still higher estimates of the defense costs attributable to Soviet acquisitions of Western technology.

46. See Mastanduno, 261–62, 273. The NAS report found no evidence to support this charge, however; see *Balancing*, 160.

47. National Academy of Sciences, 45.

48. See Esther Dyson, "Micro Capitalists: Eastern Europe's Computer Future," *Harvard Business Review*, January–February 1991, 26–38.

49. Steven Dickman, "Schwere Weg in die freie Wissenschaft," *Die Zeit*, May 1, 1992, 20.

8

Money, Credit, and Debt

> Bankers learn very slowly and forget very quickly.
>
> Klaus Schröder[1]

> A great deal has already been done to organize programs of assistance to eastern Europe. However, it is not clear, with a multiplicity of programs and organizations involved, whether these add up to a coherent program and are commensurate with the problems they are intended to solve.
>
> Economic Commission for Europe[2]

The ability of Eastern Europe to expand its imports of Western technology, to rebuild its infrastructure, and to carry out market reforms will depend heavily on the amount and terms of credit that Western nations make available to it. The GDR, Poland, Hungary, and Bulgaria all emerged from Communist rule with debilitating burdens of hard-currency debt, owed to both public and private creditors. Much of this debt has now been rescheduled or, in the case of Poland, forgiven; the GDR's debt is now the responsibility of the Federal Republic and the new east German states.[3] Western governments and multilateral lending agencies have already extended substantial new credits to the countries of the region to reward their efforts at building democratic institutions and to promote economic reform and restructuring; private Western lending, however, has dwindled. There can be no doubt that Eastern Europe will need massive financial assistance in the years ahead. The questions of who (if anyone) will provide it, in what form, for what purposes, and under what terms and conditions, however, raise a number of difficult policy issues.

RAISING CAPITAL AT HOME

The attraction of foreign lending and investment for Eastern Europe is especially understandable because of the acute shortage of domestic capital. The public sector needs capital for rebuilding the economy's infrastructure, stabilizing the currency, and much else. Capital is equally essential for those who want to start their own private businesses, purchase part or all of state-owned businesses, and modernize and/or expand either. It is the necessary prerequisite for entrepreneurship.

What domestic capital there is, however, is often found in unsavory hands. Members of the old Communist *nomenklatura* were sometimes in a position to accumulate substantial resources, or to take advantage of their insider status or knowledge to acquire ownership rights in the first stages of privatization. Successful black marketeers have also been among the first purchasers of small state businesses that have been put on the block. The stock of more legitimate private savings is small, and has been further devalued by inflation. In Hungary, for example, in 1990 domestic savings were estimated to be sufficient to buy only about 10 percent of the state's assets.[4]

Borrowing money is also difficult. Private banks are only now being established in most countries, and banking practices are severely underdeveloped. "A Polish or Bulgarian banker is more like a bookkeeper in a small company than a modern financier," writes one commentator.[5] Existing state-owned banks often have resources tied up in nonperforming loans to economically troubled but politically still influential state enterprises.[6] Pressures to make more such loans have by no means disappeared; in any case, in the absence of adequate financial data and accounting practices and in a highly volatile economic environment, the soundness of a given loan is difficult for banks to judge. In such circumstances—as recent Polish financial scandals suggest—and in the absence of effective regulatory mechanisms, the potential for corruption is great.[7]

Stock and bond markets are still largely insignificant. The stock market that opened in Warsaw in April 1991 (following the creation of a stock market in Budapest in 1990) initially offered shares in just five recently privatized companies.[8] Potential investors have reason to be cautious, and the large institutional investors who play so large a role in Western markets are virtually nonexistent. The Prague Stock Exchange, which opened in April 1993, may prove an exception, with 650 stocks listed and more than 400 investment funds (the offspring of voucher privatization) expected to participate in trading. New capital, however, is expected to come largely from foreign traders.[9]

East European governments are not by themselves in a position to raise sufficient capital for public purposes or to provide or underwrite much credit for private ventures. They face severe budgetary stringency, enforced in part by IMF demands that they curb inflation and by their own impaired capacity to collect, much less increase, taxes. One form of domestic lending that has flourished, however—and that frustrates IMF efforts to control credit through traditional means—is the granting of credits between enterprises, as they seek to keep one another afloat.[10]

Hence Eastern Europe has a strong interest in attracting foreign capital, through loans, joint ventures, and other means. Western banks and companies have begun to move into the region, although usually not in the anticipated numbers, and it is hoped that Western investors will begin to enliven the region's new stock markets. In the face of worldwide competition for capital and Western economic sluggishness, however, such external involvement is bound to be limited and/or expensive. The role of foreign public lending, both by individual governments and by multilateral institutions, will be critical.

THE USES OF WESTERN LOANS

In order to analyze the problems of credit and debt and to lay the groundwork for policy recommendations, we need first to distinguish among three major types of loans Western creditors extend to East European borrowers. In any given case, of course, there may be some overlapping or ambiguity among the three categories. Short-term credits, often extended by the supplier to purchasers of his or her exports, are widely used to facilitate "normal" international trade. While usually unproblematic, a large number of such credits, especially if their maturity dates coincide with those of longer-term credits and/or a drop in the importing countries' cash reserves, can bring liquidity problems. The absence of such credits, however, would sharply curtail East-West trade.[11]

The second category of loans comprises those intended to support economic stabilization, especially to rescue countries with balance-of-payments and related fiscal difficulties, and simultaneously to protect Western creditors. Eastern Europe's needs here are acute, owing to inherited debts, strong inflationary pressures, the costs of reform, and the collapse of CMEA trading patterns. Loans in this category are the special province of the International Monetary Fund (IMF), but other multilateral, bilateral, and bank loans granted to prevent default or rescheduling, to underwrite efforts to restore the integrity of the national currency, or to roll over existing debt or facilitate rescheduling also belong here. Many of the new loans offered to Eastern Europe are aimed at stabilization; while necessary, if previous debt is not to be written off or forgiven, these loans do not, even when fairly stringent conditions are attached to them, normally address the underlying economic problems. They may, however, help create the preconditions for doing so—IMF loans are usually intended to do precisely that, and the organization has explicitly justified several of its recent loans to Eastern Europe as support for economic reform.

Such loans thus edge into the third category, ones made for the purpose of promoting economic development and restructuring. World Bank loans, targeted for specific projects and purposes, are the prototypical examples, but many loans from the European Community, the Community's European Investment Bank (EIB), and the European Bank for Reconstruction and Development (EBRD) also belong in this category. So may tied bilateral government or private loans, although sometimes the tie is really to the products or services the lender wishes to sell, and primarily serves the interests of domestic producers. The needs of East European countries for new investment, improving export capacity, reducing costly pollution, and so on, make such loans vital to them; the alternative, trying to squeeze the needed resources out of tightly constrained domestic economies, is all but precluded at present on political as well as economic grounds. Countries whose external debt burden is already great and whose existing exports go largely to pay debt service have few attractive alternatives to additional borrowing.

Both sides, however, recognize at least in the abstract the danger that new loans, if used imprudently, will only deepen the debtors' predicament. But the new, like the old, East European regimes are prey to short-term calculations of survival as they try to cope with mounting economic problems and tenuous authority. Official Western lenders in particular thus feel compelled, with good reason, to demand reforms as a condition of their loans. For their part, recipients typically argue that they need such loans just to make reform *possible*, even if the funds do not go directly for investment, for example, to shore up the local currency as it moves toward convertibility or to support the incomes and provide retraining for those who would be most severely affected by painful restructuring policies.

THE RISE AND PERSISTENCE OF EAST EUROPEAN DEBT

Both East and West discovered some of the perils of East European participation in the international financial system at the beginning of the 1980s. During the 1970s, Western loans flowed freely, but in the wake of the Polish crisis of 1980–1981, and the discovery that no comprehensive "Soviet umbrella" of responsibility for the region's debts existed, Western banks and governments abruptly halted virtually all lending to the East European countries. Even lines of credit previously granted were withdrawn, and the banks required the East Europeans to repay some $5 billion in short-term credits in a brief span of time.[12] Poland and Romania were forced to reschedule their debts, and Hungary and the GDR barely escaped

Table 8.1
East European Credit Ratings (1980–1992)

country	1980	1983	1986	1989	Sept. 1992
GDR	**61.4**	**41.3**	**53.9**	**58.7**	___
Czechoslovakia	**60.7**	**43.1**	**51.8**	**54.4**	**46.1**
Bulgaria	**47.4***	**39.1**	**48.4**	**46.5**	**19.8**
Hungary	**59.4**	**45.5**	**51.6**	**44.5**	**42.3**
Romania	**52.6**	**16.1**	**31.1**	**32.7**	**24.8**
Poland	**41.6**	**8.3**	**14.7**	**18.1**	**24.7**
for comparison:					
Austria	**86.3**	**81.1**	**83.5**	**83.1**	**84.3**
Mexico	**71.8**	**36.9**	**36.4**	**29.3**	**42.6**
Brazil	**58.0**	**48.1**	**31.9**	**29.1**	**27.1**
Global Average	**53.5**	**42.2**	**40.6**	**38.7**	**35.9**

*1981
Source: Institutional Investor, March 1980, March 1983, March 1986, March 1989, September 1992.

doing so, thanks in part to the help of the IMF and the West German government, respectively.[13] Western banks ultimately had to write off much of their Polish debt or sell it at a discount.

Yet by the middle of the decade Western loans had again begun to flow; by early 1989 three of the Eastern European countries had regained credit ratings nearly as favorable as those they had enjoyed prior to the crisis, while a fourth, Hungary, although dropping somewhat, remained at a respectable level.[14] National credit ratings published semiannually by the *Institutional Investor,* based on a survey of leading international banks, placed the GDR, Czechoslovakia, Bulgaria, and Hungary all well above the international average of 38.7 on a 100–point scale (see Table 8.1). Only Poland and Romania remained beyond the pale; the latter had in any case halted foreign borrowing as a matter of policy.

The political transformation of late 1989 and 1990 brought an end to this brief resurgence of creditor confidence; private Western lenders fled in the face of the new uncertainties, notwithstanding the new regimes' commitment to building capitalist economies. By the end of 1990, with the region's visible economic distress mounting, private lending to Eastern Europe had once again come virtually to a halt.[15] Public lending, on the other hand, especially by multilateral institutions, dramatically increased.

There are important lessons in Eastern Europe's earlier acquisition of hard-currency debt that the changes in political regimes have not erased. The accumulation of this debt by Eastern Europe's Communist governments goes back to the import-led development strategy of the 1970s, although some of the borrowing also supported consumption, as the regimes sought to maintain the "social contract" with their populations.[16] This import-led strategy, pursued with success by several of the NICs,[17] failed in Eastern Europe, due in part to the Western economic slump and interest rate explosion brought about by OPEC price increases. The failure also reflected systemic problems, some of which have yet to be resolved: the declining competitiveness of East European exports, inefficiency in the absorption and diffusion of new technology, and so on. While both sides have learned lessons from the experience of the 1970s, the need of the East for capital, of Western banks for borrowers, and of Western producers for markets can at any time combine with one another and with government pressures on behalf of such interests to again constitute a powerful force in support of undisciplined lending.

Most of the massive increase in East European debt in the 1970s can be attributed to the lending of private banks, with West German banks playing the largest role, followed by American banks. Imprudently, the banks demanded little information on the economic situation or even the total indebtedness of the recipient nations, in part because of the bankers' belief in a Soviet umbrella and their, in retrospect, naive faith in the capacity of planned economies to discipline their financial behavior.[18] A growing proportion of bank credits were arranged on Eurocurrency markets, not subject to direct regulation by individual governments.[19] Some 20 percent of the total debt was guaranteed by Western governments, however,[20] evidence that they made little effort to restrain the private sector. Indeed, some new bank loans, notably in West Germany, came in response to government pressures.[21]

In March 1981, Poland suspended payment on its debts; Romania followed suit in July. Eventually, Western banks sold at a discount or wrote off much of their Polish debt.[22] As a result, by 1991 the bulk of the country's Western debt, some $33 billion out of a total gross debt of $48.5 billion, was owed to governments.[23] The size of the debt continued to grow throughout the 1980s, as seen in Table 8.2, in spite of the country's success in slashing its hard-currency imports and building sizeable trade surpluses; the costs of debt servicing and/or rescheduling (including the capitalization of interest payments) simply exceeded the country's export capacity. While

Table 8.2
Net Debt of East European States (1982–1991)
(1982–1989: millions of dollars at 1989 exchange rate
1990–1991: at current exchange rates)

country	1982	1985	1987	1988	1989	1990	1991
Bulgaria	**3,912**	**3,443**	**5,706**	**6,823**	**7,957**	**10,000**	**11,100**
Czecho-Slovakia	**4,097**	**4,065**	**5,156**	**5,548**	**5,724**	**7,000**	**6,100**
Hungary	**10,344**	**12,650**	**17,064**	**18,015**	**19,440**	**20,200**	**18,800**
Poland	**27,033**	**29,994**	**34,896**	**35,890**	**37,469**	**44,000**	**44,800**
Romania	**9,581**	**7,342**	**4,689**	**1,843**	**-1,254**	**0**	**1,500**
total five	**54,969**	**57,495**	**67,512**	**68,120**	**69,337**	**81,200**	**82,300**

Note: The GDR's net debt at the end of 1989 was estimated to be $11 billion and its gross debt $21 billion. However, a later estimate of the GDR's new democratic government put the gross figure as of the end of May 1990 at $33 billion.

Sources: "The International Financial Situation of the Central and Eastern European Countries," [OECD] *Financial Market Trends,* February 1991, 20, 22; Economic Commission for Europe, *Economic Bulletin for Europe,* No. 42 (New York: United Nations, 1990), 70; ibid., No. 44 (1992), 139.

the Paris Club of fifteen Western governmental creditor nations agreed in early 1991 to reduce, conditionally, Poland's debt to its members by half, no such agreement was reached with private creditors (the London Club). Poland had suspended interest payments to private creditors in 1990.

Romania's balance of payments deteriorated sharply in the latter part of the 1970s, even prior to the second oil price shock, leaving it with a net debt of $9.3 billion in 1980. Even though the IMF granted the country a $1.4 billion standby credit in 1981, Western banks curtailed their lending and withdrew deposits; by the end of the year Romania's arrears had reached $1.1 billion.[24] In 1983, after two years of difficult rescheduling negotiations, President Ceauşescu announced a plan to eliminate Romania's debt entirely by 1988;[25] this goal was met, and the Romanian parliament in 1989 passed a law forbidding the acceptance of new foreign loans altogether.[26] The new government reversed this policy; while Romania's debt is still relatively small, its exports have dropped and the country's creditworthiness remains correspondingly low.[27]

By 1981 Hungary's debt on a per capita basis exceeded that of Poland.

Table 8.3
Debt-Service Ratios in Eastern Europe (1981–1990)

Country	1981	1985	1986	1987	1988	1989	1990*
Bulgaria	21	14	31	30	35	48	77
Czechoslovakia	17	20	20	21	18	23	25
Hungary	42	58	67	52	57	49	65
Poland	163	96	63	79	68	76	71
Romania	36	28	28	26	20	19	10
Total five		43	42	42	40	43	50

*projected
Note: Debt service ratio = all interest and amortization on medium- and long-term debt as a percentage of one year's exports.
Sources: "The International Financial Situation of the Central and Eastern European Countries," [OECD] *Financial Market Trends*, February 1991, 26; Vlad Sobell, "OECD Report on Financial Situation of CMEA Countries," *Radio Free Europe Research* BR/51, March 17, 1989, 2.

Its membership in the IMF in 1982 enabled it to obtain "bridge credits" from the Bank for International Settlements (BIS) and bank credits enabling it to avoid rescheduling until it could obtain standby loans from the IMF itself. The IMF and World Bank, Western governments, and commercial sources continued to grant Hungary loans throughout the decade, partly in recognition of its commitment to economic reforms that were then the most far-reaching in the CMEA; the economy, however, continued to stagnate. Hungary's debt at the end of 1990 exceeded $20 billion—about double the 1981 figure. Debt servicing costs for that year amounted to 65 percent of total export earnings. Some three-quarters of Hungary's debt is owed to commercial banks; thus forgiveness of its governmental loans on the model of the Paris Club's agreement with Poland would help it far less.[28]

Bulgaria, after overcoming a more limited debt crisis at the beginning of the 1980s, rapidly increased its Western borrowing in the latter part of the decade and now owes some $10 billion, most of it to commercial banks. Its debt-service ratio is the highest in Eastern Europe (see Table 8.3). As noted earlier, Bulgaria suspended payments of principal in March 1990; in June, interest payments also fell into arrears.[29] The Paris Club's April 1991 agreement to reschedule the country's official debt did not affect the almost

85 percent of the debt owed to commercial creditors.[30] Only Czech and Slovak debt (divided on a 2–1 basis between the two) still appears to be of manageable proportions, in spite of its significant growth in recent years; at the end of 1991 Czechoslovakia's annual debt service costs remained at 25 percent of its exports.[31]

Commercial bank lending to Eastern Europe is now largely in abeyance, but may well revive once the most painful stages of institutional transition are completed. The growth of the East European private sector will probably encourage such a revival: banks hesitant to loan new funds to East European governments may be more ready to do so to private ventures, especially those with some Western participation. A number of Western banks are establishing branches themselves or entering joint ventures in the region; these may become channels for loans from the parent institutions. Another phenomenon of interest is the appearance in Western markets of funds for investment in Eastern Europe, although to date such funds have found it difficult to find a sufficient number of attractive investment projects.[32] What all this suggests is that the diversification of Eastern European borrowing that was already evident under the old Communist regimes is likely to continue. This development has its virtues, but it implies that Western governments will lose some of their ability to control, or even monitor, a new expansion of East European debt. The East European governments, too, will lose influence over their countries' debt as they relinquish their control over foreign exchange transactions. Yet another danger is that Western governments and multilateral agencies themselves will compete with one another in such a way as to encourage a new spiral of private as well as public lending.

THE CONFLICT OVER CREDIT TERMS

In the 1970s and again in the 1980s, one of the major forces propelling the expansion of lending to Eastern Europe was the competition among Western exporters and governments in offering favorable credit terms, guarantees, and sometimes subsidies. Western governments use a variety of measures to support exports: the United States offers Export-Import (Exim) Bank loans and guarantees, CCC loan guarantees for agricultural products, and Overseas Private Investment Corporation (OPIC) investment insurance. Europe and Japan have comparable credit and insurance agencies, including Hermes (West Germany), "Coface" and "Sofaris" (France), and the Export Credit Guarantee Department (Britain). U.S. policy, however, restricted the use of such agencies to facilitate trade with Eastern Europe during the cold war, while nearly all of West Germany's Eastern trade was insured through Hermes, and France openly subsidized its East bloc trade.[33] These conflicting policies led to disputes among the Western nations that paralleled those over strategic export rules.

The Berne Union gentlemen's agreement, dating to 1934, had sought to limit government insurance to loans with a maximum maturity of five years, unless the lending country informed its partners of any deviation and justified it. In the late 1950s, the agreement began to break down. CMEA countries turned to Japan—not a Berne Union member—for longer-term loans, and, one after another, Britain, Italy, France, and West Germany sought to meet the competition by extending their own credit terms beyond the five-year limit. The United States might have followed suit had not Congress resisted efforts to liberalize the rules for Exim Bank credits; it subsequently sought to persuade its allies through discussions within the OECD to harmonize their interest rates and loan maturities. These produced a 1978 Arrangement on Guidelines which, as the name suggests, was not legally binding.[34] In 1982, the OECD group agreed to treat the GDR and Czechoslovakia (along with the Soviet Union) as relatively "rich" countries to be charged a substantially increased minimum interest rate, while other East European countries were classified as "intermediate" and thus deserving of lower, but still increased, rates. The agreement was accepted by the Europeans apparently because it did not (as the United States wished) really slow the granting of credits[35]; indeed, in the mid-1980s most terms were highly favorable by international standards.[36]

Now that American objections to loan and investment guarantees rooted in cold war concerns have largely faded (although not ones based on free trade arguments), there is a renewed possibility of a harmful public-private symbiosis, in which governments concerned primarily with export promotion compete with one another to support and subsidize private lending, with little regard for a broader strategy of economic support for Eastern Europe. The present caution of commercial banks toward lending to the region could give way and, in the worst (but not implausible) case, unleash a new cycle of rising indebtedness, without the assurance that the money borrowed would be used productively.

Averting this possible danger would require at least voluntary coordination among countries and between governments and private lenders. In the past, such measures seem to have worked reasonably well once crises have arisen, but maintaining cooperation in more normal, that is, pre- or postcrisis, circumstances in the face of international competitive pressures appears to be more problematic.[37] The search of individual companies and nations for expanded export markets, sanctified by the political ideal of assisting Eastern Europe, could again lead to competition in government loan guarantees and insurance and in the relaxation of trade barriers, interest rates, and other credit terms.

THE IMF AND THE WORLD BANK

The International Monetary Fund, which makes financial assistance available to its members suffering balance-of-payments difficulties, and its sister institution, the World Bank (officially, the International Bank for Reconstruction and Development), which makes development loans, have come to occupy center stage on questions of East European borrowing and its use by the West as a lever of reform. Prior to the 1980s, however, they played only a secondary role. As United Nations agencies, the Fund and Bank are supposed to avoid using political criteria in granting aid. But voting in the two organizations is based on financial contributions, and is thus dominated by the leading capitalist powers; the United States has exercised a de facto veto over their actions.[38]

Thus in practice any IMF or World Bank assistance to Eastern Europe was hostage to cold war calculations. While Poland and Czechoslovakia were among the IMF's original members, Poland withdrew in 1950 and Czechoslovakia was expelled four years later. Apart from nonaligned Yugoslavia, the first Communist country to join subsequently was Romania in 1972; probably because of its maverick status in the Soviet bloc, Romania received considerable support in the 1970s from the two organizations in spite of its resistance to economic reform and its reluctance to supply adequate (or accurate) statistical data. The Fund and Bank assisted both Romania and Hungary, which joined in 1982, in dealing with the liquidity crisis of the early 1980s. Poland, whose application for readmission was blocked by the United States after the imposition of martial law, finally was permitted to rejoin in 1986; in 1990, Czechoslovakia returned and Bulgaria joined for the first time. Romania, which had broken off dealings with the Fund and Bank in 1984, resumed them.

In the post-Communist era, and especially with the precipitous drop in private lending, the role of the two organizations in shaping Western assistance has become pivotal. The IMF, for example, approved loans totalling $8.5 billion for the five East European countries in the first four months of 1991 (see Table 8.4), but its influence is still greater than this impressive figure implies. The World Bank announced $2.9 billion in loans over the period between July 1990 and June 1991, including support for such things as energy and telecommunications projects, banking and financial reform, and industrial training and job relocating programs.[39] Cumulative World Bank commitments to the region had reached $5.6 billion by late 1992.[40]

Commitments, however, are not always equalled by actual disbursements. As in the case of its other clients, the IMF conducts protracted negotiations with East European governments over the budgetary and macroeconomic policies they must promise to pursue as a condition of the "standby credits" or other loans they are to receive. Once approved, the

Table 8.4
IMF Loans to Eastern Europe (January–April 1991)
(millions of U.S. dollars)

date	country	total	standby credit or extended arrangement	length
1/7	Czecho-slovakia	1783	883	14 mos.
1/16, 2/21	Hungary	2563	1621	3 yrs.
3/15	Bulgaria	634	394	12 mos.
3/15, 4/11	Romania	1033	518	12 mos.
4/18	Poland	2487	1665	3 yrs.

Note: "Standby credits" or "extended arrangements" are meant to support economic reform; the rest of the credits were to offset higher oil and gas prices.

Source: IMF Survey, 20 (January 21, 1991), 23–24; (March 4, 1991), 74–75; (April 1, 1991), 101; (April 29, 1991), 137–40.

loans are usually distributed in installments, payment of which can be suspended or cancelled if the recipient country fails to live up to the terms of its agreement or fails to achieve specifically targeted economic and budgetary results; for example, disbursements to Poland and Hungary were suspended in 1991 and 1992, respectively, because of excessive deficits. World Bank loans are tied to more specific projects and purposes, whose conditions are also negotiated in detail. IMF conditionality emphasizes, as elsewhere, austerity measures—bringing budgets into balance, stabilizing the currency, slashing subsidies—but in Eastern Europe the IMF now also seems to require a broader commitment to marketization and privatization, preferably through a "big bang" approach, that was not demanded when the countries were under Communist rule. On the other hand, both the Fund and Bank seem ready to endorse social safety net programs (in recognition of the fragility of the new regimes) and certain *dirigiste* measures, notably wage freezes, that they have traditionally viewed with distaste in dealing with Third World clients.[41] The indirect financial mechanisms usually favored by the IMF in capitalist countries, for example, raising interest rates, often appear to be ineffective in transitional East European economies.[42]

Critics charge that with these policies the IMF and World Bank are acting as instruments through which "Western capitalism" is seeking to impose its own economic agenda—indeed, its own economic system—on Eastern Europe.[43] There is undoubtedly some truth to this charge, but it must be said that there are few indications of strong resistance to these efforts on the part of the post-Communist East European governments, for whom the "market" and "privatization" have become all-purpose shibboleths.[44] To be sure, where there are internal differences over the pace and modalities of reform, as there often are, IMF pressures are likely to tip the scales in favor of more ambitious measures. Reportedly, the arrival of an IMF team in Prague in March 1990 helped Václav Klaus win his struggle over economic strategy against his former boss Valtr Komárek, an advocate of more gradual, organic reform.[45] The shortage of expertise in market economics in most East European countries serves also to strengthen the influence of IMF and other Western advisors. (Both the Fund and Bank see the provision of such technical assistance as an important part of their mission.) The East European governments perhaps also recognize, as many Third World ones have recognized, the usefulness of the two organizations as scapegoats for unpopular measures and levels of economic deprivation that they themselves privately believe to be unavoidable.

What makes IMF lending particularly significant in shaping East-West economic relations, apart from its sheer size and multilateral character, is the dependence of assistance from other sources on its approval. IMF sanctions have long been seen in the international financial community as something of a "seal of approval" that governments and banks look to before going ahead with their own credits. Now, however, World Bank, EBRD, European Community, and individual-country assistance is often made explicitly conditional on the recipient's reaching agreement with the IMF; the agreement of Western governments to forgive half of Poland's debts, for example, is so conditioned. World Bank loans are now often extended with cofinancing by private lenders, suggesting a similar dependence of at least some private financing on the decisions of such international agencies. A World Bank affiliate, the International Finance Corporation, is devoted directly to private sector financing, seeking to find foreign capital, and providing some of its own capital, for Eastern Europe's new private businesses.[46]

IMF influence means that a remarkably uniform set of measures for economic restructuring has been prescribed for Eastern Europe, even though there is as yet no compelling evidence that they will be successful. The IMF, for example, was closely identified with the Balcerowicz reforms in Poland, which in turn became something of a yardstick for assessing the reform efforts of other countries. But IMF influence tends to be stronger over central governments than over Eastern Europe's activist, quarrelsome parliaments or over regional or local authorities—or over the enterprises themselves, where market motivations will have to take hold if such reforms are to succeed. To that extent, the fund's ability to secure implementation of its designs is less certain than it might appear.

The dominant role of the IMF and World Bank may, in any case, eventually come to be challenged by the growing importance of the European Community and its European Investment Bank, and especially by the European Bank for Reconstruction and Development. Funding for the European Bank, unlike the Washington-based IMF and World Bank, is dominated by European Community members; its first head was a French socialist. To the extent that American and European agendas for Eastern European reconstruction diverge, so may ultimately the lending practices of the different institutions, in spite of their professed commitment to cooperation.[47] The U.S. Treasury Secretary, Nicholas Brady, in 1992 accused the European Bank of going beyond its mandate, which he described, inaccurately, as limited to helping the private sector.[48] A year later, the EBRD came under sharp attack for spending more on its London headquarters than it had actually disbursed to Eastern Europe, and Jacques Attali, its director, resigned. Projects worth some $2.5 billion had been approved (but not disbursed), however, and if the bank survives the controversy it seems poised to become a major player in the region.[49]

Bilateral lending may also be extended in pursuit of objectives other than the IMF's. The EC, Japan, the United States, and other G-24 nations committed sums totalling $32 billion to Eastern Europe between January 1990 and June 1991; the American share was just 8 percent.[50] Some of the commitments were spread over several years, and experience suggests that not all the promised sums will actually be disbursed. The larger part was in the form of trade credits and credit guarantees, not all of which will be taken up. Often such credits are tied to the purchase of the lending countries' goods and services, which may contribute little to the recipients' economic development. The United States has strongly objected to this practice in international trade negotiations (in spite of its own use of credits tied to American agricultural sales).[51]

The fact that most new international assistance, whether through the IMF or otherwise, comes in the form of credits or loan guarantees, not grants, has some disquieting implications. Even though such loans may provide for long maturity periods and (rarely) below-market interest rates and include provisions delaying the repayment of principal, their effect will be to increase the volume of the region's already formidable existing debt. The continuing problem of East European debt will thus be left unresolved, if for the moment postponed.

CONCLUSIONS

A large proportion of the Western credits currently being offered to Eastern Europe are being used as levers to promote a particular, surprisingly uniform vision of economic reform. The de facto veto power that the IMF now exercises over the disbursement of these funds, and thus over the economic policies of the recipient nations, is in some respects undesirable. As I shall argue in the next chapter, there is no assurance that the IMF's preferred reform formula will succeed economically or be workable politically. At this juncture, encouraging a greater diversity in approaches to reform might well be more fruitful. Eastern European governments must also be, and must appear to their publics to be, full participants in developing reform strategies, rather than alms recipients reluctantly acceding to Western pressures to mend their ways.

On the other hand, the experience of the 1970s makes it imperative that all major loans (and grants) be conditional in some sense. They should be tied to specific projects or clearly enunciated purposes. These should be worked out in some detail, as is done in the case of World Bank loans, through a joint Western–East European assessment of the needs and possibilities of the recipient. Projects already enjoying such funding include the support of currency convertibility, specific infrastructure projects, environmental repair, and assistance to small and medium-sized businesses. Where possible, such projects should cross East (and Central!) European borders and require the cooperation of two or more of the region's governments. However, conditions tying loans to the exports of industry and agriculture of individual Western countries should generally be avoided. The United States should also abandon its ideologically inspired and economically counterproductive insistence on emphasizing private sector projects. The private sector will not flourish until public sector capacities are strengthened.

While private lending is now in the doldrums, we can expect it to revive. With its revival will come the danger of a new competitive spiral of lending and the creation of still greater debt burdens. There is a triple problem of coordination here: of private banking decisions and public policy, especially in the United States; among the disparate departments of the U.S. government sharing responsibility for the international financial and commercial sphere; and among Western nations and multilateral institutions. For the first, Benjamin Cohen's proposals for regularized forms of consultation and "prudential supervision" would appear to be apposite.[52] The second problem could be reduced (though not eliminated) by a firm presidential commitment to a specific set of policies. For the third, some sort of permanent, multilateral, and relatively high-level body for economic relations with Eastern Europe, building on existing G-7 cooperation[53] and EC mechanisms, may be desirable—a point I shall return to.

The West also needs to give high priority to assisting the development of domestic financial markets. Here, too, cooperation between the public and private sectors will be imperative. In the "wild West" atmosphere encouraged by the rapid expansion of banking facilities, investment funds, and the like, Eastern Europe has a special need for international help in the creation of effective systems of financial regulation. Western experts have a good deal of bitter experience at home to draw on in this sphere.

Finally, there is the question of dealing with the accumulated and future burden of East European debt. As matters stand, there is some danger that, as the economist Paul Marer has warned, the next years will see a net transfer of resources *from* Eastern Europe *to* the industrial West; in the former Soviet–East European region there has in fact been a net capital outflow since 1989.[54] The debt forgiveness already granted Poland will almost unavoidably have to be extended to Bulgaria and probably to Hungary as well; in these two cases, however, much of the relief will have to come from the private sector, perhaps along the lines of the Brady Plan, in spite of its likely effect on future commercial loans. Every effort should be made to shift future bilateral and EC assistance in the direction of grants rather than credits, difficult as that may be politically. The IMF, World Bank, EIB, and EBRD by their nature can only extend loans, but it must be understood that the ability of Eastern Europe to repay probably lies decades, rather than years, in the future.

NOTES

1. Klaus Schröder, quoted in *Wall Street Journal*, March 19, 1985, 32.

2. Economic Commission for Europe, *Economic Bulletin for Europe*, vol. 42 (New York: United Nations, 1991), 6. Hereafter cited as *Economic Bulletin*.

3. "Das Vertrag zur deutschen Einheit," *Frankfurter Allgemeine Zeitung*, September 5, 1990, B2.

4. David Stark, "Privatization in Hungary: From Plan to Market or from Plan to Clan?" *East European Politics and Societies* 4 (Fall 1990), 370–71.

5. David Fairlamb, "So Far So Good," *Institutional Investor*, September 1990, 73; see also "Bank Restructuring in Central and Eastern Europe: Issues and Strategies," *Financial Market Trends*, February 1992, 15–30.

6. Paul Marer, "The Transition to a Market Economy in Central and Eastern Europe," *OECD Observer*, April/May 1991, 5.

7. Ben Slay, "Financial Scandals and the Evolution of the Banking System," *Report on Eastern Europe*, September 27, 1991, 21–27. Slay notes that in spite of the presence of some eighty banking institutions in Poland as of mid-1991, "it is still virtually impossible for private entrepreneurs to obtain bank credit." Ibid., 25.

8. Stephen Engelberg, "Warsaw Turns On the Stock Ticker," *New York Times*, April 17, 1991, C1, C6. In May 1991, the stock of nine companies was traded on the Budapest exchange. *Business Eastern Europe* 20 (May 20, 1991), 153.

9. Richard W. Stevenson, "Czech Capitalism Gets Stock Market," *New York Times,* June 21, 1993, C1.

10. Erik Ipsen, "A Safety Net for Eastern Europe," *Institutional Investor,* September 1990, 28.

11. Iliana Zloch-Christy, *Debt Problems of Eastern Europe* (Cambridge: Cambridge University Press, 1987), 137.

12. Zloch-Christy, 89; Klaus Schröder, "Die Ost-West Finanzbeziehungen vor neuen Herausforderungen," *Osteuropa* 38 (March 1989), 190.

13. See Zloch-Christy, 89–90.

14. Przemslaw T. Gajdeczka, "International Market Perceptions and Economic Performance: Lending to Eastern Europe," *Eastern European Politics and Societies* 2 (Fall 1988), 558–64.

15. "The International Financial Situation of the Central and Eastern European Countries," [OECD] *Financial Market Trends,* February 1991, 15–45.

16. See Zloch-Christy, 72, 75.

17. See Kazimierz Poznanski, "Competition between Eastern Europe and Developing Countries in the Western Market for Manufactured Goods," in Joint Economic Committee, *East European Economies: Slow Growth in the 1980s,* vol. 2 (Washington, D.C.: U.S. Government Printing Office, 1986), 64–65.

18. See Klaus Schröder, "Credit," in Reinhard Rode and Hanns-Dieter Jacobsen, eds., *Economic Warfare or Détente* (Boulder, Colo.: Westview Press, 1985), 39.

19. See Zloch-Christy, 35–38.

20. See Zloch-Christy, 38, 40.

21. Benjamin J. Cohen, *In Whose Interest? International Banking and American Foreign Policy* (New Haven: Yale University Press, 1986), 187–89.

22. See Gabriel Eichler, "A Banker's Perspective on the Polish Debt Problem," in Paul Marer and Włodzimierz Siwiński, eds., *Creditworthiness and Reform in Poland* (Bloomington: Indiana University Press, 1988), 212; Paul I. McCarthy, "Poland's Long Road Back to Creditworthiness," in Marer and Siwiński, 229; Zloch-Christy, 48–49, 53.

23. Steven Greenhouse, "Poland Is Granted Large Cut in Debt," *New York Times,* March 16, 1991, 1, 19.

24. "Eastern Europe Faces Up to the Debt Crisis" (by Central Intelligence Agency analysts), in Joint Economic Committee, vol. 2, 168.

25. Valerie J. Assetto, *The Soviet Bloc in the IMF and the IBRD* (Boulder, Colo.: Westview Press, 1988), 154.

26. *Frankfurter Allgemeine Zeitung,* May 3, 1989, 6.

27. At the end of 1991, Romania's gross debt was estimated to be $2.9 billion, with a debt-service ratio of 100 percent. *Business Eastern Europe,* March 2, 1992, 100.

28. *Business Eastern Europe,* March 25, 1991, 96. Hungarian officials were said to be divided over the desirability of seeking debt forgiveness.

29. See "The International Financial Situation," 43–44. Bulgaria's Ministry of Finance is also said to have ruled out debt forgiveness, "citing the belief that it could actually slow the pace of economic reform." *Business Eastern Europe* 20 (April 29, 1991), 136.

30. Rob Whitford, "Bulgarian Outlook Better, but Rescheduling Still Needed," *Business Eastern Europe* 20 (May 6, 1991), 137–39.

31. "The International Financial Situation," 41–42; *Business Eastern Europe,* February 17, 1992, 76–77.

32. "International Financial Situation," 32–33. "The various funds set up with much fanfare to exploit new opportunities East of the Elbe have suffered great embarrassment trying to find suitable investments. For example, the bulk of the $100 million raised by John Gavett & Co.'s Hungarian Investment Co. is reportedly still held in London because of the dearth of Hungarian opportunities." Fairlamb, 75.

33. See Hanns-Dieter Jacobsen, *Die Ost-West Wirtschaftsbeziehungen als deutsch-amerikanisches Problem* (Baden-Baden: Nomos Verlagsgesellschaft, 1986), 221–27.

34. Beverly Crawford, "Western Control of East-West Trade Finance: The Role of U.S. Power and the International Regime," in Gary K. Bertsch, ed., *Controlling East-West Trade and Technology Transfer* (Durham, N.C.: Duke University Press, 1988), 300.

35. Crawford, 306–8.

36. "By early 1987," writes Gajdeczka, "the average margins above interest rates [LIBOR?] charged for international loans extended to East European borrowers was about one third lower than the overall average, and slightly lower even than those offered to OECD borrowers." Gajdeczka, 562.

37. See Cohen, 253–80.

38. See Assetto, chap. 1.

39. *New York Times,* June 13, 1991, 9.

40. *Economic Bulletin,* vol. 44 (1992), 101.

41. Ipsen, 27–28.

42. See Paul Marer, "What Role for the IMF and World Bank in Poland?" in Marer and Siwiński, 273–77.

43. Peter Gowan, "Western Economic Diplomacy and the New Eastern Europe," *New Left Review,* July/August 1990, 63–82; Gowan, "Old Medicine, New Bottles: Western Policy Toward East Central Europe," *World Policy Journal* 9 (Winter 1991–1992), 1–34.

44. See, however, the criticism of IMF demands by (then) Polish Prime Minister Olszowski, however, which preceded his government's acceptance of the organization's conditions for resuming aid in March 1992. *New York Times,* March 2, 1992, 4.

45. *Economist,* March 10, 1990, 62, as cited in Gowan, "Old Medicine," 31.

46. Amy Koslow, "Eastern Europe 1 Year Later," *Europe,* November 1990, 7. The Bush administration pressured the World Bank to shift its lending still more to private undertakings. *New York Times,* June 28, 1991, C1.

47. *Business Eastern Europe* 20 (April 22, 1991), 128.

48. *New York Times,* April 13, 1992, 5. Up to 40 percent of EBRD loans can go to the public sector. See Article 11 of the "Agreement" establishing the Bank. *Basic Documents of the European Bank for Reconstruction and Development* ([London: 1991]).

49. See Mark Milner and Ruth Kelly, "Euro-banker Who Fell to Earth," *Manchester Guardian Weekly,* July 4, 1993, 19; Karoly Okolicsanyi, "Eastern Views of the EBRD," *RFE/RL Research Report,* June 4, 1993, 50–52.

50. *Economic Survey 1991–1992,* 180–84.

51. *New York Times,* June 6, 1991, C7.

52. See Cohen, 257–63; 298–305.

53. See " 'Strengthen Policy Coordination,' Says Former G-7 Deputy," *IMF Survey* 20 (April 15, 1991), 120–22.

54. Marer, "The Transition," 10; *Economic Survey 1991–1992*, 184; Karoly Okolicsanyi, "Private Sector Gains Little from High Hungarian Savings," *RFE/RL Research Report*, April 9, 1993, 51.

PART III

OVERCOMING OBSTACLES TO SUCCESS

9

Dilemmas of Reform

> You do need to have a comprehensive approach, what has been called a "big bang." Piecemeal reform does not work.
>
> Unidentified IMF official[1]

> We want a decent market, not just a market. The market is becoming a kind of idol. Instead of the leading role of the party, now we have the leading role of the market.
>
> Jan Urban, May 1992[2]

> We listened to the West, and we made too big a leap.
>
> Lech Wałęsa, October 1991[3]

The economic predicament facing Eastern Europe in the wake of Communism's collapse was so serious, commentators agreed, that the countries of the region had no alternative but to undertake measures fundamentally transforming their economic systems. Western economists and officials argued with unaccustomed unanimity that a commitment to far-reaching reforms should be the prerequisite to the granting of any Western economic assistance. Eastern European economists, some of them proclaiming their allegiance to the ideas of Friedrich Hayek or Milton Friedman,[4] often outdid their Western colleagues in their insistence that their countries' economies had to be thoroughly "marketized" and "privatized" if they were to halt economic decline.

Yet no successful models of economic reform in countries emerging from the rule of central planning exist, and while there now appears to be a growing consensus over the principles and goals of reform, there is disagreement over the way in which it should be carried out. The economic disarray of those countries that pioneered in reform—the former Yugoslavia, Hungary, and, in some measure, Poland—does not seem significantly less severe than that of those whose Communist governments resisted it until the moment of their collapse. Those countries that have received the largest infusions of Western aid in support of their reform efforts have yet to turn the corner toward becoming successful market economies; the miseries of the former GDR, in fact, make it a cautionary example of the perils of extreme "shock therapy."[5] The former Czechoslovakia, a late starter on the path of reform, experienced with a brief lag the sharp drop in production, falling living standards, and rising unemployment of its neighbors; Bulgaria and Romania, on the other hand, began their reforms already in deep economic crisis.

The Western decisions that will shape future relations with Eastern Europe will thus be inextricably bound up with the question of economic reform in the region. Western governments have all sought to condition their trade and assistance on the adoption and implementation of reforms, but have not always agreed on which ones to require. Many such reforms entail painful economic, social, and political costs; the West must accordingly calculate the risks entailed in pressing for such changes, and decide whether, and how, to help the region's states bear their costs. The West must also decide whether the adoption of particular reforms ought to be the primary criterion of overall policy differentiation toward the area.

I argue in this chapter that, while close attention to both the reform intentions and the reform capabilities of East European elites must be an unavoidable component of Western economic policy-making, the West needs to rethink the kinds of reforms that might be desirable for Eastern Europe and serve Western interests. A rigid and uncritical insistence on the overnight creation of full-scale market economies and on rapid privatization could deepen Eastern Europe's economic predicament rather than resolve it. The West needs to place greater emphasis on the problems of implementing and administering economic reform and be willing to accept a much larger role of the state in the reform process than its own ideological reflexes might normally dictate. The problem, I suggest, is not just the familar one of fostering East European entrepreneurial skills and incentives; it is also a matter of enhancing administrative and political ones.

THE REFORM DEBATE

The debate over economic reform in Eastern Europe has shifted dramatically since the fall of the old Communist regimes. Of the three alternative objectives that earlier shaped the debate—"plan perfecting," that is, organizational reform of the central planning system[6]; market socialism, or a pure market economy—only the last now enjoys respectability in the West and, with a few exceptions, in the East. No one should regret the passing of the first alternative, but there may be some reason to wonder whether the impatient dismissal of the second, as a utopian "third way" that serious reformers need not consider, may not have been premature, given the great variety of ways, most of them untested, in which elements of socialist and market systems might conceivably be mixed.[7] The debate now, however, focusses largely on questions of pace and methodology.

On these questions, economists frequently are arrayed against politicians. Economists tend to favor the "big bang," or shock therapy, approach in which fundamental reforms of virtually every aspect of economic life are introduced more or less simultaneously, on the grounds that all are interdependent and that the unavoidable pains of transition are best gotten over with as quickly as possible.[8] (The economists, of course, are unlikely to experience much of the shock personally.[9]) Politicians are more frequently inclined to urge caution, often out of fear that the severe economic dislocation reform entails will bring social and political turmoil and their own expulsion from office.[10] A subtheme of the debate revolves around the question of social protections for the potential victims of reform—the new armies of unemployed, the poor, the elderly. All agree that there should be some sort of safety net, but there are major disagreements over how tight and thus costly the webbing should be and how to resolve conflicts between the demands of reform (and of monetary stability) and those of social protection.

In order to evaluate the debate, we need to consider the variety of economic measures that may or may not be included in reform programs. The sheer number of such measures and the complex interrelationships among them underline the difficulty of the reform process. Putting together a coherent and workable reform package is an exacting economic exercise even in the abstract; in practice it is also a delicate political undertaking.

We first need, however, to consider the goal that the reforms are meant to achieve. Commonly, Eastern Europeans say that they want a "normal," Western European economy. (Interestingly, the United States economy is rarely held up as a model, in spite of the widespread admiration for American democracy and popular culture.) This answer begs the question of which West European model ought to be pursued: Should it be that of Thatcherite Britain, West Germany, France, Spain, or possibly Sweden or Austria? More generally, it neglects the intensity and great variety of state–private sector relationships that exist in the capitalist world. The reply of the prominent Hungarian economist Janos Kornai to such a charge has some justice: After years of state domination of the economy, with catastrophic results, we know that we want to move toward a market system; we can debate the *kind* of market economy we want and the possibility of a renewed state role later.[11] Still, ambiguity in defining the ultimate goal is bound to produce disagreement over the means appropriate for reaching it.

COMPONENTS OF REFORM

In considering the means, a number of broad categories are required to encompass the possible components of a reform package.[12] Most have been widely discussed in the vast literature on reform, but one or two have escaped the attention they deserve. Within each category, reforms may be more or less far-reaching. Different combinations of the measures discussed in each could be incorporated into either a radical or a more gradualist reform strategy.

The centerpiece of the reforms undertaken by East European countries while still under Communist rule was the attempt to *decentralize* economic decision making to individual enterprises or groups of them organized in "enterprise associations" or "combines." Such reforms sought to narrow the responsibilities of the state planning commission and/or individual economic ministries ("narrowing" sometimes meant streamlining in order to allow the central bodies to concentrate on more basic decisions, and sometimes meant genuinely reducing their significance). Unhappily, management was sometimes decentralized without financial discipline and responsibility being imposed, and the hoped-for boost in performance did not occur.[13] Now the old central planning authorities and ministries have been abolished, but the issue itself remains, in somewhat altered form. How much of a role in making fundamental economic decisions should the now-democratic state maintain—in directing investment so as to promote needed industrial restructuring, for example, or in subsidizing and rationalizing unprofitable enterprises that might one day be made profitable and/or be sold? Such firms tended under Communism to be very large and to monopolize their branch of production; to what extent should they be broken up, given the still larger size of the multinational entities with which they will be competing? How are the firms remaining in state hands to be administered? Generally, decentralization is meant to place greater economic authority in the hands of those best able to judge production and market needs and potentials. Its success presumes the presence of well-trained and appropriately motivated decision makers at that level. Such managers, however, are more the exception than the rule in Eastern Europe.

A related class of reforms thus seeks fundamentally to alter the system of *incentives* motivating managers and workers. The now-departed Communist regimes sought through a variety of devices to make managers more attentive to profit and cost cutting; by and large they failed, because of soft-budget constraints, that is, the readiness of the state to bail out firms in difficulty, and because the managers were unable to fire unneeded or indolent workers, control supply, or set their own prices. Now managers are to be stripped of their subsidies and loss-making firms genuinely threatened with bankruptcy (for years a theoretical possibility in Hungary and later elsewhere, but rarely carried out). Workers are now to be motivated by the very real threat of dismissal, and by revisions of the wage structure.

Economists all but universally view *price reform* as the key to successful economic reform overall. If profit or related incentives are to produce the behavior desired, the prices charged by enterprises must reflect the actual costs of production *and* be responsive to consumer demand. With some exceptions, consumer and producer prices have either been freed in Eastern Europe or sharply increased by administrative decision. But simply allowing prices to be set by the producing entity in response to the interaction of supply and demand is laden with risk in what are still in some cases shortage economies and in settings where there is little or no effective competition. To curb resultant inflation, the new regimes have sought to limit increases in wages. So doing, as one might expect, has fed public discontent over the higher prices. The discrepancy, as the experience of Poland shows, can lead to a slump in consumption, then to a fall in production, then to more unemployment, and then to strikes and social unrest.

Still another need is to reform the systems of wholesale *distribution* and retail trade. Under Communist rule, distribution was carried out by the state; in several cases these mechanisms, never very efficient, decayed or collapsed before new, effective, and competitive wholesaling networks arose to replace them. Hence the now-familiar East European street scene in which small (and some large) producers offer their goods directly to the public from the back of trucks.

In order to make firms and individuals responsive to price and cost incentives, reformers must find means of introducing or strengthening *competition* in economies previously dominated by state-owned monopolies. Such state enterprises can be broken up in the course of privatization or even without it. New private undertakings competing with former state monopolies can be encouraged. Especially in fields in which the small size of the East European economies and considerations of productive efficiency make the introduction of domestic competition impractical, the domestic market may be opened to foreign sellers.[14] This course, as we have seen, has been chosen by the East European countries with varying degrees of domestic enthusiasm and foreign response.

Still another class of reforms are those designed to rationalize the *financing* of investments and make credit available for the creation of new firms.[15] The intention of such reforms has generally been to break the monopoly over the granting of credit once enjoyed by the central state bank, usually by creating additional banks, which are required to be profitable and must do so by competing with one another for borrowers. The formation of private commercial banks, or joint investment banks established with Western partners, may also be encouraged. Broader capital markets may also be created for enterprise bonds and stocks.

State *budgetary*, *fiscal*, and *legal* reforms are indispensable. The large government deficits that we now know to have been run by several Communist regimes, and financed essentially by printing more money, contributed to an excess of demand over available goods that produced actual or suppressed inflation. Since the deficits threatened the success of any effort to subject production and distribution to market forces or to move the local currency toward convertibility, the IMF has pressed the new regimes to eliminate them quickly. All now agree, at least in principle, that the heavy subsidization of consumer staples, transportation, and housing; of inefficient enterprises; and of goods produced for foreign trade, for example, certain priority items promised to CMEA partners, must be curtailed or halted if waste is to be eliminated, not only in the interest of slashing budget deficits but also to assure that resources are allocated more rationally. Existing tax systems also need to be overhauled to ensure adequate revenues and eliminate disincentives to efficient performance, and a whole new body of commercial law must be formulated and passed (and administrators and lawyers trained to apply and litigate it).

Reforms are also needed to ease the conditions and strengthen the benefits of *foreign trade*, particularly with the industrial West. Most East European Communist regimes moved to decentralize export functions to major individual firms or groups of enterprises, and post-Communist governments have permitted individual firms to make import agreements and have made hard currency available for the purchase of foreign inputs. Among other things, liberalized foreign trade, in conjunction with currency convertibility, is expected to bring about the importation of world prices and thus provide reliable measures of domestic economic performance. Hungary, Poland, and the Czech Republic have moved furthest toward internal convertibility of their currencies and have sought to establish exchange rates for them that undercut the black market and favor exports over imports. New trade agreements with the EC are in force and negotiations over associate membership in the Community have been completed. Other steps toward liberalizing trade, including agreements with EFTA and the Visegrad Triangle trade pact between Poland, Hungary, and the former Czechoslovakia, are underway.

A longer-term dimension of reform is concerned with the basic *restructuring* of production facilities. In effect, such restructuring seeks to overcome the legacy of the Stalinist pattern of industrialization. Reforms of this type may include the immediate closure or phasing out of "rustbelt," obsolete, or highly inefficient (and/or highly polluting) enterprises or even entire industries; introducing new ones better suited to domestic resources and needs and/or international markets; and narrowing the range of goods produced while emphasizing those for which the country enjoys a significant comparative advantage. In the agricultural sector, such reforms might entail the downsizing (not just the privatization) of huge collective farms or, in the case of Poland, combining small private farms into more efficient units better able to utilize advanced machinery and methods of cultivation. As in Western controversies over industrial policy, the place to be assigned to the state and the market in effecting structural changes ("picking winners") is a critical and controversial matter.

A final, rather different class of reform widely discussed and in some cases introduced in the waning days of Communist rule contemplated the expanded participation of employees in the decision making of enterprises or other economic entities. These could entail the election of managers by workers (as implemented in the USSR and Hungary) or the establishment of something akin to the Yugoslav workers' councils. Such schemes came under discussion in virtually every CMEA country that considered broad economic reforms, not because they were widely expected to increase efficiency—some feared just the opposite—but because they were seen as necessary to give the workers a stake in reforms that were expected to have otherwise painful short-term consequences. Now dominant liberal economic opinion opposes or seeks to roll back such measures on the grounds that they give the workers all-too-effective means for resisting the more painful changes and tend to undermine managerial authority and wage discipline.[16] Poland's workers' councils, given significant powers during the first Solidarity period (1980–1981), are viewed as particularly serious obstacles to change.[17] Proposals for employee stock ownership, however, still enjoy some support, partly as a shortcut to privatization.

PRIVATIZATION

Almost all of these issues, in fact, are implicated in the wide-ranging East European privatization debate. Economic reformers have come to view a massive shift to private ownership as indispensable to successful marketization. Contrary to the idea of market socialism, once popular in many of the same circles, most reformers are now persuaded that markets can only function properly when economic actors have acquired a strong personal stake in maximizing profits and lowering costs. Privatization sales also promise revenues badly needed for hard-pressed state budgets. Actually carrying out the privatization of economies heretofore dominated by state ownership, however, is an enormously complex and difficult task, and it is around the question of implementation that the debate now rages.[18]

Commonly a distinction is made between "small" and "large" privatization. The privatization of small-scale enterprises is seen as desirable because it promises to increase quickly the quality, range, and number of goods and services available to citizens and also because it will create the basis for a badly needed entrepreneurial class and culture.[19] Small privatization is seen as comparatively easy, since small private businesses were tolerated in several countries even under Communist rule,[20] and the former black marketeers of the "second economy" in all six countries are viewed as possessing many of the necessary instincts of successful legitimate businessmen (if not always the desired ethical standards). Small privatization also requires only moderate amounts of capital. The Czechs and Slovaks have auctioned off thousands of small businesses, and in Hungary and Poland the number of newly registered small firms runs into the hundreds of thousands (most of them, to be sure, one-person operations). The principal drawback of small privatization may be the high rate of failure of such firms, aggravated by depressed living standards, which could contribute to a disillusionment with free markets.[21]

"Large" privatization—of massive state-owned firms—is another matter. Western precedents, such as that of Thatcher's Britain, have not proven helpful because of the deliberate pace and relatively small scale of such undertakings as well as the presence in Western countries, but not in the East, of a large stock of domestic capital. Only a few of the large East European state enterprises have obvious attractions for any investors, domestic or foreign, in their present form; some will not be viable in market economies in any form. Placing an appropriate valuation on such properties has also proven to be a formidable problem, given the absence of a well-established real estate market and of Western systems of accounting. East Europeans differ over whether state properties should be sold at "fire-sale" prices, but often it may not be clear what a fire-sale price would be.

The proper mode of privatization is a central issue. Although privatization is sometimes treated as an end in itself, the real goal, presumably, is to produce competitive, efficient businesses whose performance is driven by a strong orientation to profit.[22] Widely diffused ownership among individual stockholders, Western experience suggests, may afford little control over managers and thus impose little financial discipline.[23] This problem may be even greater, critics argue, if the stock is provided at little or no cost to firm employees or to citizens at large through a voucher system like Czechoslovakia's.[24] Such an approach also does not provide any of the new capital needed for restructuring and modernization.

The creation of public or private investment funds to manage such small individual holdings has its own risks, as do other proposals to create the equivalent of Western institutional investors by putting large blocs of stock into the hands of banks, other firms, and nonprofit entities (hospitals, universities, and so on, which would then be required to finance many of their operations from their returns). They are likely to falter to the extent that they assume that such institutions will function just as they do in the West, in spite of very different economic histories and cultures and the consequent danger of fraud or incompetent financial management.[25] Foreign buyers and joint-venture partners would presumably be more attentive to profits and efficiency and better able to infuse fresh capital, but, for reasons suggested earlier, are unlikely to present themselves in sufficiently large numbers. Foreign investors could, however, acquire the choicest properties, leaving more troubled ones for domestic investors or the state.

If large privatization is apt to be protracted, the question of the status of state firms in the interim becomes a critical one. If they are left in limbo while awaiting buyers, or put under the control of a giant trusteeship agency such as the German *Treuhand*, there is a danger that they will receive neither the individual attention, the skilled management, nor the investment they need to contribute positively to the economy. In such circumstances pressures to close the firms in question will mount, with all the attendant hardships and negative multiplier effects throughout the rest of the economy. Kornai and Szelenyi are surely correct in acknowledging that the Hungarian and other East European economies will remain dual state-private ones for decades to come—in spite of some official optimistic projections of a rapid sell-off; any workable economic strategy must therefore concern itself with rationalizing the state sector's performance.[26] To that end, enterprises likely to remain in state hands must be clearly identified and separated from those that are realistic candidates for quick and not merely nominal privatization.

OBSTACLES TO REFORM

This formidable list of components of reform is not exhaustive. It does, however, suggest the complexity of the choices facing the architects of economic renewal. It implies that facile slogans about removing the heavy hand of the state and speeding up privatization do not in themselves offer much guidance toward assembling a workable combination of appropriate measures. It is also quite possible that different combinations of measures will be suited to the circumstances of different states. In reform as in other questions, differing levels of development and the diverse policies pursued in the last years of Communist rule should dictate different responses. Hungary is far readier for markets and for some degree of immersion in the international economy than Bulgaria or Romania because of its long history of reform experimentation and exposure to Western economic influence. Czechoslovakia's (comparatively) superior technological base and standard of living must be balanced against the long isolation of most of its economists and managers from Western influence and its limited experience with reform. Eastern Germany presents a special case because of the availability of west German funds; on the other hand, the abruptness of its immersion in the west German economy has made both the material and psychological costs of transition exceptionally high.[27]

Broad explanations for the failure of the major East European efforts at reform to bear much fruit to date often fall along two lines. One blames the resistance of the *nomenklatura*, former Communist (or Communist-appointed) officials who stand to lose influence and material benefits if reforms are successfully enacted. This charge contains elements of scapegoating, but also reflects the more prosaic reality of deeply ingrained bureaucratic habits and, on the enterprise level, managerial timidity and patterns of dependence on state support and/or captive markets, habits and patterns that are hard to break. The second explanation stresses the partial and inadequate character of the reforms thus far enacted; the only cure for the ills of reform, this view insists, is more reform, and in particular more privatization.

There is surely much truth in both explanations. But there are also vexing structural obstacles to reforming planned economies of the East European type that are unlikely to bend readily to the enthusiasm of the most enlightened bureaucrats or to the most drastic and comprehensive formulation of reform strategies. Most can be described as problems of transition from unreformed to reformed states, although that term does not fully capture the immensity of the difficulties, which are at once economic, social, cultural, and political.

A particularly troublesome problem is that of the sequencing and pace of reforms.[28] It is by no means self-evident which reforms are prerequisite to others and should therefore take precedence; moreover, the most desirable sequence in purely economic terms may not be the most feasible politically. Should price reform, for example, precede the decentralization of managerial authority and the creation of a system of wholesale trade? Realistic prices, it is argued, are needed to give managers the criteria they need to make rational decisions and to assure that inputs go where they are most needed and are not needlessly stockpiled. "Enterprises cannot be trusted with their autonomy," Ed Hewett has written, "unless the price system provides accurate and fair judgments on the economic contribution each enterprise is making to total economic welfare."[29] But freeing prices before a competitive market can be created may produce distorted judgments, and can bring other unhappy consequences: hyperinflation (as in Poland in 1989), followed by desperate government measures to curb it, followed by deep recession.

The view is now widespread that early privatization, large as well as small, is necessary to release the entrepreneurial drive required to make markets work effectively. The accurate valuation of the properties to be privatized, however, is impossible without price and accounting reforms and the creation of a real estate market. The shortage of capital, unclear titles, and the general climate of uncertainty make the marketing of large numbers of state firms within a short time frame a risky undertaking. Moreover, a study of the first firms to be privatized in Poland suggests that little change in management style or performance can be expected from privatization alone.[30] Another question is the timing of financial and foreign currency reforms: a rush to full convertibility, a Princeton economist has argued, could jeopardize reform by forcing governments to pursue excessively stringent monetary policies.[31]

It is now often argued that major reforms must all be implemented simultaneously,[32] in effect begging the question of sequencing. Such a course, to the extent that it is feasible at all, places an enormous burden on the officials who must carry it out and the citizens who must absorb the consequences. The initial model along these lines was the "leap into the abyss" proposed for Poland by the Harvard economist Jeffrey Sachs and adopted, under the pressures of hyperinflation, by that country in modified form. On January 1, 1990, the Zloty was made internally convertible and exchange controls were lifted, most price regulation and many (but not all) subsidies were eliminated, a wage tax (a form of incomes policy) was introduced, and barriers to foreign trade and the formation of private firms were removed.[33] Overall, however, the Balcerowicz reforms were less comprehensive and uncompromising than they were initially advertised as being; Lech Wałęsa was able to base part of his presidential campaign on the demand that reform be "accelerated."

In general, the success of such measures depends on the performance of economic structures that can be reformed or rebuilt only over an extended period of time. As we have seen, the meaningful privatization of large state-owned firms, or at least their restructuring to force them to behave in accordance with market rather than bureaucratic imperatives, the creation of modern financial institutions, the renewal of the infrastructure, and the reconstruction of the system of distribution are all lengthy undertakings. Yet other reforms cannot be expected to function as intended until these institutional changes are well advanced. To suggest, as many commentators have, that a measured or incremental approach to reform is unworkable is to demand in effect a "revolution from above." It is difficult to concieve of any but the most powerful and autocratic government carrying out such a revolution successfully; governments of that sort no longer exist in Eastern Europe. The fragile governments that do exist, so long as they remain democratic, are doomed to incrementalism.

A second problem is that most East European economies have little of the economic (or political) slack they need in order to absorb some of the inevitable costs of a reform that drastically decentralizes authority and exposes poorly prepared managers and workers to the uncertain disciplines of a newly created market. The absence of slack was a central characteristic of the command economy; it persists under the new regimes. A new round of reckless or unrealistic investment decisions, more banking and securities fraud, or the emigration of skilled personnel in the wake of mass unemployment are costs Eastern Europe cannot easily bear, but they may be unavoidable. One of the primary functions of Western assistance will have to be to supply the slack; the less such assistance is available, the less flexibility reformers will possess.

I have already referred to the difficulty of introducing competition in major industries in small countries. The large economic units created under the traditional planning systems, and claimed to be one of its primary advantages, cannot be expected to perform at optimal levels while enjoying monopoly status. But the experience, for example, of the German *Treuhand*, suggests that breaking such enterprises up into smaller units capable of successful independent operation can be a difficult task with uncertain results. In many sectors, newly launched private firms are unlikely to be able to mobilize the resources to compete effectively. Opening up the domestic market to external producers without restriction can destroy domestic producers before it makes them competitive.

As Josef Brada has noted, the very uncertainty inherent in the reform process itself—concerning not only the content but the pace, effectiveness, and longevity of reforms—makes it extremely difficult for the state or public and private firms to make rational individual investment decisions or to undertake large-scale economic restructuring.[34] Reform uncertainties inhibit the risk-taking behavior on the part of domestic entrepreneurs and foreign investors that the reformers would like to stimulate.

Economic reform, we also know, is not possible without serious social dislocation, although it is by no means obvious which reform strategy will produce the most devastating consequences, and which the least. Reforms tends to subvert, or at least are perceived as subverting, the social values East European Communist regimes were most successful in instilling in their populations, those of economic security and egalitarianism. The long official celebration of stable prices, full employment, and modest income differentiations as core achievements of socialism has left its mark. The new regimes must find ways to justify their abandonment in the interest of what to many citizens must appear to be utopian promises of a better but distant economic future.

The design of an adequate social safety net to mitigate the hardships of reform presents both administrative and budgetary problems. The old regimes offered generous, even exemplary, programs in such areas as paid maternity leaves and day care, but provided no unemployment insurance or poverty programs, since they claimed that neither of these social ills existed. The new economic and social environment thus calls for the construction of social benefit systems radically different from their predecessors. At the same time, the need for a safety net collides with pressures on the new governments from the IMF and domestic reformers for fiscal responsibility and the avoidance of taxes that might dampen entrepreneurial enthusiasm.

The social costs East Europeans attribute to reform—sometimes correctly, sometimes not—are daunting. These costs include unemployment ranging from moderate (in the Czech Republic) to massive (in the former GDR); exploding crime rates and right-wing extremism; double-digit and in some cases triple-digit inflation, especially devastating to those on fixed incomes; a growing chasm between the ostentatiously (and often newly) rich and the many poor; and the disappearance of many accustomed social services. Reform, it is widely believed, particularly benefits the dishonest and the greedy, including former Communist party functionaries who were well positioned to take illicit advantage of opportunities for privatization and the formation of joint ventures ("*nomenklatura* privatization").[35] Thus it is hardly surprising that popular attitudes toward specific reform measures are often hostile even when the abstract principles and goals of reform are applauded.

More broadly, experience with reform in Eastern Europe and the former Soviet Union to date suggests that to remake an economic system in fundamental ways, it is not sufficient merely to change economic institutions and legal rules. "The most difficult part is the human software," the Hungarian-American manager of Tungsram, acquired by General Electric, has remarked.[36] A successful market economy requires that a congruent market *culture* take hold among its managers, bureaucrats, workers, and consumers.[37] Such a culture cannot be expected to emerge overnight in the place of a state socialist culture oriented toward quantitative production goals, economic security, and pervasive bureaucratic regulation. Creating a market culture is one of the most difficult tasks reformers face.

ECONOMIC REFORM AND POLITICAL RECONSTRUCTION

Culture may ultimately be the most formidable obstacle to successful economic reform, but the more concrete and immediate impediments, apart from the economic ones discussed above, are political. Central elements of the traditional political system now put to rout in every East European country—above all, the "leading role of the party" and its control over the principal economic posts on all levels through the *nomenklatura* system—were of course incompatible with full-scale market reform. The sacrifices and hardships of reform also place acute strains on democratic polities, however, especially in the trial-and-error phase of their emergence.

Even in the last phase of Communist rule, East European reformers came to believe that political reforms would have to precede or accompany serious economic reforms. To enlist the energies of ordinary citizens, they concluded, required a level of identification with the state and its policies that would only be possible through some form of recognition of the diverse groups and interests present in society ("socialist pluralism"), competitive elections to significant public offices, and protections for individuals grounded firmly in law and a new (or drastically revised) constitution. In Hungary and Poland, efforts to initiate such reforms set a process in motion that quickly led not to the Communists' salvation but to their fall, and the assumption of the tasks of political restructuring by their inexperienced successors.

To undertake the uncertain task of reinventing pluralist democracy in a form appropriate for societies accustomed to one-party rule while simultaneously seeking a fundamental reordering of the economy would seem in the abstract reckless if not foolhardy. But history appears to be offering the East European regimes little choice. The reservoir of authority available to the new, non-Communist governments is not sufficient to allow them the time to make the mistakes that are virtually unavoidable in such circumstances. Disillusionment with the inability of post-Communist governments to deal with inherited economic dilemmas has given life to authoritarian alternatives, and has even begun to revive the fortunes of the former Communists.[38] Even if these possibilities are contained, the transition period required to complete political reform is apt to be nearly as long as that needed for economic reform.

Political democratization, even when successfully carried out, almost unavoidably wars with economic reform.[39] New regimes claiming to be responsive to popular sentiments are under strong pressure to demonstrate quick results, an objective likely to be achieved only at the expense of effective long-term economic strategies. The legitimization of interest representation increases the ability of firms and unions to resist those reform measures that appear to disadvantage them. Expanding the powers (and accountability) of local government officials is apt to strengthen resistance to layoffs and/or the closing of inefficient local enterprises. The strengthening of East European parliaments has already slowed the timetables of reform in several countries; Kornai's hope that parliamentary controls could be used to discipline the performance of enterprises still in state hands seems under present circumstances (and in the light of Western experience) unjustified.[40] The bargaining and compromise that are routinely required to achieve policy agreement in pluralist democracies imply a degree of incrementalism that economists have attacked as entirely inadequate, and possibly detrimental, to the needs of East European economies.

THE NEED FOR A STRONG STATE

What follows from the realities I have presented is that successfully implementing economic reform demands above all a *strong state*.[41] It must, of course, be very different from the strong state of traditional Communist rule. Rather, it must be a state that enjoys a firm basis of popular authority and possesses a well-trained, capable, honest, and depoliticized—in other words, a thoroughly rebuilt—bureaucracy. Such a state might well come to resemble the neocorporatist states of Western Europe, the *dirigiste* and technocratic French state, or the Japanese state, with its close interlocking of corporate industry, ruling party, and state bureaucracy, rather than the more pluralist democracies or anything like a pure free market model.[42]

A strong state is needed to make the difficult and sometimes unpopular decisions that economic transformation necessarily entails. It must be in a position to carry out such decisions consistently and over an extended period of time. Scarce public investment funds must be allocated; state budgets and current accounts must somehow be balanced; new legal codes and regulatory systems must be created. Economic sacrifices must be imposed and enforced, and painful structural reforms carried out, even against determined resistance. The state must be able to formulate and administer programs of benefits offsetting the cruelest social effects of reforms; it must be able to raise the resources necessary to pay for them.

The prospect for creating such states in Eastern Europe—at least ones that remain democratic in some sense—may appear to be wildly utopian. The former GDR has been fortunate in receiving a proven state structure as part of its incorporation into the Federal Republic. For many eastern Germans, however, it is an alien structure, and their own new *Länder* governments (some of whose personnel are Western imports) are gravely short of funds and influence. Elsewhere, the new national governments suffer from severe deficits of legitimacy; in Hungary, Bulgaria, and Romania, public opinion quickly shifted away from governments elected only in 1990, resulting in the replacement of those of Bulgaria and Romania. The fourth new government of Poland fell in May 1993, while the new Czech and especially the Slovak state face serious political uncertainties. Disputes between the executive and parliament reign almost everywhere. Calls for emergency powers by Wałęsa and, earlier, Havel suggest their frustration at parliamentary squabbling and stalemate. The political opposition in most countries is divided and contentious, and does not offer a clear alternative to the present government, however great popular disaffection is with the latter. The fact is not lost on East Europeans that in the past the strong states that have carried out economic modernization have generally been authoritarian; the Korean model is sometimes cited, not always unfavorably.

What, in these circumstances, can the West do to help? Western governments and universities have developed a number of cooperative programs intended to raise the level of managerial skills and stimulate entrepreneurial behavior among East European enterprise officials. Western officials and experts (sometimes with little knowledge of local conditions) have descended upon East European capitals offering advice on the ways of market economies. Such measures are useful, in part to begin to create the market culture referred to earlier. But perhaps still more helpful would be programs designed to strengthen the skills and performance of East European administrators—those who must plan reindustrialization, guide investment priorities, modernize and regulate the financial system, reform tax structures and tax incentives, and devise means for effective enforcement of the state's economic decisions. The French, whose own experience with elite administrative training and long *dirigiste* traditions equip them peculiarly well for the task, have begun to offer such assistance.[43] Germans, Japanese, Austrians, and others may be able to offer similar help rooted in their own largely successful experience. Such an approach goes against the grain of the United States' verbal devotion to free enterprise, but in fact agencies such as the Treasury Department and the Office of Management and Budget as well as leading schools of public administration have relevant experience to offer.[44]

The West can also serve the broader need of strengthening the authority of the newly emerging governments of Eastern Europe, if only in limited ways. Verbal support must be accompanied by appropriate economic assistance—to ease acute shortages of food or medicine where needed, to reduce the financial pressures resulting from existing hard-currency debt, to provide backing for currency stabilization and convertibility, and to support well-conceived plans for industrial restructuring and modernization. Reform must ultimately become a cooperative East-West venture; the West can not micromanage it, but neither can it provide large sums of money merely in the hope that the new leaders, however attractive in Western eyes by comparison with their predecessors, are prepared to use it effectively.

What the West—including the United States—should *not* do, in my estimation, is continue to insist on unforgiving deflationary policies, uncompromising marketization, or the instant privatization of the East European economies. "The market," as an American economist has written, "is a powerful and rational economic mechanism. At the same time it is a fragile one, likely to produce unexpected and undesirable outcomes in the wrong environment."[45] Given the absence of many of the necessary preconditions for an efficiently and equitably functioning market, the precipitous abandonment of all public instruments of influence over prices, wages, investments, and currency exchange could produce a degree of economic turmoil and perceived injustice that might well gravely discredit fledgling democratic and/or reform governments. Under such circumstances, there are no guarantees that new forms of authoritarianism in Eastern Europe might not ultimately replace the old ones. "There are limits," the Hungarian economist András Köves has argued, "to what society can bear, and violating such limits might have sociopolitical consequences that would thwart the whole economic policy and preclude (democratic) management of the crisis."[46]

The West needs also to be wary of any efforts to apply a single reform model to the very different levels and characteristics of the economic problems of the six East European CMEA states. The needs and expectations of the Romanians, wrestling with the legacy of poverty and technological backwardness left by the Ceauşescus, are quite different from those of the

Czechs, with their comparatively high level of industrial development and relatively comfortable standard of living. Everywhere, the task is daunting, and demands utmost sensitivity to the political dimension of reform.

NOTES

1. Quoted in *New York Times,* April 19, 1991, C5.

2. Quoted in *New York Times,* May 3, 1992, F11.

3. Quoted in *New York Times,* October 25, 1991, C4.

4. See Václav Klaus and Tomáš Ježek, "Social Criticism, False Liberalism, and Recent Changes in Czechoslovakia," *East European Politics and Societies* 5 (Winter 1991), 26–40; cf., however, János Mátyás Kovács, "From Reformation to Transformation: Limits to Liberalism in Hungarian Economic Thought," in ibid., 41–72; Kovács argues that the triumph of economic liberalism at least among Hungarian "transformers" has been greatly overstated.

5. See Thomas A. Baylis, "Transforming the East German Economy: Shock without Therapy," in Michael G. Huelshoff, Andrei S. Markovits, and Simon Reich, eds., *The New Germany in the New Europe* (Ann Arbor: University of Michigan Press, forthcoming 1993).

6. See Thomas A. Baylis, " 'Perfecting' the Planning Mechanism: The Politics of Incremental Reform in the GDR," in Donna L. Bahry and Joel C. Moses, eds., *Political Implications of Economic Reform in Communist Systems* (New York: New York University Press, 1990), 295–321.

7. See Alec Nove, " 'Market Socialism' & 'Free Economy,' " *Dissent* 37 (Fall 1990), 443–46; Mark Levinson, "Reforming the Economies of Eastern Europe," ibid. 38 (Winter 1991), 127–30; Wojciech Gielzynski, "There's No Other Way but the Third One," *East European Reporter,* November–December 1992, 29–31.

8. There are a growing number of exceptions, however. See, for example, András Köves, *Central and East European Economies in Transition* (Boulder, Colo.: Westview Press, 1992), 17–36.

9. "The citizen so afflicted will not be as easily convinced as are those who, from a distance or from positions of some personal comfort, see virtue in hardship. And the political consequences are far from attractive." J. K. Galbraith, "Why the Right Is Wrong," *Manchester Guardian Weekly,* February 4, 1990, 10.

10. Similar disputes, Susan Woodward has noted, have broken out between East European presidents and their prime ministers, who in several cases have been economists. See her comments as cited in "Seminar Explores Sequencing of Reforms in Former Socialist Economies," *IMF Survey* 22 (January 11, 1993), 11–12.

11. János Kornai, "Socialist Transformation and Privatization: Shifting from a Socialist System," *East European Politics and Societies* 4 (Spring 1990), 261.

12. For a succinct and astute review of the central issues of East European economic transition, based on the discussions at an OECD/World Bank conference held in November 1990, see Paul Marer, "The Transition to a Market Economy in Central and Eastern Europe," *OECD Observer,* April/May 1991, 5–10.

13. Marer, 5.

14. See Ellen Comisso, "Market Failures and Market Socialism: Economic Problems of the Transition," *Eastern European Politics and Societies* 2 (Fall 1988), 438–51.

15. See "Financial Reforms Essential in Eastern European Economies," *IMF Survey* 20 (January 7, 1991), 11–12.

16. See, e.g., János Kornai, *The Road to a Free Economy* (New York: Norton, 1990), 98–100.

17. On the councils' resistance to privatization, see Wojciech Bienkowski, "Poland's Bermuda Triangle," *RFE/RL Research Report,* April 24, 1992, 22–25.

18. For an illuminating account of the debate as it has unfolded in Hungary, see David Stark, "Privatization in Hungary: From Plan to Market or from Plan to Clan?" *East European Politics and Societies* 4 (Fall 1990), 351–92. See also "Privatization: A Special Report," *RFE/RL Research Report,* April 24, 1992.

19. See Ivan Szelenyi, "Alternative Futures for Eastern Europe: The Case of Hungary," *East European Politics and Societies* 4 (Spring 1990), 231–54.

20. See Anders Aslund, *Private Enterprise in Eastern Europe* (New York: St. Martin's Press, 1985).

21. Alice H. Amsden, citing an unpublished World Bank study of private Polish manufacturing firms that experienced a high rate of failure, points out that "most died because they were dependent for either their final demand or their inputs on state-owned enterprises that were themselves going bust." Thus, the fate of much small privatization would appear to depend on a solution to the problems of large public sector firms. Alice H. Amsden, "Beyond Shock Therapy," *The American Prospect,* Spring 1993, 94.

22. "It is not greatly important as to where ownership resides. . . . What is important is that the producing firm, not less than the individual, be the expression of its own personality, with the reward of its own success and the penalty of its own failure." Galbraith, 10.

23. "With widely dispersed stock ownership, the owners are not in a position to exercise much control over managers. . . . Investment funds don't do that either. Investment funds in the USA always vote with management, and that's the end of it." Josef Brada, in Ben Slay, ed., "Roundtable: Prospects for Reform," *RFE/RL Research Report,* March 20, 1992, 28.

24. Stark, 382–88. On the Czech scheme, see Jiri Havel and Eugen Kukla, "Privatization and Investment Funds in Czechoslovakia," *RFE/RL Research Report,* April 24, 1992, 37–41, and Josef C. Brada, "The Mechanics of the Voucher Plan in Czechoslovakia," ibid., 42–45.

25. Stark, 370–79; on some of the perils of the Czech approach, see Havel and Kukla, 40–41.

26. Kornai, "Socialist Transformation," 304; Szelenyi, "Alternative Futures," 238.

27. See, e.g, Roger de Weck, "Nichts bleibt, wie es ist," *Die Zeit,* April 26, 1991, 1.

28. See Marer, "Transition," 5, 9.

29. Ed A. Hewett, *Reforming the Soviet Economy* (Washington, D.C.: Brookings Institution, 1988), 350.

30. Conrad J. Kasperson and Krzysztof Obloj, "Training Polish Managers in a New Economic Era," *RFE/RL Research Report,* March 13, 1992, 64–67. The authors particularly blame the inadequacies of enterprise managers, nearly all of whom remained in their positions after privatization, for this disappointing finding.

31. See "Currency Convertibility is Not an End in Itself, Says Kenen," *IMF Survey* 20 (April 1, 1991), 97–98.

32. Tamás Bauer, "Hungarian Economic Reform in East European Perspective," *Eastern European Politics and Societies* 2 (Fall 1988), 427–28; Kornai, *Road,* 158–63.

33. See the translation of part of the original program with accompanying commentary in Janusz Bugaski, "Poland's Anti-Communist Manifesto," *Orbis* (Winter 1990), 109–20.

34. Josef C. Brada, "Is Hungary the Future of Poland, or is Poland the Future of Hungary?" *Eastern European Politics and Societies* 2 (Fall 1988), 471.

35. See Jacek Rostowski, "The Decay of Socialism and the Growth of Private Enterprise in Poland," *Soviet Studies* 41 (April 1989), 209–10; Jadwiga Staniszkis, " 'Political Capitalism' in Poland," *East European Politics and Societies* 5 (March 1991), 127–41.

36. Cited in Karoly Okolicsanyi, "Tungsram: A Case Study," *RFE/RL Research Report,* April 24, 1992, 36.

37. Stark (389–91) points to the importance of established informal "networks of interaction" among managers and small-scale producers in facilitating or, more likely, impeding, marketization.

38. In Romania, there are reports of a posthumous Ceauşescu cult; in Poland in June 1991, 43 percent of the Poles surveyed said they were better off two years earlier, when the Communists were in power. Dan Ionescu, "The Posthumous Ceauşescu Cult and Its High Priests," *Report on Eastern Europe,* May 31, 1991, 23–28; *Financial Times,* June 14, 1991, 2.

39. See Ellen Comisso, "Property Rights, Liberalism, and the Transition from 'Actually Existing' Socialism," *East European Politics and Societies* 5 (Winter 1991), 179–88.

40. See Kornai, *Road,* 60–62, 173–74.

41. See ibid., 206–8.

42. Marer cites the recommendation of several participants at the OECD/World Bank conference that tripartite government-business-labor "councils" be established for the support of reform, a proposal with evident neocorporatist overtones. Marer, "Transition," 8. See also George Schöpflin, "Obstacles to Liberalism in Post-Communist Regimes," *East European Politics and Societies* 5 (Winter 1991), 193–94.

43. See Daniel Schneiderman, "France in Quandary Over the Best Way to Help Poland," *Manchester Guardian Weekly,* November 5, 1989, 14 (translated from *Le Monde,* October 24, 1989).

44. In October 1992 the Joint Vienna Institute, co-sponsored by the IMF, EBRD, World Bank, OECD, Bank for International Settlements, and European Community Commission, opened, offering courses in public administration and economic management for officials from former Soviet bloc countries. *IMF Survey* 21 (November 9, 1992), 352. Also, in Warsaw a new National School of Public Administration has opened with international support.

45. Brada, "Is Hungary," 480.

46. Köves, 46.

10

The Dangers of Divergence: The United States and the New Europe

> The Americans believe in sticks, the Germans in carrots and the French in words.
>
> Pierre Hassner[1]

> As the world's biggest debtor nation, the U.S. has at last begun to accept that it is simply too poor to undertake the kind of foreign policy it would prefer.
>
> Martin Walker[2]

> I have not lost interest; we have not lost interest in what's going on in Eastern Europe.
>
> George Bush, February 1991[3]

Recurring tensions between the policies of the United States and those of its West European allies colored Western economic relations with Eastern Europe during the years of the cold war. In the post–cold war era we can expect such disagreements to continue, although the specific objects of discord may change. Arguably, they could become still deeper, as the fear of a common enemy that earlier enforced cooperation between the two loses its relevance.

Within Western Europe the leading actor is without question the German Federal Republic, which even prior to unification dominated Western trade and the granting of credit and other economic assistance to Eastern Europe. Now it finds itself redefining its identity partly in terms of its relationship to the East. Well behind it in significance is France, followed by Britain, Austria, and Italy. The French government, especially under de Gaulle, Giscard d'Estaing, and Mitterrand, has been the most creative and independent in its East European initiatives, but critics have rightly pointed to inconsistencies between its rhetoric and its economic practice. The European Community as a corporate entity, however, has taken on pivotal and rapidly expanding responsibilities in Eastern Europe, reflecting in part the preferences of the German-French consortium that has become the Community's driving force. The tensions between the German and French visions of the Community's future lends some ambiguity to the role of the EC, however.

Overall, the policies of France, the other West European states, and the EC have been closer to German views than to American ones.[4] The economic involvement of Western European countries apart from Germany in the East is proportionately greater than that of the United States, although with the partial exception of Austria their economic and political stake is smaller than the Federal Republic's. The West German approach was long conditioned by the primacy of relations with the GDR in its calculations; in the future, we can expect it to be shaped in large part by the multiple strains that unification has produced.[5] The policies of other European countries, especially France, will be driven in no small measure by their desire to contain German influence—which, ironically, seems to require that they support basic German goals.

The still broader issue with which American policymakers must contend is the prospect of the economic incorporation of Eastern Europe into an enlarged European Community. The Community has already taken the first steps toward incorporation; it has extended West Germany's EC membership to the territory of the former GDR (with certain transitional provisions), granted formal association status to three of the other states, and initialled similar agreements with Bulgaria and Romania. Most present EC members support full membership for Eastern Europe in principle, although the timing remains in question. Governments concerned with easing the unavoidable strains of integrating, however gradually, their poor, technologically underdeveloped, debt-ridden neighbors into the emerging single European market (and ultimately, perhaps, into a single polity) will naturally be motivated by very different considerations from those that move an external power like the United States. Community measures designed to facilitate the integration process can also be expected to complement the advantages European firms (along with American firms that already have a strong EC foothold) enjoy in developing markets and production facilities in the East. Below the official level, the long-standing resentment of many Europeans of what they see as excessive American economic and cultural influence in Europe will undoubtedly lead them to view the integration of Eastern Europe into the EC as a way of furthering the "Europeanization" of the continent on especially favorable economic turf.[6]

All parties nevertheless share an interest in maintaining some sort of official United States economic presence in Eastern Europe: Europeans concerned over the influence of the Germans and nervous over the political vacuum an American departure might leave, Americans fearful of a new domestic isolationism and alarmed at the prospect that their country might cede the opportunity to help shape the post–cold war European order. The tortured course of American and European efforts to find a common policy toward the Bosnian crisis suggests the ambivalence of both in seeking to define the future place of the United States in European affairs. But the logic of European integration and the likelihood that American interest in the area will decline as that of Western Europe grows does not bode well for the congruence and coordination of future Western policies. The United States will need to make extraordinary exertions and policy concessions if it is to remain an influential economic force in the region.

PAST DISAGREEMENTS AND THEIR SOURCES

Several persistent themes characterized the conflict between the United States and Western Europe over their economic policies toward Eastern Europe during the postwar decades. Perhaps most fundamentally, Americans and Europeans differed over the likely political results of their economic strategies. The United States on various occasions sought to employ economic sanctions to punish what it viewed as East European or Soviet misbehavior; while it did not claim that sanctions would force immediate reversals of policy, it did contend that they would send a useful signal that would yield longer-term benefits. Europeans tended to doubt the effectiveness of such measures, however, and were reluctant to make the commercial sacrifices they would require.[7] This conflict led to a near crisis in U.S.-European relations early in the Reagan years over the issue of sanctions against the Soviet Union and Poland in the wake of the invasion of Afghanistan and the Polish declaration of martial law. The clumsy attempts of the administration to punish European firms supplying natural gas pipeline equipment to the USSR led to tensions that were only resolved when the new American Secretary of State George Shultz engineered a compromise that amounted to a United States withdrawal on the issue.

On the other hand, the belief that positive political change in the East might be promoted by relaxed trade and credit policies and other forms of economic assistance, although viewed with skepticism in many quarters, seemed to be shared by Americans (e.g., with respect to Poland) and Germans (especially with respect to the GDR). The United States, however, was willing to reward only signs of change that were already overt and substantial; the Federal Republic, more patient, was ready to extend aid even to relatively unreformed countries in the hope that it might ultimately stimulate change.

Thus the Germans did not subscribe to the persistent American emphasis on differentiation among the East European states on the basis of their deviation from the Soviet model or from Soviet foreign policy guidance. Not only the GDR but Czechoslovakia and Bulgaria, countries consigned to the bottom three places on Washington's priorities list, enjoyed considerable favor with West German business and the Bonn government. In so far as the West Germans differentiated their policies at all (beyond their preoccupation with the GDR), it was on the basis of the East European states' treatment of their German minorities.[8] Thus while the Federal Republic became the leading Western exporter to all six countries and the leading Western importer from five of them, U.S. East European trade was dominated by Romania and Poland; the United States did not even rank among the top five Western countries in trade with Czechoslovakia or the GDR.

Americans and Europeans also disagreed over the question of strategic export restrictions and the terms of Western lending to Eastern Europe. Any history of COCOM would show its deliberations to have repeatedly revolved around American efforts to expand or maintain the list of proscribed exports and to tighten enforcement and European efforts to reduce the list and resist zealous enforcement.[9] Similarly, American efforts to limit the size and length of Western credits to the East and to prevent them from being offered at below-market rates were rewarded at best with grudging European acceptance and at worst with efforts at circumvention.[10]

Both economic and political factors account for these recurring policy disagreements. The Federal Republic, like the other West European states and Japan, is far more dependent on trade for its economic prosperity than is the United States, and it carries on a larger (although still modest) proportion of its trade with the East European countries. In 1991, 3.0 percent of its exports went to Eastern Europe, not including the former GDR, as opposed to 0.3 percent for the United States.[11] Prior to the Second World War, Germany dominated trade with Eastern Europe, and this traditional pattern is reinforced by geographical proximity and German cultural influence. History and geography also give Austria, Italy, and—in lesser measure—France and Britain more compelling commercial interests in Eastern Europe than the United States has, and a corresponding reluctance to sacrifice these interests for the sake of ideological principle.[12]

Institutional differences have also contributed to policy divergence. Especially important is the considerable influence of Congress over foreign economic policy in the United States, and Congressional responsiveness to the pressures of ethnic, economic, and ideological interest groups, which has the effect of subjecting U.S. policy decisions to greater swings of political emotion than is usual in Europe. Congress's penchant for intervening in foreign policy matters is inevitably reflected in the policies of the executive branch, which is constrained by what it believes Congress will be willing to accept. Such legislative influence has no real parallel in the parliamentary systems of Western Europe, not even in the presence in the *Bundestag* of spokespersons for the Federal Republic's vocal refugee groups from the "lost territories" in the East. Intrabureaucratic conflict notably the struggle among the Defense, State, and Commerce Departments over trade issues, also appears to have played a larger role in the United States than in Europe.

The pronounced ideological cast lent to American politics by the rise of the conservative movement and its triumph in the 1980 national elections also set the United States apart from the more pragmatic style of European governments. Reservations over the ritualized American invocation of the Soviet "threat" undoubtedly contributed to Western European impatience with American-sponsored restrictions on trade with the East. American insistence on giving priority to assisting the private sector in multilateral aid ventures has also met with European (notably French) resistance.

The force of these sources of American-European divergence has not diminished with the breakup of the Soviet–East European bloc, although the direction of Congressional influence is now more ambiguous. At the time of the breakup, at least some Congressional pressures were applied on behalf of liberalized trade and more generous economic assistance to those countries Congress believed to have genuinely abandoned their Communist pasts. But the distrust in Congress and the executive of the European Community over trade issues, and of Germany over defense questions, is likely to spill over and foster new conflicts over policies toward Eastern Europe. Americans, in calling for burden sharing during the Gulf war, were notably unsympathetic to German protestations that cited the high costs of unity and of the country's other East European commitments. Another element contributing to potentially greater divergence is the United States' self-created budgetary corset, tightened by its foreign trade deficit, the legacy of the Gramm-Rudman Act, and the political constraints on raising taxes.

In the past, the ability of the United States to obtain the acquiescence of Western Europe in its economic policies toward the East depended in significant part on its military and political dominance in NATO. The inevitable decline of NATO's importance, in spite of fervent American efforts to resuscitate the organization by reinterpreting its mission, thus stands to weaken American influence. The implementation of proposals, promoted particularly by the French, to develop a separate European defense structure through the Western European Union or the CSCE (Conference on Security and Cooperation in Europe) would have similar effects.[13] While Western disarray over the Yugoslav civil war has underlined the need to reconstruct U.S.-European military relationships, there are as yet few signs of progress toward that objective.

Moreover, the changes wrought by unification in the German psyche as well as in the country's economic and geopolitical position have heightened the prospect that the Federal Republic's policies will, over time, depart further from those of the United States *and* from those of its West European partners. All three—the United States, the Federal Republic, and the other states of the European Community—now face difficult choices concerning their fundamental priorities in Eastern Europe. The choices they make could bring them closer together, but on present evidence are more likely to drive them further apart.

UNITED STATES CHOICES

The United States can choose to expand its economic involvement in Eastern Europe through aid, technical assistance, the vigorous promotion of trade and investment, and the elimination of barriers to economic, technical, and scientific exchange, as part of a broader adherence to the ideals of what Walter Russell Mead dubs "Wilsonian internationalism."[14] Alternatively, it can elect largely to disengage economically from Eastern Europe, leaving the field to Western Europe, Japan, and the newly industrializing countries. There are reasons to fear that the latter, if only by default, is the more likely course.

These reasons include the pressing demands on American attention and American resources at home and in other parts of the world. The massive U.S. foreign debt, continuing foreign trade and budgetary deficits, and strong political resistance to spending on foreign assistance all strengthen the sentiment among Americans that the "rich" Europeans and East Asians ought to assume the primary responsibility for helping Eastern Europe. The fact that Eastern Europe can no longer be seen as either contributing to or substantially inhibiting any sort of Soviet (or Russian) threat and the widespread perception that the post-Soviet states no longer constitute much of a threat anyway—remember that American policy toward Eastern Europe in the past has been almost entirely a function of its policy toward the Soviet Union—reinforce the attractions of withdrawal. Indeed, American interest in helping the former Soviet republics out of their economic crisis is apt to work to Eastern Europe's disadvantage.[15]

There are some countervailing forces. They include the influence of ethnic interest groups and some residual Wilsonian idealism stimulated by the efforts of the former Communist states to build democratic institutions, although the idealism may well diminish as media attention shifts elsewhere and to the extent that democratic experimentation in the region is overwhelmed by political disorder and ugly outbursts of nationalism. American commercial interests fearful of losing potential markets and investment opportunities to European and East Asian rivals can be expected to lobby for continued or expanded official U.S. involvement. The State Department is not oblivious to the danger that withdrawal from Eastern Europe would mean reduced influence in Western Europe and ultimately a smaller world role for the United States. Nevertheless, on balance I would judge the forces favoring withdrawal to be stronger; it will take considerable determination to overcome them.

GERMAN CHOICES

As Wolfram Hanrieder has noted, for years international economic policies have served the Federal Republic as the "extension of politics by other means."[16] Unable because of its past to employ the threat of military force and consigned (until recently) to a secondary diplomatic role, the Federal Republic made use of its economic strength and technological prowess, along with its prominence as a trading power, to buy support for its Eastern (and other) policies and to win concessions in the Soviet bloc itself. We can expect a united Germany to continue to use its economic leverage and to replace the Soviet Union as the dominant economic force in Eastern Europe, and there are already indications that it will use its economic strength to justify a greater political assertiveness. But the Germans face their own difficult choices among economic priorities. How much emphasis, relatively, should they give (1) to overcoming the material and psychological gap between the old Federal Republic and its new eastern states, (2) to West European integration, including monetary and political union, (3) to economic relations with the former USSR and the rest of Eastern Europe, and (4) to prosperity at home?

The Kohl government, characteristically, has insisted that it is firmly committed to all four priorities—and to NATO and a new European security order as well. (Another Kohl commitment, to avoid new taxes, fell by the wayside after the December 1990 German elections.) There are, however, serious tensions among these goals. Even German financial resources are not inexhaustible. Unification has proven far more costly than anticipated: the Federal Republic spent some $100 billion in 1991 and again in 1992 to support the former GDR, but no broad upturn is yet in sight. Another $50 billion has been committed to the former Soviet states, much of it in effect payment for Soviet acquiescence in German unity.[17] In spite of the efforts of the German government to present itself as an advocate for Eastern Europe (especially Poland) within the EC and for Russia in the councils of the G-7 nations, there is apt to be little additional money left for these countries, and for easing the path to Western European integration. In the past, it should be recalled, German financial concessions have often been the grease permitting the EC to resolve its disagreements. But a German public already worried about the costs of unification is likely to balk at expensive new commitments to the Community.[18]

The escalating costs of unity have produced large budget deficits and high German (and thus European) interest rates; these have contributed to a severe economic slump in Germany and the rest of Europe, a stalling of European plans for monetary union, and new economic tensions with the United States. For Eastern Europe, the Western recession threatens to shrink export markets and stall foreign investment. For Germans, the economic crisis, coupled with political scandals, the rise in right-wing violence, and the controversy over asylum-seekers, has undermined the country's capacity to excercise leadership in Europe and has reinforced pressures on it to turn inward. Whether the new Germany can recover its confidence and economic health while balancing its competing priorities remain the country's critical dilemmas.

EUROPEAN CHOICES

For the European Community, the choice in the broadest terms is whether it will become necessary to amend its goals and/or timetable in order to accommodate the Eastern European states within an all-European framework. The EC's present members differ over the treatment of Eastern Europe according to the strength of domestic economic interests and their broader view of European integration. Completion (more or less) of the single internal market at the beginning of 1993 allowed the Community to return to the question of expanding its membership. Shortly after the East European revolutions, the Community had proclaimed its intention of accelerating the integration process in response to the changes there.[19] As so often in the history of the EC, however, political idealism collided with shorter-term calculations of economic interest by its members, which in turn shape the political strategies of their negotiators. The EC has decided to consider the applications of EFTA states first, citing the high costs of bringing in Eastern Europe. The ideal embraced by the Community of encouraging the development of the fragile democracies of the East will also have to be reconciled with the older and still controversial vision of a politically united Europe. The two goals are not necessarily incompatible, but combining them will raise questions, for example, concerning future relations with the former Soviet Union, that will complicate still further the integration process. The EC will have to face up to the implications of the fact that the admission of Poland, Hungary, the Czech Republic and Slovakia—and later Bulgaria and Romania—will shift the balance in the former "rich man's club" still further toward its poorer, and politically less stable, members.

There are more immediate economic questions. Will Community development aid to Eastern Europe come at the expense of aid to the less developed regions of Southern Europe and Ireland?[20] How generous can the EC afford to be with "transitional" requirements for Eastern Europe in general? The reduction of import barriers to East European goods and the relaxation of EC rules with respect to pollution, product standardization, and so on inevitably cause economic harm to some present members. In its aid policies, how is the EC to work out the difficult triangular relationship between itself, Eastern Europe, and the former Soviet states? More generally, will the complexity and costs of the arrangements necessary to open the EC's doors to Eastern Europe offer reluctant present members (such as the British government) new reasons and opportunities for resisting monetary union and progress toward common social policies and greater political integration?

ON THE PATH TO AMERICAN ISOLATION?

The potential conflict between the integration of Eastern Europe into the European Community and the other goals of the EC, while not unrecognized, has thus far remained largely below the rhetorical surface in the public statements of European leaders, who vaguely endorse both a "wider" and "deeper" Community. Any tension between German interests and those of the Community as a whole have been similarly minimized. American differences with Europe have been less well concealed, however. They emerged openly in several instances in the wake of the stunning changes in Eastern Europe of 1989.

Characteristically, Western European initiatives have been met by American hesitancy or resistance. In mid-1989 the United States appeared to concede to the European Community the leadership role in organizing assistance to Poland and Hungary as those two countries moved toward non-Communist rule. At the Western economic summit held in Paris in July, President Bush agreed that the EC should coordinate emergency food aid to Poland, organize an international conference on aid to both countries, and act as a broader clearing house for policies toward Eastern Europe. Promises of American assistance to Poland and Hungary, while substantially increased by Congress over the modest figures proposed by the administration (in part in response to the lobbying of Polish-American organizations), amounted to somewhat less than met the eye. Besides economic stabilization assistance and food aid for Poland, which supplemented larger sums from the EC, they emphasized private sector investment (through a special "private enterprise fund" and OPIC guarantees) and trade liberalization.[21] Future American assistance to the region will have to compete with the demands of traditional, politically weighty U.S. aid recipients like Israel and Egypt, desperately needy Third World claimants, and the former Soviet Union, as well as domestic needs.

American reluctance to relax its traditionally rigid stance on "strategic" trade even in the face of the disintegration of Communist rule in Eastern Europe led to its finding itself in isolation in votes in COCOM in February 1990. The restrictions the United States continued to defend on exports to Eastern Europe were more severe than those applied to China even after the Tiananmen Square crackdown. In June 1990, COCOM accepted a United States proposal for the liberalization of export rules with respect to telecommunications equipment and such other items as computers and precision machine tools; additional liberalization was delayed until May 1991 after the United States toughened its position on items that had proven critical during the Gulf war.[22]

The negotiations carrying the strongest symbolic overtones for the future of Western policy, however, were those surrounding the creation of the European Bank for Reconstruction and Development (EBRD). The bank, initially proposed by French President Mitterrand—partly, it is said, to counter potential German domination of relations with Eastern Europe—offers loans to both private and public undertakings in the region; it opened for business in April 1991. Unlike the U.S.-dominated World Bank, the EBRD, based in London, is largely controlled by Western Europeans; its first director was Jacques Attali, an advisor to Mitterrand. The United States, with a 10 percent stake, is the largest shareholder of the forty-two members of the bank, but the EC countries together control 51 percent of the bank's $12 billion capital (and thus 51 percent of its votes). U.S. objections led the Europeans to agree to limit loans to the Soviet Union to its own contribution of capital ($216 million in the first three years), and to require that at least 60 percent of the loans go to private undertakings; up to 40 percent can go to support public infrastructural projects that will presumably also benefit the private sector.[23] Even so, conservative Republicans (including Senators Dole and Kasten), the Heritage Foundation, organized labor, and other groups threatened to block Congressional approval of American membership.[24]

PROBLEMS OF COORDINATION

The great number and many types of economic initiatives being undertaken toward Eastern Europe, and the variety of institutions involved in them, make the already difficult task of Western policy coordination especially challenging. An important development that came in the wake of the East European revolutions of 1989, however, was the emergence of the European Community as a critical body for shaping and channelling both its own and bilateral assistance to Eastern Europe; it acts not only for its own 12 members but also on behalf of the EFTA countries, the United States, Japan, Australia, New Zealand, Canada, and Turkey. The EC Commission and its bureaucracy, in spite of inexperience in dealing with Eastern Europe, provide relatively disinterested expertise in the necessary process of defining the region's needs and formulating technically and politically feasible programs. The summits of EC leaders held two or three times a year offer a forum for resolving more fundamental differences of policy among its member states.

The European Community's authority, however, does not extend to the United States and other nonmember nations except in so far as these choose to comply with its recommendations. Neither does it extend to the decisions of multilateral lending agencies or to multinational corporations and banks partially or entirely outside its borders. Although the Community can develop a common European policy, and thus a strong bargaining position, on such matters as export controls and public debt rescheduling or forgiveness, it cannot impose them on non-EC actors. Even within its own borders, it cannot readily control private entrepreneurial ventures that can profoundly influence the development of the East European economies.

Nevertheless, the emergence of the EC as a central coordinating force for economic policies toward Eastern Europe significantly changes the framework within which the United States must consider its own course. From the American perspective, the EC's new role reduces the number of partners with which it must deal in coordinating its policies, but on the other hand it can also accelerate the decline of U.S. influence. In February 1990, concerned over potential U.S.-European divergence, Secretary of State Baker persuaded the Community to agree to hold twice-annual summit meetings between the American president and the current president of the EC, supplemented by semiannual meetings between the secretary of state and the twelve EC foreign ministers.[25] At such meetings, however, or at the annual seven-power (G-7) economic summits, the United States will continue to suffer from its own internal coordination problems. It cannot, for example, make unqualified financial commitments prior to winning Congressional approval of corresponding appropriations.

In arenas such as COCOM, the International Monetary Fund and the World Bank, and the Paris Club of East Europe's governmental creditors, the United States has a strong voice and a potential veto, although it is generally less and less in a position to insist on its own policies. COCOM remains a voluntary organization, and a COCOM veto can also be effectively overridden by lax or nonexistent enforcement; in any case, most of the restraints it once imposed on trade with Eastern Europe are being dismantled. Credits denied through the World Bank because of an American veto could, in theory, now be granted by the European Bank for Reconstruction and Development, in which, as noted, EC governments hold the majority, although at least initially the EBRD has promised to work together with the World Bank and IMF. The United States holds only a small proportion of total Paris Club debts, but used its position in the Club to persuade other creditors to agree to reduce Polish official debt by a larger proportion than they might have independently.

An additional dimension of the coordination problem is presented by the emerging role of East Asian nations in Eastern Europe. Japan is included among the twenty-four nations whose aid is coordinated through the EC, is a participant in the seven-nation summits, and belongs to COCOM and the Paris Club; it does not participate in any regular overall discussions of policy toward Eastern Europe, however, and its policy influence thus far does not match its growing financial involvement in the region. South Korea and Taiwan are in most respects outside the present circle of arrangements.

FUTURE DIRECTIONS FOR U.S. POLICY

In the past, the divergence of American policies toward Eastern Europe from those followed by Western European states could be attributed to the conflicting interests and perceptions of the two. Now American and European policies threaten to diverge primarily because traditional American interests—first of all strategic ones—in the region are declining while those of Western Europe have expanded. There is a serious possibility that the loss of perceived U.S. interest will be followed by the drying up of funds, and that future U.S. economic relations with Eastern Europe will come to be largely mediated through Western Europe.

American interest in the region will not entirely disappear. The emotional ties of Americans of East European descent will be reinforced by the substantial number of new emigrés, particularly from Poland; American concern for the emergence of democratic institutions and human rights will continue; American business will still seek to exploit opportunities in the region. But East Europe's loss of strategic relevance for the United States will mean that more than token government appropriations will be hard to come by. The course of least resistance for the United States will be to leave most of the financing of East European reconstruction to the West Europeans and East Asians, and that will all but inevitably mean a far smaller voice in policy decisions as well.

Will it matter if the United States no longer plays an influential and independent role in Eastern Europe? It will for the East Europeans themselves, who still admire the United States and look upon it as something of a political and cultural model, and who see it as a potential counterweight to overwhelming German influence.[26] Western Europeans who are also nervous about the disproportionate weight of a united Germany in the new Europe, or who recall the baleful effects of earlier American withdrawals and fear the uncertainties that would be created by the departure of a now disengaged and inward-looking Atlantic ally from the continent, will be likely to agree. From the perspective of the United States, economic withdrawal from Eastern Europe would mean a reduced ability to influence events in Western Europe and the loss in particular of a lever that might help keep an enlarged European Community outward looking; it could also mean a loss of American influence over the still unpredictable evolution of the former Soviet republics.

But only an unusually forceful presidential commitment is likely to halt the decline in the American role. Such a commitment must be to a multilateral approach to reconstructing Eastern Europe; neither American resources nor the logic of European integration will permit a separate U.S. course. The United States must call for the creation of joint U.S.–European Community mechanisms for shaping policy toward Eastern Europe, but it can hardly expect to have much of a voice in them without making a significant financial contribution. The Bush administration's strategy of relying on "other people's money"—advocating the forgiveness of debt owed to other nations and private lenders and promising support for IMF and World Bank aid in place of bilateral commitments—will not be sufficient. Nor can the United States retain much influence by clinging to obsolescent cold war principles, such as those still embodied in some COCOM rules or the structure of NATO. Winning the necessary appropriations and overcoming old foreign policy thinking toward Eastern Europe will require a far higher level of presidential determination and a much more coherent and detailed program than presently exist.

NOTES

1. Pierre Hassner, "The View from Paris," in Lincoln Gordon et al., *Eroding Empire: Western Relations with Eastern Europe* (Washington, D.C.: Brookings Institution, 1987), 216.

2. Martin Walker, "Stripped for Cash, Stumped for Solutions," *Manchester Guardian Weekly*, July 25, 1989, 9.

3. George Bush, cited in *New York Times*, February 28, 1991, C15.

4. On France, see Pierre Hassner and Dominique Moïsi, "French Policy toward Central and Eastern Europe," in William E. Griffith, ed., *Central and Eastern Europe: The Opening Curtain?* (Boulder, Colo.: Westview Press, 1989), 353–65; on Britain, Italy, and Austria, see the chapters by Edwina Moreton and J. F. Brown in Gordon et al.

5. Timothy Garton Ash's 1990 comment has proven somewhat prophetic: "If I have a fear for the next few years it is not that Germany will turn outward in any sort of bid for great power (economic) domination, but rather that it will turn inward, become obsessed with the problems flowing from unification, a little self-pitying, self-protective, and with a wall on its eastern frontier which its other West European partners will only help to reinforce." Garton Ash, "Germany Unbound," *New York Review of Books*, November 22, 1990, 15.

6. See Peter Bender, *Das Ende des ideologischen Zeitalters: Die Europäisierung Europas* (Berlin: Severin und Siedler, 1981).

7. See Gunnar Adler-Karlsson, "The Effectiveness of Embargoes and Sanctions," in Reinhard Rode and Hanns-Dieter Jacobsen, eds., *Economic Warfare or Détente* (Boulder, Colo.: Westview Press, 1985), 281–93.

8. See Timothy Garton Ash, "Mitteleuropa," *Daedalus* 119 (Winter 1990), 12. Ash notes that the Federal Republic also favored states willing to accommodate its specific interests, such as the establishment of Goethe cultural institutes to offset existing cultural ties with the GDR.

9. See above, chap. 7, and Michael Mastanduno, "The Management of Alliance Export Control Policy," in Gary K. Bertsch, ed., *Controlling East-West Trade and Technology Transfer* (Durham, N.C.: Duke University Press, 1988), 241–79.

10. See Beverly Crawford, "Western Control of East-West Trade Finance," in ibid., 280–312, and chap. 8 of this book.

11. See chap. 6, Table 6.1.

12. The proportion of Austrian exports going to Eastern Europe in 1991 was 6.7 percent; for Italy the figure was 1.4 percent, France 0.9 percent, and Britain 0.7 percent. See chap. 6, Table 6.1.

13. See Henry Kissinger, "A Role for the Atlantic Alliance Today," *Manchester Guardian Weekly* (*Washington Post* section), March 8, 1992, 19.

14. See Walter Russell Mead, "The United States and the New Europe," *World Policy Journal* (Winter 1989–1990), 55–56.

15. In June, 1991, just after the United States announced a $1.5 billion credit to the USSR for the purchase of American farm products, East European officials criticized such aid as undermining their own exports to their former leading trade partner. *New York Times,* June 16, 1991, 6.

16. Wolfram Hanrieder, *Germany, America, Europe* (New Haven: Yale University Press, 1989), 225.

17. See *Wall Street Journal,* June 17, 1991, A7; *New York Times,* December 9, 1990, E3; Suzanne Crow, "Russian Federation Faces Foreign Policy Dilemmas," *RFE/RL Research Report,* March 6, 1992, 18.

18. An upsurge of German criticism of the EC has led one German writer to comment: "Just as the Americans bash Japan, in Germany it has become chic to bluster against the EC." Roger de Weck, "Deutschland wird deutscher," *Die Zeit,* March 13, 1992, 1.

19. See Leigh Bruce, "Europe's Locomotive," *Foreign Policy* (Spring 1990), 68–90.

20. See Edward Cody, "Southern Europe Fears Funding May Switch," *Washington Post,* reprinted in *Manchester Guardian Weekly,* April 8, 1990, 19.

21. "Legislation Enacted to Begin Business, Economic Aid," *Congressional Quarterly Weekly Report* 47 (November 25, 1989), 3256–3257. The largest American commitment, of $200 million, was for the $1 billion Polish economic stabilization fund, with most of the remaining $800 million contributed by Western Europe; none of the money, meant as backing for the zloty exchange rate, has been needed.

22. *New York Times,* May 3, 1990, 1, C8; ibid., June 8, 1990, 4; *Wall Street Journal,* May 28, 1991, A8. The new rules, it might be noted, incorporated the principle of differentiation by granting more favorable treatment to Poland, Hungary, and Czechoslovakia than to Bulgaria, Romania, and the Soviet Union.

23. As an EBRD official has pointed out to me, however, the line between public and private sector aid is not always clear, giving the institution somewhat greater flexibility.

24. *New York Times,* April 12, 1990, C1. Dole and Kasten proposed as an alterna-

tive the creation of a special section of the World Bank devoted to East European lending.

25. *Washington Post,* February 28, 1990, (A)14.

26. In 1990 Rita Klimova, then the Czechoslovak ambassador to the United States, appealed for United States investments to prevent the "Germanization" of the Czech economy, which she feared would result from the pure working of the market mechanism. *Report on Eastern Europe,* March 9, 1990, 58. Czechoslovak concerns over German economic dominance were also prominent in the competition between Volkswagen and a Renault-Volvo consortium for the Skoda joint venture. It is noteworthy, however, that Volkswagen's more generous offer was ultimately accepted. Jan Obrman, "Skoda Becomes Part of Volkswagen Empire," *Report on Eastern Europe,* January 25, 1991, 7–12.

CONCLUSION

11

A Marshall Plan for Eastern Europe?

> Following a number of decades when a maximal state prevailed, it is now time to take great steps in the direction of a minimal state.
>
> János Kornai[1]

> In his studies on the economic history of modern capitalism, Polanyi demonstrated that private property and markets can be produced only *as a result of state intervention.*
>
> Ivan Szelenyi[2]

Even before the collapse of the Communist regimes of Eastern Europe, the idea of launching a massive Western program of economic assistance comparable to the post–World War II Marshall Plan in order to pull the region out of its economic predicament was in the air.[3] Once the old regimes had fallen, and the magnitude of the economic crisis facing the governments that succeeded them became apparent, the popularity of the idea grew.[4] But as quickly as such ambitious proposals surfaced, they were met by a wave of criticism questioning either the desirability or the feasibility of such a project. From the perspective of this book, there can be little question but that a broad and generous program of economic assistance to Eastern Europe underwritten by the more prosperous of the world's democracies would be highly desirable. Whether it is politically realizable is much more questionable. And whether, even if implemented, it would substantially promote East European recovery would depend very much on its design.

THE IDEA OF A "MARSHALL PLAN"

The appeal of the Marshall Plan metaphor is not surprising. First of all, it suggests the scale of the assistance that would be needed to pull Eastern Europe from its economic morass. The total amount of Marshall Plan aid extended by the United States between 1948 and 1952 was $13.3 billion; the equivalent today would be well over $100 billion. Second, it suggests the unique mixture of idealism and Realpolitik necessary to make such an undertaking a success. Third (and often forgotten), it underscores the importance of an element that was a critical ingredient of the original Marshall Plan: the requirement that the aid giver and aid recipients cooperate closely with one another in planning the modes of assistance and the purposes to which it would be devoted.[5] The Marshall Plan was far from being a no-strings-attached handout from the wealthy United States to the impoverished nations of Europe. It was informed by an integrationist vision and required that the Europeans share responsibility for planning and carrying out the process of economic recovery.

The limitations of the Marshall Plan metaphor are also apparent. The original plan was very much an artifact of the cold war; without the presence of a Soviet enemy it is exceedingly unlikely that Congress would have supported it. Indeed, the rejection of Marshall Plan assistance by the East European states, on the instructions of Stalin, was probably essential for the plan's approval. In 1948, a credible argument could be made that massive economic assistance to Western Europe was necessary for the very survival of the West; no equivalent argument can be made with respect to Eastern Europe today. Moreover, the original Marshall Plan was initiated and financed by a single nation facing what it viewed as a single overwhelming threat. A 1990s' Marshall Plan would have to be coordinated among many nations whose political attention is divided among a variety of domestic and international issues. Especially the United States, although incomparably wealthier than it was in 1948, now views itself as locked in severe fiscal difficulties, and torn between the demands on public attention and public resources of drugs, crime, the health care crisis, educational failure, the Middle East, and much else.[6]

In 1948, moreover, the Soviet Union conveniently excluded itself from consideration for assistance. Today its successor states clamor for Western aid. Neither can the claims of other states, such as the former Yugoslav republics and Albania, readily be ignored. Thus what might be a financially manageable program of aid for the former East European CMEA members could be overwhelmed by the needs of a much larger recipient pool; the magnitude of Russian needs alone would dwarf those of the region of our concern.

Even if these difficulties could be ignored, there would remain the problem of implementation. What, the critics ask, would prevent large-scale

Western aid from going the same unhappy way of the credits of the 1970s? However devastated by World War II, the recipients of Marshall Plan funds had (for the most part) legitimate governments, capable bureaucracies, and well-developed private economies and capitalist instincts. The legitimacy of the new governments of Eastern Europe is at best fragile, their officials are inexperienced, and their bureaucracies remain laced with the products of state socialist education, indoctrination, and experience. Entrepreneurial skills are in short supply, and only the beginnings of a market culture can be said to exist. To put it harshly, many of the preconditions for the successful utilization of large-scale Western aid do not appear to be present.

THE CASE FOR A "MARSHALL PLAN"

Nevertheless, the case for a carefully designed, comprehensive international program of aid remains compelling. The case is apt to seem most persuasive to the nations of Western Europe, whose own economic interests and idealism are most clearly engaged by the plight of the East European states. For that reason, such a program must all but certainly be led by Europeans, and probably by the European Community. But the United States is still in a position to play a catalytic role in the process, and in doing so might contribute to halting its gradual slide into irrelevance in the region.

Problems are not solved, so we have been frequently reminded, simply by "throwing money at them," and Western governments, led by the United States, protest that in any case they have no money to throw. But the yawning economic gap between Eastern Europe and the West, and the political and social strains it produces, cannot be reduced just by token programs and good will. As the East German case shows, economies that seemed to function adequately so long as they remained insulated from world markets can rapidly fall into deep crisis once their protection is lifted. Eastern Europe's "[long-]deferred tasks of modernization"[7] now haunt its future: the backwardness of its infrastructure, including communications facilities, transportation networks, and financial institutions; the advanced age of industrial facilities and the obsolescence of the entire industrial structure; the profligate consumption of energy and the acute shortage of adequate and safe energy supplies; the massive level and costs of pollution; the shortage of entrepreneurial, managerial, and, above all, administrative, skills.

Only a major commitment of Western resources, targeted at critical problem areas, can begin to address these needs. Not merely sympathy with the peoples of Eastern Europe, but compelling considerations of Western self-interest demand that such a commitment be made. On the positive side, the economic opportunities for Western business represented by East European markets, potential production facilities, and the region's technical and scientific potential are substantial. On the negative side, the Chernobyl accident was only the most dramatic illustration of the ways in which East European pollution and the neglect of health and safety considerations can endanger Western populations. The present relative poverty of Eastern Europeans must be reduced if the large-scale East to West migration that has been the focus of violence in Germany and caused severe social problems in Austria is not to accelerate and affect other Western countries as well. Finally, the danger that East European economic and political instability and nationalist conflict might infect the West is demonstrated too persuasively by history to require elaboration.

If Eastern European opportunities seem to be concentrated in the northern tier states, the dangers listed are most apparent in Southeastern Europe. Western attention and Western economic assistance have focused on the more hopeful cases of Hungary, the Czech Republic, and Poland; German resources have been concentrated on the former GDR. The tendency to write off Bulgaria, Romania, and now perhaps Slovakia is unwarranted. Political turmoil and economic desperation in these latter states would gravely imperil the northern tier states as well; any comprehensive program must include both.

THE SHAPE OF AN AID PROGRAM: BRINGING THE STATE BACK IN

An effective program of aid must begin with the assumption that for years to come the state will need to play a preeminent role in organizing the transformation of the East European economies. Thus a significant proportion of Western assistance will have to be targeted at strengthening the capacities of East European governments and their bureaucracies to administer reform and reconstruction. Much of the remaining aid will have to be channelled through government structures whose trustworthiness and effectiveness is likely to remain suspect in the eyes of many.

Such a recommendation would appear to fly in the face of the conventional insistence that what the East European economies need above all is a drastic reduction in government intervention. But the fundamental restructuring required in these economies cannot be accomplished by their fledgling private sectors alone. In analyzing the dilemmas facing East European economies, we often forget the pivotal role played by the state in the development of most capitalist economies[8] and the continuing ubiquity of government regulation and subsidy in the advanced societies of the West. The U. S. savings and loan crisis and the BCCI (Bank of Credit and Commercial International) scandal underline the perils of trying to do without such regulation.

To be sure, the new East European governments must rebuild the administrative structures and practices inherited from the old regimes, with

Western financial and technical assistance. They will have to reduce the inflated size of the Communist-era bureaucracies. The old economic branch ministries, planning authorities, and ideological bureaucracies, now largely dismantled, will have to be replaced by new agencies more appropriate to tasks such as regulation, the stimulation of research and development, export promotion, and indicative planning, tasks that are characteristic of a mixed economy. Old personnel will have to be retrained or retired, and schools and courses of study for a new generation of public administrators established. Governments will have to resist strong pressures for a total purge of the old regime's officials, in the name of "decommunization"; it is neither feasible nor desirable. Even without a purge, there is a serious danger that capable and experienced bureaucrats will depart for private business.[9] The restructuring of the public sector is vital, however, and Western experience and expertise should be mobilized in its support.

In their economic policies Eastern European governments will have to give especially high priority to the modernization or creation of the infrastructure necessary for broader economic progress: telecommunications, transportation, and a network of modern financial institutions. Western companies have already undertaken investments and joint ventures in telecommunications, but assuring their adequacy and appropriateness will require state licensing and regulation, which in turn would benefit greatly from Western administrative experience. The large sums required for modernizing rail, air, and road facilities cannot be expected to come from private companies; loans (and appropriate guidance) from multilateral lending institutions will be needed. Private Western banks and insurance companies have exhibited varying degrees of readiness to move into Eastern Europe by themselves or through joint ventures, but extensive technical assistance in creating the necessary institutions and rules for regulating banking, insurance, and the emerging stock and bond markets is essential. The widespread banking scandals in Poland underscore the need for such assistance. A longer-term but critical infrastructural need demanding Western aid is support for East European higher education and research, now in desperate financial straits.

Another broad arena in which large-scale Western assistance is needed is that of the restructuring and modernization of East European industry. Here hard decisions face the East European regimes, which to date have been reluctant to confront them. Which enterprises can usefully be saved, and where necessary adapted to the new economic context, and which must be closed down with the attendant loss of jobs and concomitant social dislocation? The Gdansk shipyard is only the best-known example of a technologically backward but socially and politically important enterprise whose international viability might still be in doubt even after extensive modernization and rationalization of the work force. Many sizeable East European communities are wholly dependent on mammoth enterprises that may be unsalvageable; alternative providers of jobs must be found. Here too the East European governments will need solid data and disinterested counsel with respect to international markets and competition as well as to alternative strategies. However controversial industrial policies may be in the West, Eastern European governments, with their responsibility for the fate of thousands of state-owned firms, can hardly avoid formulating them.[10]

A particularly vital area in which restructuring is necessary is in the production and use of energy. Here again public sector decisions will be critical. On the supply side, the choices among imported oil and gas, highly polluting domestic fuel sources, nuclear power (produced by Soviet-designed plants), and renewable alternatives will be even more agonizing than they have been in the West; the cost of any conceivable solution is apt to be staggering. On the demand side, Eastern governments need assistance in devising workable and effective incentives for conservation—and financial support to cover the high initial costs (ultimately recoverable, however) of reducing energy consumption.

The public sector will also have to take responsibility for the daunting task of cleaning up the environment, poisoned by decades of neglect by regimes that repeatedly sacrificed it to pressures for economic growth. The need is urgent, for public health reasons and because of the devastating level of unemployment that the permanent closing of all environmentally hazardous plants would entail. Once again, the technology, the expertise and, in all likelihood, most of the money will have to come from the West.

Should Western aid nevertheless go primarily to private and privatized businesses, as the Bush administration demanded? The early experience of all the new East European regimes makes it clear that meaningful privatization of the major enterprises will take years and possibly decades to complete, in part because of the domestic shortage of capital and of willing investors who are not tainted by their roles in the old regimes.[11] With some reason, both Eastern and Western economists fear that state-owned enterprises will be as little inclined to efficient operation under the new governments as they were under Communist auspices, although Western experience (e.g., in France) suggests that public corporations are not inherently incapable of competing in the international market place or turning a profit. There are three problems: first (as in the private sector), the need to train or retrain managers capable of functioning in competitive markets; second, ensuring that state corporations are adequately insulated from day-to-day political interference so that they can operate on a strict profit and loss basis; and third, creating the competitive environment that will force state firms to improve their efficiency. While a number of programs for educating East European managers in capitalist skills are already in operation,[12] the shielding of public enterprises from political meddling and unjustified subsidization from the state treasury has proven difficult to accomplish even in the West; our expectations for Eastern Europe will have to remain modest. In some cases, competition can be stimulated in the absence of privatization by breaking up monopolistic firms and/or inviting in foreign rivals, but the feasibility of doing so varies from industry to industry.

Privatization can be speeded to some extent by the sale of state assets (either entirely or on a joint-venture basis) to foreign investors, a course particularly favored by Hungary and welcomed by most other states of the region. Such sales have the virtue of costing Western governments little, bringing needed hard currency into East European treasuries, and often bringing Western know-how and technology. But the extent of such investment to date has been disappointing.[13]

Even when encouraged by government investment guarantees, Western firms have little interest in purchasing companies whose prospects for profitability in the short run are dim. On the other hand, East Europeans worry that they will awaken to find their most attractive enterprises—and particularly vital ones in terms of national pride and cultural self-definition, such as the media[14]—under foreign control, and that a single country, Germany, will dominate them. Of course, the expansion of multinational investment and finance now limits the economic sovereignty of every Western government, but the loss of control by the small and weak new governments of Eastern Europe could be particularly damaging to their credibility and their ability to act effectively. East Europeans also fear that assets whose real value is impossible to measure in economies just at the outset of marketization will be sold at fire-sale prices; such sales can only add to the social dissension that is certain to accompany the restructuring process.

Thus the public sector will inevitably be at the center of economic reconstruction, and the West should not hesitate to assist it. The West needs also to expand investment guarantees and other measures that support private Western ventures, but should not extend them indiscriminately. For both the public and the private sectors, Western support for investment should be linked to infrastructure modernization, long-term job creation, and/or technology transfer. Joint ventures in which the Eastern partner genuinely shares both risks and benefits should be given preference over purely Western undertakings.

A final area to which the West will need to direct its aid—both technical and material—might loosely be termed "legitimacy assistance." The new East European governments are all fragile and in constant danger of being forced from office, owing to political inexperience on the part of both elites and citizens, emerging party systems that are still highly fluid if not inchoate, and the absence of popular consensus on questions of procedure as well as substance. Political instability rooted in these circumstances will threaten the continuity governments must have to implement fundamental measures of economic transformation. Such measures cannot succeed if sufficient time is not available for putting them into effect and assuring that they take hold.

Western assistance cannot guarantee political stability, but can improve its chances. It may be vital that the West provide aid for currency stabilization and generous provisions for loan rescheduling and/or forgiveness for those governments whose payments of interest, let alone principal, threaten to consume export earnings. Help in developing food processing industries and an effective distribution network can ease shortages that would otherwise undermine governmental credibility. Western assistance is also needed to design and help finance adequate safety net programs for the poor, sick, and aged, who are typically the first to suffer the effects of newly unleashed prices and rising unemployment. Such programs have been severely curtailed in the effort to curb runaway budgetary deficits. Western help in developing labor market policies, such as unemployment compensation systems and job placement and retraining measures, can also lend support to governments willing to undertake painful measures of economic change.

What cannot be readily transplanted to Eastern Europe is the "civic culture" that, however imperfectly, sustains democracy in Western societies. The values of tolerance and compromise, the complementary roles of government and loyal opposition, and the place of critical but responsible media are not, in general, well understood or appreciated by Eastern European publics and elites. Nevertheless, the West can make a contribution by strongly supporting those leaders and groups who do embody such values, and private groups and such entities as the educational foundations of the German parties and the U.S. National Endowment for Democracy can assist corresponding civic education ventures.

TRADE POLICIES

Liberalized policies toward East European trade will complement, though they cannot replace, direct assistance.[15] The United States and other Western nations should remove remaining barriers to East European imports, going beyond so-called Most Favored Nation to special preferential status if necessary (as seems likely) to substantially increase the East-to-West flow of goods. The reduction or elimination of barriers, particularly in Western Europe, to agricultural imports will be especially important for Hungary, Bulgaria, and Poland, although we can expect continuing fierce resistance to such measures from the European Community's own agricultural exporters and from other competitors for the EC market for farm products.

Because of the poor competitive position of East European exports and the strong appeal of Western goods to the region's publics, the West must be prepared to accept some asymmetry in East-West trade rules. While opening up its own markets, it will need to tolerate certain protectionist measures in Eastern Europe. These might include some continuing restrictions on currency convertibility, conditions or limitations on foreign investment, protective tariffs, and/or significant export subsidies.

Remaining COCOM restrictions on the export of dual-use technologies to Eastern Europe ought to be eliminated. Western governments will need to guarantee or grant limited credits for exports of needed capital goods (but not, generally, of consumer goods) to the region. They will need to offer protection for investments, especially so long as East European commercial creditworthiness remains low.

A novel but vital component of a recovery strategy must be Western support of trade between Eastern Europe and the states of the former Soviet Union. The former will still need the raw materials and fuels that it long imported from the Soviet Union, and markets for the agricultural products and manufactured goods (including spare parts) that cannot easily be sold in the West. The former Soviet republics need such goods but largely lack the ability to pay for them. "Triangular" Western credits to make such sales possible will not be popular in countries that normally extend such credits to support their own exports, but can be defended as an alternative to opening up domestic markets immediately to East European competition. Over the longer term, Western help in expanding oil and gas production in the former USSR will help enable it to pay for East European products.

CONDITIONALITY

The unhappy experience of Western creditors with loans to Eastern Europe in the 1970s and lack of confidence in the abilities and chances for survival in office of the new East European regimes make it certain that the West will insist that any new aid to Eastern Europe be hedged with conditions. Such an insistence is justified, but the West must carefully assess the degree and type of conditionality demanded. In general terms, the conditions demanded may be political/ideological, macroeconomic, or project-specific. In my view, the denial of assistance on the basis of political and ideological considerations should play a role only in the case of grave human rights abuses or the wholesale abandonment of democratic practices. The reluctance of the West to aid Romania because of the questionable democratic credentials of its regime only deepens the misery of the unhappy population of that country, without assuring positive political change.[16] The growing possibility that reformed post-Communist parties might join coalition governments in one or more countries should not be a justification for cutting off aid, if such governments observe democratic rules.

Demanding a highly specific set of economic reform measures (e.g., shock therapy) or confining aid to private sector undertakings is difficult to justify when no proven formula has yet been found for the sort of economic transformation the East European states are now attempting. In the macroeconomic sphere, an insistence on anti-inflation measures and limits on budgetary deficits seems justified, but demands for rigid monetarism or the slashing of social welfare expenditures do not, given the potential such measures have for political destabilization and the checkered experience of the World Bank and IMF with similar requirements in Third World settings. It does seem reasonable to insist that specific projects be prepared in some detail and serve clearly defined purposes, that they make economic sense, and that some assurance be provided that they will be competently implemented and administered. But an exaggerated emphasis on Western criteria of efficiency at the expense of popular perceptions of fairness will not be helpful.

Large-scale projects, for example, in the energy sector, might usefully be designed to benefit several countries simultaneously. A central condition of support ought then to be the development of cooperative mechanisms among the recipients. In general, where possible Western assistance should seek to encourage the East European states to move toward measures of genuine economic integration among themselves, overcoming the unhappy legacy of the CMEA.[17] In this respect the precedent of the Marshall Plan, which consciously pushed Western Europe toward integration and indirectly led to the Schuman Plan for a coal and steel community, is highly apposite.[18]

Nevertheless, the donor nations and institutions must recognize that under the exisiting political circumstances, fragile governments will sometimes have to make economically questionable decisions for politically compelling reasons. Inevitably, some assistance will be wasted. Unrealistic Western expectations and the imposition of correspondingly harsh conditions will serve no purpose if they serve to undermine the new regimes. More limited conditions can, however, prove useful, in so far as they furnish governments committed to reform with a Western scapegoat for unpopular measures they themselves recognize to be necessary.

ADMINISTRATION AND COORDINATION

Elements of a multilateral framework for Western assistance and trade policies toward Eastern Europe already exist. The most important of these is probably the European Community's coordination of aid to Poland and Hungary—subsequently extended to Czechoslovakia, Bulgaria, Yugoslavia, and Romania, on behalf of the G-24 nations. Apart from the Community's own substantial PHARE program, the International Monetary Fund and World Bank have been major lenders to the region, and the European Bank for Reconstruction and Development is beginning to play an important role. Bilateral aid tends, as always, to be tied to the priorities and domestic interests of the donor nations. It remains to be seen how well the loans of the EBRD will be coordinated with the policies of the EC, whose members hold the majority of the bank's stock. The importance of the IMF lies not only in its own loan decisions but in the fact that its stamp of approval is still the prerequiste for the release of most other assistance. The United States has a small voice in the decisions of the EC and a somewhat greater one in the EBRD, but it looms large in the decisions of the IMF and the World Bank. The Eastern European states themselves are largely in the position of supplicants with respect to all these institutions, and the influence of their own views is correspondingly limited.

We need have no illusions about the possibility, or even the desirability, of centralizing and coordinating all Western economic initiatives and policies toward Eastern Europe. But a multilateral approach to Western assistance and trade is in the interest of nearly all parties, and the EC mechanism is probably the most promising foundation on which to build. It would be desirable for the West to create some sort of umbrella body, a kind of East European Recovery Commission, with greater U.S. and East Asian participation, plus an institutionalized voice for the East European governments themselves. Such a commission should set broad strategic objectives for the region as a whole and individual countries, challenge excessive duplication and projects that work at cross-purposes, and monitor the activities of private Western banks and corporations in the region. As a self-consciously political as well as economic and financial institution, it ought to take over the function the IMF has assumed, more or less by default, of grading the economic policies of recipient states. The participation of Eastern Europeans, both government officials and economic experts, is essential if the commission's recommendations (which may entail considerable domestic sacrifice) are to enjoy some modicum of legitimacy in the recipient countries. The temptation to include Russia and the other former Soviet republics in such an entity should be resisted; East European interests would unavoidably be submerged.

THE STAKES

What is at stake in Eastern Europe is more than the economic and political fortunes of several small countries newly liberated from one-party rule. The shape of the post–cold war order in Europe (and thus the world) will depend heavily on the place occupied in it by a reemergent Germany that cannot avoid redefining its identity; a Russia still possessing much of the arsenal of a superpower but now separated from the other former Soviet republics and in political, social, and economic turmoil; and a United States debating its own putative decline and tempted to turn inward or at least to shift its attention to other parts of the world. The place of these, in turn, will depend in part on the relationship that evolves between them and Eastern Europe.

Scenarios for the future of Eastern Europe are legion and mostly pessimistic, embracing different combinations of domestic and international alternatives. Simplified, these include: political turbulence or political order? Democracy or authoritarianism? Economic stagnation and dependency or growth and relative autonomy? International integration or nationalistic fragmentation? The West's economic policies will strongly influence, though they may not finally determine, the outcome.

"Eastern Europe," it is also useful to remember, is in the process of being enlarged. The states of the former Yugoslavia, when and if they escape the horrors of their civil wars, will share many problems with their East European neighbors. Areas of the former Soviet Union with historic links to Poland or other Eastern European states, such as the Baltic states, Moldova, and Ukraine, face similar (if still more severe) political and economic difficulties in the wake of their separation from the old USSR. To that extent, the West's East European problem goes well beyond the boundaries of the states emphasized in this study.

Unhappily, the dimensions of the crisis in the former Soviet Union threaten to overshadow the still intractable problems of transformation in Eastern Europe and reduce still further the potential for Western assistance. There is, however, a good case to be made for giving priority to assisting Eastern Europe, even when we view that region, as we must, in a global context that takes account of the pervasive dangers unleashed by the Soviet collapse. However acute, Eastern Europe's problems are dwarfed by those of the former Soviet republics; the resources that will be needed to deal with the former are a fraction of those that the Soviet Union's successors will require. Aid to Eastern Europe can be monitored more closely than aid to the post-Soviet states, and there is good reason to believe that it will be used more efficiently. If measures of Western assistance can be found that lift Eastern Europe from its political and economic disarray, the lessons learned there can subsequently be applied to the former Soviet republics. A more stable and productive Eastern Europe can also furnish badly needed customers and relatively low-cost suppliers for the former Soviet Union. While there will be no avoiding the need to help the latter stave off hunger and violence or to support other vital and well-conceived projects, I suggest that the West's most productive investments for the future of the entire region are likely at this time to be in Eastern Europe.

There can be no doubt that Germany will play a highly influential role in the region in the next decades, but the intensity and nature of that role will depend in part on the choices of her EC partners and the United States, as well as on German domestic politics. For both Americans and Europeans, the willingness and ability of the United States to contribute aid, foster investment, and exert policy leadership is of paramount importance. For the United States, the alternative is to disengage from Europe as a whole and to relinquish much of its accustomed leadership role. For Europe, American disengagement would mean the loss of a still-needed external stimulus and critic, and the heightened danger of a degree of German preeminence that is likely to be unhealthy both for the continent and for Germany itself.

I have sought to argue that *economic* reconstruction in Eastern Europe will require success in building stable and effective governments there, while such *political* reconstruction will depend considerably on Western economic assistance. Western resources adequate to both the political and economic tasks will not be easy to find and mobilize in a time of economic stringency; the growing American hostility to all forms of foreign assistance will be particularly difficult to overcome. But more than is commonly realized depends upon doing so.

NOTES

1. János Kornai, "Socialist Transformation and Privatization: Shifting from a Socialist System," *East European Politics and Society* 4 (Spring 1990), 261.

2. Ivan Szelenyi, "Alternative Futures for Eastern Europe: The Case of Hungary," *East European Politics and Societies* 4 (Spring 1990), 248.

3. See Endre Gömöri, "Marshall-Plan in Verbesserte Variante," *Budapester Rundschau*, May 30, 1988, 3.

4. Zbigniew Brzezinski, "For Eastern Europe, a $25 Billion Aid Package," *New York Times*, March 7, 1990, 15.

5. See the comprehensive study by Michael J. Hogan, *The Marshall Plan: America, Britain, and the Reconstruction of Western Europe, 1947–1952* (Cambridge: Cambridge University Press, 1987).

6. A *Business Week* poll taken in November 1989 suggested that 80 percent of Americans were hostile to a new Marshall Plan. Jan Krausze, "America's New 'Marshall Plan' Mere Shadow of the Original," *Manchester Guardian Weekly* (*Le Monde* section), April 15, 1990, 16. Krausze notes, however, that in 1947 just 14 percent of the U.S. population supported the original Marshall Plan.

7. Sarah M. Terry, "The Implications of Economic Stringency and Political Succession for Stability in Eastern Europe in the Eighties," in Joint Economic Committee, *East European Economies: Slow Growth in the 1980s*, vol. 1 (Washington: U.S. Government Printing Office, 1986), 505–8.

8. See Dietrich Rueschemeyer and Peter B. Evans, "The State and Economic Transformation," in Evans, Rueschemeyer, and Theda Skocpol, *Bringing the State Back In* (Cambridge: Cambridge University Press, 1985), 44–77.

9. It is reported that some 40 percent of Hungarian professional civil servants, in many cases the "most qualified," have left public service since 1989. Valery Bunce and Mária Csanádi, "Uncertainty in the Transition: Post-Communism in Hungary," *East European Politics and Societies* 7 (Spring 1993), 259.

10. Vladimir Dlouhy, the Czech minister of Trade and Industry, has rejected

the notion that the state should "pick winners," echoing the views of Western conservatives. But his alternative is hardly reassuring: "to allow the banks to choose. You may ask whether the personnel in the banking sector is any better than my personnel. Not much, but still they should be the bankers. Are the banks technically prepared? I believe the best way to learn swimming is to jump in the water." Quoted in Martin Wolf, "Minister with a Mission: Interview with Vladimir Dlouhy," *Financial Times,* November 8, 1991, sec. 3, 2.

11. The mass distribution of vouchers planned in Poland and Hungary and undertaken in Czechoslovakia appears to place effective supervision of the industries so privatized in the hands of the directors of government-created (Poland) or independent (Czechoslovakia) mutual funds, managed in the latter case largely by banks. Whether in operation these arrangements will amount to much more than a variant form of state ownership remains to be seen.

12. In February 1991, the Bush administration announced plans for an extensive program of instruction in market economics and management for Eastern Europeans; the government was to provide $14 million for the program and expected additional private contributions. *New York Times,* February 28, 1991, C15.

13. Stephen Engelberg, "Eastern Europe Foils All but the Hardiest of Western Investors," *New York Times,* March 5, 1992, 1, C8.

14. Western investment in the Hungarian press, by the likes of Rupert Murdoch, Roger Hersant, and the Springer and Bertelsmann groups of Germany, is said to approach 80 percent of total assets. Edith Oltay, "Hungary," in a special issue on the media, *RFE/RL Research Report,* October 2, 1992, 39.

15. Cf., however, Phil Gramm, "For Eastern Europe, Free Trade, Not Aid," *New York Times,* March 30, 1990, 13.

16. See Daniel N. Nelson, "Romania Needs Help, Not Sanctions," *New York Times,* June 16, 1990, 15.

17. "By helping to finance the establishment of institutions of regional cooperation, and by insisting that these countries work together as a condition of aid, the United States will be acting in the best traditions of American foreign policy—and in the best interests of the countries concerned." Walter Russell Mead, "The Once and Future Reich," *World Policy Journal* 7 (Fall 1990), 631. See also Jan Urban, "Eastern Europe—Divided It Falls," *New York Times,* November 21, 1990, 15.

18. See Hogan, *passim.*

Selected Bibliography

BOOKS

Adler-Karlsson, Gunnar. *Western Economic Warfare 1947–1967*. Stockholm: Almquist & Wiksell, 1968.

Assetto, Valerie J. *The Soviet Bloc in the IMF and the IBRD*. Boulder, Colo.: Westview Press, 1988.

Bahry, Donna L., and Joel C. Moses. *Political Implications of Economic Reform in Communist Systems*. New York: New York University Press, 1990.

Baldwin, David A. *Economic Statecraft*. Princeton, N.J.: Princeton University Press, 1985.

Banac, Ivo, ed. *Eastern Europe in Revolution*. Ithaca, N.Y.: Cornell University Press, 1992.

Basic Documents of the European Bank for Reconstruction and Development. [London: 1991.]

Baylis, Thomas A. *The Technical Intelligentsia and the East German Elite*. Berkeley: University of California Press, 1974.

Bertsch, Gary K., ed. *Controlling East-West Trade and Technology Transfer*. Durham, N.C.: Duke University Press, 1988.

Bornstein, Morris. *East-West Technology Transfer: The Transfer of Western Technology to the USSR*. Paris: Organization for Economic Cooperation and Development (OECD), 1985.

Bornstein, Morris, Zvi Gitelman, and William Zimmermann, eds. *East-West Relations and the Future of Eastern Europe*. London: George Allen & Unwin, 1981.

van Brabrant, Jozef M. *Adjustment, Structural Change, and Economic Efficiency: Aspects of Monetary Cooperation in Eastern Europe*. Cambridge: Cambridge University Press, 1987.

Braun, Aurel, ed. *The Soviet–East European Relationship in the Gorbachev Era*. Boulder, Colo.: Westview Press, 1990.

Brown, Archie, ed. *Political Culture and Communist Studies*. Armonk, N.Y.: M. E. Sharpe, 1984.

Brown, Archie, and Jack Gray, eds. *Political Culture and Political Change in Communist States*. 2nd ed. New York: Holmes & Meier, 1979.

Brown, J. F. *Eastern Europe and Communist Rule*. Durham, N.C.: Duke University Press, 1988.

Brown, J. F. *Surge to Freedom: The End of Communist Rule in Eastern Europe*. Durham, N.C.: Duke University Press, 1991.

Brzezinski, Zbigniew K. *The Soviet Bloc: Unity and Conflict*. Cambridge, Mass.: Harvard University Press, 1960.

Campbell, John C. *Tito's Separate Road: America and Yugoslavia in World Politics*. New York: Harper & Row, 1967.

Cohen, Benjamin J. *In Whose Interest? International Banking and American Foreign Policy*. New Haven: Yale University Press, 1986.

Comisso, Ellen, and Laura d'Andrea Tyson, eds. *Power, Purpose, and Collective Choice*. Ithaca, N.Y.: Cornell University Press, 1986.

Crane, Keith. *The Soviet Economic Dilemma of Eastern Europe*. Santa Monica: Rand Corporation, 1986.

Dawisha, Karen. *Eastern Europe, Gorbachev, and Reform*. Cambridge: Cambridge University Press, 1988.

Dawisha, Karen, and Philip Hanson, eds. *Soviet–East European Dilemmas*. New York: Holmes & Meier, 1981.

DDR-Handbuch. 3rd ed. Cologne: Verlag Wissenschaft und Politik, 1985.

Eastern Europe . . . Central Europe . . . Europe. *Daedalus* (Winter 1990).

Economic Commission for Europe. *Economic Bulletin for Europe*, Vol. 44, 1992. New York: United Nations, 1992.

Economic Commission for Europe. *Economic Survey of Europe in 1991–1992*. New York: United Nations, 1992.

Evans, Peter B., Dietrich Rueschemeyer, and Theda Skocpol, eds. *Bringing the State Back In*. Cambridge: Cambridge University Press, 1985.

Fallenbuchl, Zbigniew. *East-West Technology Transfer: Study of Poland, 1971–1980*. Paris: Organisation for Economic Cooperation and Development, 1983.

Forschungsstelle für gesamtdeutsche wirtschaftliche und soziale Fragen. *Glasnost und Perestroika auch in der DDR?* Berlin: Berlin Verlag Arno Spitz, 1988.

Friedländer, Michael, ed. *Foreign Trade in Eastern Europe and the Soviet Union*. Boulder, Colo.: Westview Press, 1990.

Garthoff, Raymond L. *Détente and Confrontation: American-Soviet Relations from Nixon to Reagan*. Washington, D.C.: Brookings Institution, 1985.

Garton Ash, Timothy. *The Magic Lantern: The Revolution of '89 Witnessed in Warsaw, Budapest, Berlin, and Prague*. New York: Random House, 1990.

Garton Ash, Timothy. *The Uses of Adversity: Essays on the Fate of Central Europe*. New York: Random House, 1989.

Gati, Charles. *The Bloc that Failed*. Bloomington: Indiana University Press, 1990.

Glenny, Misha. *The Rebirth of History: Eastern Europe in the Age of Democracy*, 2nd ed. London: Penguin Books, 1993.

Gomulka, Stanislaw, and Alec Nove. *East-West Technology Transfer: I—Econometric Evaluation of the Contribution of West-East Technology Transfer to the East's Economic Growth*. Paris: OECD, 1984.

Gordon, Lincoln, with J. F. Brown, Pierre Hassner, Josef Joffe, and Edwina Moreton. *Eroding Empire: Western Relations with Eastern Europe*. Washington, D.C.: Brookings Institution, 1987.

Griffith, William E., ed. *Central and Eastern Europe: The Opening Curtain?* Boulder, Colo.: Westview Press, 1989.

Hanson, Philip. *Western Economic Statecraft in East-West Relations*. London: Routledge & Kegan Paul, 1988.

Hardt, John P., and Carl H. McMillan, eds. *Planned Economies Confronting the Challenges of the Eighties*. Cambridge: Cambridge University Press, 1988.

Harrington, Joseph F., and Bruce J. Courtney. *Tweaking the Nose of the Russians*. New York: Columbia University Press, 1991.

Hayden, Eric W. *Technology Transfer to Eastern Europe: U.S. Corporate Experience*. New York: Praeger, 1976.

Hewett, Ed A. *Reforming the Soviet Economy: Equality vs. Efficiency*. Washington, D.C.: Brookings Institution, 1988.

Holzman, Franklyn. *International Trade under Communism*. New York: Basic Books, 1976.

International Monetary Fund. *Direction of Trade Statistics Yearbook 1992*. Washington, D.C.: International Monetary Fund, 1992.

Jacobsen, Hanns-Dieter. *Die Ost-West Wirtschaftsbeziehungen als deutsch-amerikanisches Problem*. Baden-Baden: Nomos Verlagsgesellschaft, 1986.

Jeffries, Ian, and Manfred Melzer, eds. *The East German Economy*. London: Croom Helm, 1987.

Joint Economic Committee. *East European Economic Assessment*. 97th Cong., 1st sess. 2 vols. Washington, D.C.: U.S. Government Printing Office, 1981.

Joint Economic Committee. *East European Economies Post-Helsinki*. 95th Cong., 1st sess. Washington, D.C.: U.S. Government Printing Office, 1977.

Joint Economic Committee. *East European Economies: Slow Growth in the 1980s*. 99th Cong., 2d sess. 3 vols. Washington, D.C.: U.S. Government Printing Office, 1985 (vol. 1), 1986 (vols. 2–3).

Joint Economic Committee. *Pressures for Reform in the East European Economies*. 101st Cong., 1st sess. 2 vols. Washington, D.C.: U.S. Government Printing Office, 1989.

Joint Economic Committee. *Reorientation and Commercial Relations of the Economies of Eastern Europe*. 93rd Cong., 2d sess. Washington, D.C.: U.S. Government Printing Office, 1974.

Kaser, M. C., ed. *The Economic History of Eastern Europe 1919–1975*. 3 vols. Oxford: Clarendon Press, 1985–1986.

Kornai, János. *The Road to a Free Economy*. New York: W. W. Norton, 1990.

Kovács, János Mátyás, ed. "Rediscovery of Liberalism in Eastern Europe." Special issue of *East European Politics and Socities* 5 (Winter 1991).

Köves, András. *The CMEA Countries in the World Economy: Turning Inwards or Turning Outwards*. Budapest: Akadémiai Kiado, 1985.

Köves, András. *Central and East European Economies in Transition*. Boulder, Colo.: Westview Press, 1992.

Kovrig, Bennett. *The Myth of Liberation: East-Central Europe in U.S. Diplomacy and Politics since 1941*. Baltimore: Johns Hopkins University Press, 1973.

Kovrig, Bennett. *Of Walls and Bridges: The United States and Eastern Europe*. New York: New York University Press, 1991.

Levcik, Friedrich, and Jan Stankovsky. *A Profile of Austria's East-West Trade in the 1970s and 1980s*. Vienna: Institute for Comparative Economic Studies, 1985.

Linden, Ronald H. *Communist States and International Change*. London: Allen & Unwin, 1987.

Managing the Transition: Integrating the Reforming Socialist Countries into the World Economy. New York: Institute for East-West Security Studies, 1989.

Marer, Paul, and Włodzimierz Siwiński, eds. *Creditworthiness and Reform in Poland: Western and Polish Perspectives*. Bloomington: Indiana University Press, 1988.

Marrese, Michael, and Jan Vanous. *Soviet Subsidization of Trade with Eastern Europe*. Berkeley: University of California Institute of International Studies, 1983.

Monkiewicz, Jan, and Jan Maciejewicz. *Technology Export from the Socialist Countries*. Boulder, Colo.: Westview Press, 1986.

Myant, Martin. *The Czechoslovak Economy 1948–1988*. Cambridge: Cambridge University Press, 1989.

National Academy of Sciences, *Balancing the National Interest: U.S. National Security Export Controls and Global Economic Competition*. Washington, D.C.: National Academy Press, 1987.

Palankai, Tibor. *The European Community and Central European Integration*. New York: Institute for East-West Security Studies, 1991.

Poznanski, Kazimierz Z. *Technology, Competition, and the Soviet Bloc in the World Market*. Berkeley: University of California Institute of International Studies, 1987.

Pryor, Frederic L. *The Communist Foreign Trade System*. Cambridge, Mass.: MIT Press, 1963.

Przeworski, Adam. *Democracy and the Market*. Cambridge: Cambridge University Press, 1991.

Rat für gegenseitige Wirtschaftshilfe: Strukturen und Problemen. Bonn: Ostkolleg der Bundeszentrale für politische Bildung, 1987.

Rode, Reinhard, and Hanns-Dieter Jacobsen, eds. *Economic Warfare or Détente: An Assessment of East-West Relations*. Boulder, Colo.: Westview Press, 1985.

Roosa, Robert V., Michiya Matsukawa, and Armin Gutowski. *East-West Trade at a Crossroads: Economic Relations with the Soviet Union and Eastern Europe*. A Task Force Report to the Trilateral Commission. New York: New York University Press, 1982.

Rothschild, Joseph. *Return to Diversity: A Political History of East Central Europe Since World War II*. New York: Oxford University Press, 1989.

Shafir, Michael. *Romania: Politics, Economics and Society*. London: Frances Pinter, 1985.

Smith, Alan H. *The Planned Economies of Eastern Europe*. New York: Holmes & Meier, 1983.

Smith, Gordon B., ed. *The Politics of East-West Trade*. Boulder, Colo.: Westview Press, 1984.

Sobell, Vladimir. *The Red Market: Industrial Cooperation and Specialisation in Comecon*. Aldershot, Hants, England: Gower, 1984.

Spulber, Nicolas. *The Economics of Communist Eastern Europe* (Cambridge, Mass.: Technology Press, 1957.

Staniszkis, Jadwiga. *The Dynamics of Breakthrough in Eastern Europe: The Polish Experience.* Berkeley: University of California Press, 1991.

Stares, Paul B., ed. *The New Germany and the New Europe.* Washington, D.C.: Brookings Institution, 1992.

Statistisches Amt der DDR. *Statistisches Jahrbuch der Deutschen Demokratischen Republik '90.* Berlin: Rudolf Haufe Verlag, 1990.

Stent, Angela, ed. *Economic Relations with the Soviet Union: American and West German Perspectives.* Boulder, Colo.: Westview Press, 1985.

Terry, Sarah Meiklejohn, ed. *Soviet Policy in Eastern Europe.* New Haven: Yale University Press, 1984.

Vienna Institute for Comparative Economic Studies. *COMECON Data 1990.* Westport, Conn.: Greenwood Press, 1991.

Vine, Richard D., ed. *Soviet–East European Relations as a Problem for the West.* London: Croom Helm, 1987.

Wallace, William V., and Roger A. Clarke. *Comecon, Trade, and the West.* New York: St. Martin's, 1986.

Wienert, Helgard, and John Slater. *East-West Technology Transfer: The Trade and Economic Aspects.* Paris: Organisation for Economic Cooperation and Development, 1986.

Wilczynski, Jozef. *The Economics and Politics of East-West Trade.* London: Macmillan, 1969.

Wolchik, Sharon L. *Czechoslovakia in Transition: Politics, Economics and Society.* London: Pinter, 1991.

Wolf, Thomas A. *U.S. East-West Trade Policy: Economic Warfare versus Economic Welfare.* Lexington, Mass.: Lexington Books, 1973.

Wörmann, Claudia. *Der Osthandel der Bundesrepublik Deutschland.* Frankfurt: Campus Verlag, 1982.

Zaleski, Eugene, and Helgard Wienert. *Technology Transfer between East and West.* Paris: Organisation for Economic Cooperation and Development, 1980.

Zloch-Christy, Iliana. *Debt Problems of Eastern Europe.* Cambridge: Cambridge University Press, 1987.

PERIODICALS

Acta Oeconomica

The American Prospect

Business East Europe

(U.S.) *Department of State Bulletin*

Deutschland Archiv

DIW *Economic Bulletin*

DIW *Wochenbericht*

East European Politics and Societies

East European Reporter

Economist Intelligence Unit, *Country Reports*

Economist

Euromoney
Financial Market Trends (OECD)
Financial Times
Foreign Policy
Foreign Broadcast Information Service (FBIS), *Daily Report*
Frankfurter Allgemeine Zeitung
IMF Survey
Institutional Investor
Joint Publications Research Service (JPRS), *Daily Report*
Manchester Guardian Weekly
New York Times (All citations are from the National Edition)
PlanEcon Report
Problems of Communism
Radio Free Europe (RFE) Research Reports
Report on Eastern Europe
RFE/RL Research Report
Soviet Studies
Studies in Comparative Communism
Südosteuropa
Wall Street Journal
World Policy Journal
Die Zeit (All citations are from the North American Edition)

Index